FEDERAL TAX REFORM
The Issues and a Program

DAN THROOP SMITH

*Professor of Finance, Harvard Graduate School
of Business Administration*

Former Deputy to the Secretary of the Treasury

New York
Toronto
London

McGRAW-HILL BOOK COMPANY, INC.
1961

FEDERAL TAX REFORM

PREFACE

The prospects for general tax reduction have dwindled in recent years under the pressures for new and enlarged government expenditures. Tax reform has taken the place of tax reduction as a limited but attainable goal. This book presents the issues and advances a program for reform of the existing Federal tax structure.

Virtually any proposal for a reform in the tax law will be opposed by someone. Those who would lose a favored position will object to a change and reiterate such reasons as they can find to justify their special treatment. Those who are anxious to create political issues may object even to a change which will remove an unfair and unsound tax discrimination against some form of investment or activity, if the taxpayers receiving relief are among the groups against whom emotions may be aroused.

The analysis in this book recognizes the political difficulties of tax reform. The proposals made are less ambitious and fundamental than would be appropriate if it were possible to start with a clean slate to draft an "ideal" tax system. In some areas, however, the law seems so bad that a rather extreme reform is suggested even though its adoption seems improbable for many years. This is notably the case in the tax treatment of trusts.

Most tax specialists will probably find this book inadequate from the standpoint of their respective professional points of view. The analysis does not push into new areas on theories of tax incidence or countercyclical economic policy; it does not even review systematically the extensive literature in the field. Nor does it fully indicate the refinements which are important to tax practitioners in the interpretation and application of the law. The objective is rather to bring together the differing points of view. Those usually concerned with broad generalizations will find here examples of the many specific provisions of the law involved in actual tax legislation. Those usually concerned with specific provisions will find them presented in a broader perspective. The objective above all is to present to those who are not tax specialists enough background in both theory and application to enable them better to appreciate the issues involved and to judge proposals for new legislation. The emphasis throughout is on public policy.

Some of the principal points presented here were developed for a paper given to the American Economic Association in December, 1959, before the manuscript for this book was written. In that brief paper, there was a feeling of regret that the recommendations for changes in the tax law had to be advanced as assertions rather than as demonstrated conclusions. It was expected that a longer discussion in a book would permit a full development of the analysis. Regretfully, it must now be recognized that there still seems to be more assertion than proof, but broad coverage is more important here than thorough discussion of a few topics. Professional specialists are already familiar with the literature on most of the topics covered.

The opinions given here as to what is good and bad in the existing tax law and in proposed changes in it may help to sharpen the issues and focus attention on many of the important points which must be considered in a tax reform program. This is so even if the conclusions are not acceptable to many readers as, inevitably, they will not be.

Full acknowledgment for the background on which this book is based cannot be adequately or appropriately given in individual terms. I want, however, to state my grateful appreciation for the opportunity to participate in the development of the tax law during six years in Washington and for the stimulating and pleasant associations with colleagues in the Executive Departments and the Congress—and with representatives of taxpayers' and public groups interested in changes in the tax law. Participation in government, in spite of its frustrations, can be fascinating and satisfying and should indeed be regarded as a privilege.

Specific acknowledgment may be made, however, to Messrs. Thomas F. Leahey and Laurence N. Woodworth, who were kind enough to read most of the manuscript, and to Arthur S. Fefferman and Richard E. Slitor, who read parts of it. The comments of each of them were helpful and saved me from some errors in both fact and presentation. A fuller acceptance of some of their suggestions might have improved additional aspects of emphasis and content, which have been left as they are as a matter of individual taste. On all matters of opinion, coverage, and factual research an author has the satisfaction of making his own decisions, and for them he must assume full responsibility.

Dan Throop Smith

CONTENTS

Chapter 1   THE NATURE OF TAXATION AND THE OBJECTIVES OF TAX POLICY

The purpose of this book is to present the issues of Federal tax policy in nontechnical terms and to recommend a program for reform.

One must assume, though with regret, that substantial tax reduction is not in prospect in the foreseeable future; an increase in total tax burdens may indeed become necessary. With a continuing high level of taxation, it is important to have a tax system which is as fair and simple as possible and which imposes minimum restraints on economic growth. Our present tax system is conspicuously bad by all these standards. In spite of substantial improvement made in the tax revision of 1954, more fundamental reforms are needed, as was recognized at that time.

Specific items of tax reform may involve either increases or decreases in revenue. In view of the need for government funds, a realistic plan for tax reform should be essentially self-financing; the gains should substantially balance the losses in revenue. Statistics are not used extensively in this book, however, nor is there any attempt to draw up a final table of balancing items. Many of the reforms discussed do not have major revenue significance and should be accepted or rejected on qualitative grounds.

Though the language used here is not technical, many of the concepts are abstract and involved, especially in some aspects of corporate income taxation. The topics range from such familiar ones as expense accounts, pensions, charitable contributions, and medical expenses to the tax treatment of corporate mergers and family trusts

1

running over several generations. Inclusion here is based on social and economic importance. Most of the subjects covered have become familiar through frequent discussions, but some of the most obscure provisions of the law have far-reaching implications and have not yet received the attention they deserve.

The point of view throughout the book is that of public policy. Proposals to change or to maintain the existing law are given at the end of each section. These proposals unavoidably involve subjective judgments, but the opposing arguments are presented and others may draw different conclusions. The objective is to help in securing a wider appreciation of the fundametnal issues involved in tax policy and of the pressures under which members of Congress and Treasury officials work in trying to resolve these issues.

The reform proposed here is a limited one. Hopefully, it is within the range of what may be politically feasible regardless of total revenue requirements. It is assumed that income taxation will continue to be the major source of Federal revenue and excise taxation a very minor one. In current theory, proposals for net wealth taxes and progressive consumption or expenditure taxes receive much attention, either as supplements to or partial substitutes for existing income, excise, and property taxes. Discussions of fundamental changes involving the use of such taxes are interesting and important. Some of these taxes may become useful to permit reductions in the rates of existing taxes or to provide additional revenue if that becomes necessary. But whatever new taxes may be adopted, we shall continue to use our existing ones to a substantial extent for the foreseeable future. Reform in these taxes as proposed here is itself a major goal, even though it falls short of the completely new structure which may be desirable and may ultimately be developed.

This chapter deals with taxation in very general terms. It includes a discussion of government expenditures which make taxation necessary and of the broad and conflicting objectives of tax policy. In doing so, it provides background for the specific issues of tax reform which occupy the rest of the book.

Taxation—The Price for Government Services

Taxes are compulsory payments which individual citizens make, directly and indirectly, for services provided by the government.

Each citizen will have his own doubts and reservations about what he regards as the excesses or deficiencies of government programs and the spending thereon and about the distribution of the burden of the taxes which pay for them. But for better or worse, the existing program of expenditures and taxes at any time represents the consensus of national opinion as it is resolved, perhaps inadequately, through the entire process of government.

Taxes, by themselves, are generally bad because they tend to discourage economic activity and investment. They also divert attention away from productive effort to maneuvers to save on taxes rather than to acquire income. At a 90 per cent income tax rate, it is as useful to an individual to save $1,000 in taxes as to make $10,000 of income.

High taxes also lead to complicated tax laws. High tax rates make Congress particularly susceptible to pleas for special relief by groups of people or industries, and relief provisions are inevitably complicated. Other complicating provisions are necessary to close loopholes, which often arise even within special relief provisions.

Complicated laws increase taxpayers' annoyance. And special relief provisions, though welcome to those who benefit from them, are likely to make those who do not get special treatment still more resentful of the additional tax burdens which they must carry. Ultimately, resentment can rise to the point where taxpayer morale breaks down.

We still have in this country a tradition among most people that tax fraud is morally reprehensible. But this attitude is strained by high taxes, especially if there is doubt as to the fairness of the distribution of the burden. If we ever reach a stage where outright tax fraud is socially acceptable, public corruption of other sorts will be condoned and our form of government will be truly in danger. The fact that a conviction for tax fraud does not prevent election to public office is disheartening and a frightening sign of deteriorating tax morality. Tax reform is needed to prevent further deterioration.

Taxation is the method by which we pay for government activities, which are presumptively good. Private incomes are diverted from private consumption to joint or public consumption. The good effects of wise government expenditures should more than offset the bad effects of the taxation which pays for the outlays. Thus, though taxes are bad by themselves, they become acceptable as the only available way of financing the basic governmental process which is necessary and the supplemental government services which may be very good. But the higher the general level of taxes, the greater the chance that the inherent bad effects of taxation may outweigh the advantages of the government expenditures which they finance.

It has sometimes been said that there is some universal point at which any tax system breaks down. Taxation at some such figure as 25 per cent of the national income has been mentioned as the bearable limit. There is a further implication that tax burdens below this point can be imposed without concern. Neither the general proposition nor the implication is correct. A bad tax system can produce great damage even though the total tax burden is not great, while a wisely designed tax system can support a high level of government expenditures without significant damage. The greater the total tax burden, the more important it is that the tax structure be critically reviewed to keep its inequities, its repressive effects, and its complexities at a minimum and the more important it is that expenditure programs be really justified.

The tax burden in this country is heavy. Our tax structure in many respects is bad. The possibility of serious and lasting damage to public morale and to prospective economic growth is real. In this book, on the regretful assumption that we shall continue to have high taxes, various suggestions are made as to how the tax laws can be made fairer, less repressive, and simpler—in brief, more bearable. Only with tax reform can we expect to continue to carry the tax load which is the price we must pay for survival in this time of peril and for public improvement in this time of opportunity.

Though this is a book about the ways in which the tax system might be changed to keep its bad effects at a minimum, some preliminary comments will be made about the government expenditures which make taxes necessary. Adequate defense expenditures are basic for the very existence of a society; government defense expenditures are necessary for survival. So are nondefense expenditures for certain basic functions, such as those for police, the judiciary, and general government. These are essential for the existence of a complex society. Other government expenditures such as those for education, public health, a system of highways, and the conservation of natural resources, if made wisely, can greatly increase the base for private production activities and the national income. And still other government expenditures can also provide a better basis for the "good life"—outlays such as those on the cultural aspects of education, aesthetically pleasing public buildings, national parks, and municipal cleanliness are forms of consumption which can be provided more effectively, and in some instances exclusively, by governmental action. They are features of our life and community which we would be sorry to forego. As we become more prosperous individually and as a nation, we can reasonably afford more of the amenities provided publicly as well as more of our privately purchased luxuries. But this does not mean that all government expenditures are good.

Many critics in our society advocate new and ever-larger government functions and outlays as the cure for most problems. Such undiscriminating advocacy of spending is irresponsible in ignoring the damage which is likely to be inflicted by ever-higher taxes required to pay for the enlarged scope of government activity. And it is fundamentally wrong in the assumption that larger government expenditures automatically make a better society. In fact, public expenditures seem as likely to be made extravagantly as are private expenditures, especially when they are not directly related to the taxes which must be imposed to support them. Public extravagance can undermine a society and the individuals of which it is composed in the same way that private extravagance can undermine a single individual or family.

The gross inadequacies of our education system, for example, appear to arise more from wrong standards and objectives than from inadequate funds. The use of taxes to pay for "life adjustment" courses in schools seems as silly as private spending on items of conspicuous consumption. Such a use of taxes is a good deal more harmful to our society, since it diverts time from real education and creates an undesirable standard of conformity at the expense of individuality and differences in personal achievement. Nor is public spending necessarily the solution for bad housing. Attractive public housing is quickly turned into a slum by slovenly occupants, while individually responsible citizens with decent standards will make good homes in inferior buildings.

More fundamentally, increasing reliance on government programs is likely to sap individual initiative and responsibility. The presumption that government action represents an idealized joint effort for mutually desired objectives is too often a naïve misconception. A religious community or a neighborhood group may do things collectively with a reasonable chance to balance efforts against results, but large-scale representative government is subject to pressures which lead to results different from those which would be achieved in a small group where both effort and results can be appraised simultaneously.

Public assistance can degenerate into handouts and even rackets, protected by the anonymity of the recipients and their families who in many cases should be responsible for those who are actually in need. If not adequately supervised, it can attract to a community people who are at best parasitic. The belief that society owes everyone protection even against his own misdeeds and negligence contributes to the sort of softness and personal irresponsibility which is the cause of so much concern to those who recall the pattern of degeneration of other civilizations.

It is not appropriate in this book on taxation to review the specific expenditure programs which make the taxes necessary. Every citizen has his own individual judgment as to which ones are handled extravagantly and which ones stingily. The government has in it at one extreme men obsessed with increasing their own status by enlarging the scope of the activities under them regardless of their value (the so-called empire builders) and at the other extreme dedicated men who are frustrated by inadequate funds. Publications of trivial value and rivalries among agencies with duplication of efforts and unnecessarily large staffs arise from the former. Ridiculously small expense allowances for our representatives abroad and inadequate funds for tax collection—larger appropriations would pay for themselves several times over and give greater public confidence that the laws are being applied fairly—are examples of the latter.

Those who criticize waste in government should examine their own attitudes concerning proposed reductions which affect their own group or locality; the almost universal objections to closing an unnecessary government facility or office dishearten the people in government who are concerned with efficiency and economy. Sometimes it seems that there is political realism in the facetious remark,

"We must reduce expenditures drastically, but we must be careful not to affect anyone's constituents."

In the traditional New England town meeting, with everyone voting on all major items in the budget and aware of what each $10,000 of town expenditures means in terms of his own taxes on his home, there is a fair chance that the allocation between private and public expenditures will be rational or at least will represent a consensus of opinion. But as the decisions concerning government expenditures move further and further away from the people concerned, and as the connection between expenditures and taxes becomes more and more tenuous, the chance for rational decisions or even a true consensus of opinion becomes less likely. The arguments, logical and emotional, for particular expenditure programs are appealing, and strong pressure groups build up around them. The balanced judgments present in a town meeting because everyone knows that an expenditure means a specific, identifiable, and immediate personal tax burden are hard to attain in larger scale governments. In our national government, different Congressional committees deal with appropriations and taxes. There is a multiplicity of taxes with no identifiable relation between specific taxes and specific expenditures. And, unhappily, at times there may not be any real concern about balancing the budget anyway. Unofficial comments of municipal officials to state officials and of state officials to Federal officials testify to the decreasing discrimination with which programs are appraised as they reach higher levels of government and become more remote from the people. Thoughtful proposals to improve the processes of budget review and control in both the legislative and executive branches of the government have been made in the Congress and by the Bureau of the Budget. They deserve attention and action. They would improve the control over expenditures and thus minimize tax burdens and the need for tax reform.

In striking a balance between the bad effects of taxation and the good effects of wise government expenditures, the standard must not be based solely on materialistic terms. Just as an individual may decide that his conception of a good life does not include a maximum attainable personal income, so the good life for the individuals who make up a society may involve a combination of public expenditures and taxation which actually impedes the development of a maximum national income. Even if the combination of taxation and public expenditures has a net repressive effect on total national production, the amenities derived from the government programs may add more to individual satisfaction than would the production which is foregone because it is, on balance, repressed by the level and nature of the tax system.

In summary, it is not true, as is sometimes presumed, that government activity is inherently and inevitably a drag on the economic system. Some of the government activities financed by taxation provide the very basis for the existence and operation of the private economic system, and others represent rational decisions in favor of forms of consumption which can be provided only through joint action. But it is also not true that all government activity is either indirectly productive or gives generally desired satisfactions available only by joint action; too much government expenditure is for the special benefit of limited groups who have been effective in investing their selfish interest with distorted sentimentality or masquerading it under a public purpose. It must further be remembered that the mere fact that a government program is good or that a government expenditure is for a worthy purpose does not mean that it should be undertaken. Even a prosperous society cannot afford all outlays which might be desirable any more than can a prosperous family.

Choices must be made between public and private spending; these decisions determine what fraction of the country's total income must be taken in taxes to pay for the expenditures made through government agencies. Everyone will have his individual judgment as to what is wise and what is foolish in both private and public spending, but there seems to be no very good reason to suppose that a shift to more public spending with less private spending would necessarily result in a wiser allocation of the total.

It is currently fashionable among critics to deplore what they regard as public penury amid private profligacy. There is justification for this judgment when one notes the relative outlays on liquor and tobacco as compared with those on education, on cosmetics as compared with public health, or on ornamentation and gadgets on new automobiles as compared with highways on which to drive. But there is little reason to suppose that joint decisions through government would be much wiser than the sum of individual decisions made privately.

Those who advocate a shift to the public from the private spheres might be disappointed to find that the public outlays would, in fact, turn out to be on foolish things or for selfish groups, on balance no better than the sort of private outlays which they hoped to supplant. Also, the higher taxes required for additional government spending might make people reduce what the advocates of the change regarded as important individual family expenditures while frivolous and ostentatious private consumption is maintained. Over all, the generally repressive effects of higher total taxes would have impeded growth of the total national income, with little net gain in the wisdom with which it is spent. Though reform of our tax structure may reduce the bad effects of taxation and even permit a somewhat higher total tax burden than we now have without serious repressive effects, it by no means follows that larger government expenditures would produce a better society or even that the present level is justified, constituted as it is and is likely to continue to be of the same sort of allocations, wise and foolish, extravagant and stingy, which we all make in our personal affairs.

Objectives of Tax Policy

A tax system should be as fair as possible, as simple (and certain) as possible, and impose minimum restraints on economic growth, at the same time fostering maximum economic stability. There would probably be general agreement that each of these three objectives is important in appraising a country's tax system. But though these concepts appear simple, there is much controversy on at least two of them. Opinions differ on matters of fairness and on the best way to raise revenue with minimum economic damage. Furthermore, agreements on each of the separate objectives would not assure agreement on the proper structure of a tax system because the objectives frequently conflict with one another and judgments differ as to the relative emphasis to be given to each. This section outlines the nature of the conflicts among objectives and then reviews the controversies concerning fairness. The next section considers the economic objectives of a tax system. The issues raised

here in general form will be discussed more fully in the remainder
of the book.

Conflicts among Objectives. A simple tax system may not be
regarded as fair, and provisions of the law intended to facilitate
economic development may be criticized as being too complicated
or as unfair. Virtually all the deductions and exemptions allowed in
the individual income tax, for example, are intended to ease the
burden of the tax and bring it more into line with the abstract and
imprecise concept of ability to pay, and yet every deduction and
exemption complicates the law. Tax forms and tax computations
would be much simpler if the tax were based solely on income
received during the year with no deductions for interest or for state
and local taxes, medical expenses, charitable contributions, or casualty losses or even for personal exemptions with the complicated
rules concerning the definition of a dependent.

Each deduction in computing taxable income is presumed to add,
at least superficially, to the fairness of the income tax, and yet each
one adds a line or a schedule to the tax form and requires record
keeping and calculations to support it. Worse yet, the existence of
any deduction is an invitation to create artificial transactions to
come within the letter, though not the spirit, of a simple allowance.
The simple allowance must then be hedged around with restrictions
and qualifications to prevent abuse until it becomes so complicated
that it is criticized even by those who benefit from it.

The deduction for charitable contributions, for example, is consistent with our tradition of private philanthropy and is probably
necessary to maintain private charitable activity, but it is subject to
serious abuse by people who attempt to claim deductions for ficti-
tious values of property contributed to charities. Abuses in connection with claims for the original purchase price of discarded
furniture or artificially high values for art objects as charitable contributions require tightening of the law at present. Interest deductions have been abused through unnatural if not altogether artificial
claims for interest payments on so-called insurance policies which
are designed almost entirely to provide taxpayers with current
interest deductions against ordinary income, offset to some extent
and in some instances by a much later tax on an eventual capital
gain. An abuse of this sort is unfair to the vast majority of taxpayers
who are not in a position to take advantage of the loophole—and

one hopes might not be disposed to do so anyway. But if this loop-hole in the interest deduction is completely closed, the law will be made more complicated, and attempts to close it by statute have thus far been successfully obstructed by irrelevant but emotion-ally appealing talk of widows and orphans and small business-men.

Conflicts may also arise between the economic objective of mini-mum restraint on growth and the other two objectives of simplicity and fairness. The sections of the tax law dealing with corporate reorganizations, for example, are among the most complicated in the law, but they have been adopted because the simple rule under which all exchanges of securities and property are treated as tax-able events would impose serious barriers to transactions which occur in the ordinary course of business without giving rise to any immediately disposable funds with which to pay a tax.

Some allowance for the carry-over of business losses is also neces-sary to prevent an annually imposed income tax from penalizing new or fluctuating businesses which by their nature are especially risky and toward which, in all fairness and in the national economic interest, the tax system should be at least neutral. But the calcula-tion of loss carry-overs is inevitably complicated and their allowance is subject to abuse when the benefit of a carry-over goes not to those who incurred the original loss but to a predatory financial manipu-lator who buys a corporate shell at a nominal price.

Exemptions of particular categories of income also lead to prob-lems and abuse, even in the case of the basic personal exemption. The definition of a dependent had to be tightened, for example, because under a previous definition it was possible to claim as dependents the entire membership of a foreign orphanage, with a tax saving in excess of the actual cost of support. It was not only possible; it was done. Tax exemption of most scholarships and fellowships has been long recognized as a matter of equity because they are gifts and, as a matter of social policy, to ensure that the limited amount of funds for such purposes should go as far as pos-sible. But the objective tests for such exemptions established in 1954 with the hope of clarifying and simplifying the law have been eagerly noted by some faculty groups as a basis for converting a regular salary payable during a sabbatical leave into a partly tax-exempt "fellowship," if university authorities would only alter the formal arrangements and methods of payment of sabbatical salaries. If this practice actually developed, the inequities arising from the abuse would certainly require complicating restrictions if not actual repeal of the basic exemption of fellowship grants.

In addition to the three principal objectives of fairness, simplicity, and minimum restraint on economic growth, other considerations enter into policy decisions. An awareness of the nature and extent of tax burdens, for example, is desirable in a democracy, though it is repugnant to a dictatorship. This point is significant in the discussions of effects of tax withholdings on tax consciousness.

Tax policy may also be influenced by a multiplicity of social and political objectives. Differential rates and special depreciation allowances give preferences to particular products, activities, or forms of investment. Small business, foreign investment and residence, and various aspects of farming are among the favored categories now in the law. A list of proposed differentials would be endless; it sometimes seems as though a first approach to all problems is a suggestion for a special tax allowance or rate.

Neutrality in taxation is assumed to be a desirable objective in this book. As a general proposition, taxation should not be used to influence consumption, personal activity, or investment. The free play of prices, consumer choices, and investment decisions will, it is believed, produce better results than can be secured from a directed economy. If one favors a controlled economy, taxation can be used as a powerful factor among the controls, but that is not the approach adopted here.

Inevitably, however, with high tax rates and a large total tax burden, complete neutrality in the tax law is impossible. In the following analysis of specific issues, there are doubtless many instances where a personal bias on a social or economic policy will be apparent; this is true in such unrelated subjects as homeownership, corporate mergers, or business entertainment expenses. This brief reference to social, political, and special economic objectives, other than the main one of healthy economic growth, is made in recognition of the fact that they cannot fail to influence anyone's judgment on tax policies. It is hoped that, when present, they are forthrightly stated in the following pages.

"Fair" Taxation—An Uncertain Standard. Not only are there conflicts among the criteria of tax policy, but neither the objective of

fairness nor that of minimum restraint on economic growth is clear and unambiguous in itself. What may seem fair to one person will seem grossly unfair to another. The concept of "ability to pay" is widely used as setting a standard of fairness in taxation; actually it is little more than a phrase. The concept has not been reduced to objective or scientific standards, and there does not seem to be any basis for so reducing it. Comparisons of relative "abilities" to pay taxes involve measurements of psychological units of pleasure and displeasure, and as yet, psychologists have not provided a standard or means for such calculations. A brief digression into some abstractions of economic theory will indicate why actual political decisions on the distribution of the tax burden have to be made on practical or intuitive rather than scientific grounds.

Most theorists agree that the standard of ability to pay should lead in practice to progressive taxation. This is based on what is referred to as the diminishing utility of income. Diminishing marginal utility is a familiar and well-established concept in economic analysis; when applied to single products or groups of products, it it readily comprehensible and even measurable. It is a theoretical abstraction for the commonly observed fact that one can be surfeited with even the most attractive of commodities. An orange a month is a luxury, an orange a week a treat, an orange a day an agreeable item in a diet, but an orange an hour, with its associated stomach upset, would be thoroughly distasteful and something to be avoided. So it is with other items, both necessities for physical existence and luxuries. Successive units provide diminishing satisfaction or utility, with an eventual point of satiation beyond which there is actual repugnance for additional amounts.

The supposed sequence of logic from the diminishing utility from successive units of a single commodity to progressive income taxation runs as follows. First, the diminishing utility of additional amounts of a particular item of consumption is generalized to apply to income as a whole; each additional hundred or thousand dollars of income is considered as providing less satisfaction, having less utility, than the equal amount of income preceding it. There is thus a diminishing utility of successive amounts of income, with the utility of the last segment referred to as the marginal utility. The marginal utility is measured by the satisfaction secured by the use of the unit of income, the hundred or the thousand dollars, which is used in the least important way and hence gives the least satisfaction.

The concept of diminishing utility of income is the theoretical basis for distributing the tax burden in accordance with the so-called ability-to-pay principle, but at this point there are at least two alternative standards which have been advocated as providing the fairest distribution of the total tax burden. Both "minimum aggregate sacrifice" and "equal marginal sacrifice" have their advocates. Each has a logical basis, but neither can be measured or practically applied. Abstractly, the concepts can be described as follows.

"Minimum aggregate sacrifice" means that the total burden of taxation should be so distributed that the total sacrifice involved is at a minimum for the population as a whole. If one accepts the proposition that additional amounts of income represent less and less utility, then the amount by which the largest income in a country exceeds the second largest income is the income with the least utility and hence should be taxed away before any of the second largest income is taxed. And on the same assumption, the amounts by which the largest and the next largest incomes exceed the third largest income should be taxed away before the third largest income is touched by taxation. Thus, the tax system would proceed through an equalizing process until the total desired revenue was secured, with all incomes above a certain level reduced to that level below which no incomes would be taxed at all. This would be equalization with a vengeance; a certain figure would be the breaking point, above which all income would be taxed away and below which no income would be touched by taxation. This is the extreme application of ability to pay, it would be rejected on practical grounds by most of those who undiscriminatingly advocate the abstract concept, but it is nonetheless a result which they may unintentionally support.

"Equal marginal sacrifice" means that the total burden of taxation is so distributed that the last increment of taxation for each person has the same burden. It implies that everyone will pay some tax, in contrast to the preceding concept of minimum aggregate sacrifice. It is intended to equalize tax burdens in such terms as would be represented in a conversation in which a man with a smaller income would say to a richer man, "But a dollar—or ten dollars—or a hundred dollars—is as important to me as a thousand dollars is to you." And the tax law would be fair only if it so distributed the burden that the last hundred million dollars of taxation is taken 10 cents from one, 25 cents from another, and $1 from still another, so that the sacrifice involved in the payments of the respective dimes, quarters, and dollars is the same for each taxpayer. The concept is a simple one, but its application is confused by the innumerable arguments over whether one man's 10 cents represents the same in satisfaction to him as another man's 10 cents or 20 cents or $1 or $10. Only if there could be agreement on such comparisons of the utility of successive segments of different incomes to different people could the concept of equal marginal sacrifice be applied with any assurance.

Now the fact remains that there are no ways of comparing one person's satisfaction with another's. Nor is there any very solid basis for generalizing from the diminishing utility of a single commodity to the diminishing utility of total income. As one's scale of income increases, the manner of expenditure may change substantially. Some people may be so unimaginative that they simply consume more of the same thing or get more frequent models of the same products. Others will modify their standard of living, moving to a different sort of community or adopting new hobbies which afford them great pleasure of an entirely different sort from that which they experienced before.

Likewise the satisfactions from an income may vary with the duration of its receipt and the direction of change. A temporary large increase may mean only "more of the same" or fringe luxuries, whereas a person who is accustomed to a high standard of living would feel greatly deprived to give up items of consumption to which he has been accustomed. In any case, the satisfaction from larger incomes seems to increase by steps rather than smoothly. Everyone will have his own sequence of steps which he hopes to take, a larger house, a second house, more family cars, more expensive vacations, travel, different schools, more leisure, a different residential community, more help in and around the household. All these are real objectives for some, just as flashier and more frequent cars, larger televisions, more numerous items of high-style clothing, and more conspicuous consumption of various sorts are objectives for others.

Important though the subject of standards of consumption is for social improvement and in an appraisal of the ultimate significance of increasing productivity beyond a subsistence level, the varied nature of man's economic wants is beyond the scope of this analysis. The objective of maximum economic growth, herein assumed, is itself questionable from many standpoints, especially if it ignores or conflicts with qualitative improvements. But here it is sufficient to recognize that the differences in tastes among people and irregular decreases in the utility of successive increments of income for any one person make any assurance about measurements of the "ability" to pay taxes impossible. Though there will be broad agreement that a dollar to one family is more important than a dollar to another, there will not be agreement as to how much more important or, more precisely for tax purposes, how many dollars from the one will involve the same sacrifice as one dollar from the first. And so we are left to the play of political pressures and prejudices in the distribution of the tax burden, on which there will be more discussion in a later chapter.

In spite of the widespread acceptance of progressive taxation in both theory and practice, proportional taxation, though an arbitrary standard itself, has some theoretical support and the great practical advantage of certainty. James McCulloch effectively made the pragmatic argument in favor of proportional taxation in the middle of the last century when he wrote that departure from it, to progressive taxation, left one "at sea without rudder or compass" in the determination of specific standards. He noted further than once one adopts progressive taxation, "there is no amount of injustice and folly you may not commit." The experience of the intervening generations has fully confirmed McCulloch's judgment. The equitable argument for proportional taxation is derived, in a sense, from the pragmatic one. In the absence of any solid basis for determining a fair degree of progression, should not the services of government be presumed to be desired and hence priced, through taxes, in accordance with each citizen's general capacity for consumption? Would not proportional taxation in fact be consistent with the basic objective of ability to pay? Are not capacity and ability to pay taxes almost implicitly related proportionately to one's financial status? The ancient custom of tithing for churches might be thought of as in a sense sanctifying the proportionate standard with the wisdom of the ages.

In the actual evolution of our tax system, progressive taxation was not feasible until the introduction of individual income taxation in 1913, if one ignores the Civil War income tax and the brief attempt to establish it in 1894. Support for progressive taxation and the Sixteenth Amendment authorizing the Federal income tax were interrelated. The maximum of 7 per cent in 1913, a 6 per cent surtax added to a normal tax of 1 per cent, was thought by some to be extortionate and revolutionary. Emphatic assurances at the time that the tax would never exceed 10 per cent, when compared with the present 91 per cent, attest to McCulloch's prescience.

Originally the income tax was superimposed on the existing structure of customs and excises in order to provide the element of progression then deemed appropriate. It has since become the largest single source of revenue. In the process the basic income tax rate, not the progressive element, has inevitably come to provide well over 80 per cent of the total yield of the individual income tax. Repeal and reductions of various excise taxes have increased the importance of income taxation. Though the income tax is still the source of progression in our tax system, the total revenue demands have become so great that the progressive element, extreme though it is, is of very minor importance in terms of the entire tax yield. But in spite of its relatively minor revenue significance and the lack of any objective standard in its application, progressivity seems firmly embedded in our national tax system on social as well as economic grounds. Practical reform should be directed to make progression more rational, to curb its excesses, and to prevent the unfair escape of some categories of income from it.

"Benefit" Taxation—A Good Standard of Limited Application. The benefit principle of taxation is altogether different from the ability principle. It has limited application but, where appropriate, makes very good sense. When government services are of a quasi-commercial character, and especially when those who use the services can well afford to pay for them, it seems unfair to impose the burden of payment on general taxpayers. And with the general tax burden so heavy that it is repressive, it is uneconomic not to give what relief is possible by making special projects pay their own way.

The highway program is the most clear-cut example of benefit taxation. It could be and has been argued that some part of the cost should be attributed to defense and charged against the general

revenue through the Defense Department. A network of highways
no doubt has great military importance, just as it also has general
economic value of significance even to those who do not drive on it
or consume products transported over it. But no accurate basis has
been suggested to allocate the benefits and the costs. Even the
allocation of cost between the passenger cars and trucks which
actually drive on the roads has not yet been resolved. However, the
Congress is aware of the problem, and the report required by it
from the Bureau of Roads in January, 1961, may lead to better legislation.

Though there are unmeasurable benefits to nonusers, the fact
remains that direct users of the highways can pay the entire cost
through a gasoline tax and other charges related to use which are
modest compared with those in other countries and with the total
expenses of automobile ownership. The special highway trust fund,
with the gasoline and other taxes related to highway use paid into
it and expenditures limited to available funds, puts the highway
program on a sound basis and prevents it from becoming a runaway
charge on the general revenues.

The policy of tying particular expenditures to particular sources
of revenue is generally undesirable because it may lead to mis-
allocation of total resources, as changes in the designated revenues
will not be likely to correspond to desired changes in the associated
expenditure program. But when there is a clear case of particular
benefit, a ready source of revenue related to use, and an opportunity
to relieve the already overburdened general revenue from a charge
that is likely to rise substantially over the years, the advantages of
taxation on the benefit principle are overwhelming. The only misfortune is that there are not more programs with equally appropriate user charges. Additional special charges for all aviation fuel
or other user charges to help finance the airways program would be
equitable in relieving the general taxpayer of a charge which gives
special benefits to those who can afford to pay for them. Benefit
taxation or user charges would also help to redress the competitive
disadvantage of railroad transportation, which is subject to heavy
property taxes, in contrast to the Federal subsidies to air transportation.

Certainly quasi-commercial functions should be carried on a self-
sustaining basis, either by direct user charges or by taxation imposed

on the benefit principle. Opinions differ as to what should be considered a quasi-commercial function. In some countries many public
utilities are deemed to be noncommercial in character, and where
they are constructed to provide a foundation for economic development, in advance of an immediate pecuniary demand for them, their
temporary deficits may properly be a charge on the general budget.
But our own experience with private taxpaying utility companies in
this country should convince us that government activity in this
area should be of limited duration and that tax-absorbing functions
should be made taxpaying or income-producing activities as soon as
possible. Since most government functions cannot be financed by
user charges, it seems really wasteful to divert general revenue, so
urgently needed for general functions, to activities which could be
self-financing. The post office is a good example of a function which
should pay for itself; the effective lobbying of some commercial and
other users to thwart the imposition of reasonable charges shows the
difficulty of maintaining a sound principle.

Our social security system provides a special case of taxation
according to the benefit principle. The fact that it is on a con-
tributory basis has thus far been associated with restraint in its
scope. Comparisons with welfare programs in other countries, in
both Europe and Latin America, show how they may discourage
employment by their excessive benefits and costs when they are
financed entirely by taxes on employers. In this respect, the inclusion of self-employed people who are fully conscious of their own
tax payments may be useful; the self-employed are more aware of
the cost of their ultimate benefits than are employees whose contributions are made through payroll deductions. The combination of
quasi-insurance and quasi-benefit taxation should be rigorously
maintained, though even this method of financing will not necessarily assure moderation in the extension of the system.

Tax Policy for Economic Growth and Stability

Before turning to specific provisions of the tax laws and details of tax reform in subsequent chapters, we shall in this section
conclude the discussion of objectives of tax policy by considering
the two economic objectives of tax policy. The first question is the
influence of taxation on economic growth. Is there such a thing as

incentive taxation? Can taxes ever be a positive inducement to productive action, or is taxation always a deterrent, so that minimum restraint of economic growth is the highest attainable goal? The second problem is the proper role of tax policy in economic fluctuations, in alternating periods of boom and recession. To what extent should the policy of paying currently for government expenditures by taxation, which was presumed in the preceding section, be modified in the interests of economic stability? Just as there are conflicts between the objectives of fairness and simplicity, there are also conflicts between these first two objectives and the economic objectives; there are even conflicts between the two economic objectives themselves.

From the standpoint of long-term growth, the first issue turns on the relative importance of maintaining income for consumer purchases and maintaining incentives for work and investment. This is a subject of perennial controversy. Unfortunately, it is also one which lends itself to political distortion, since an emphasis on consumer buying power can be associated with people with small incomes while emphasis on incentives can be related to those with higher incomes.

Actually both consumer buying power and incentives for work and for investment are important. The United States owes much of its prosperity and growth to the concept that all the people can and should share generously in the national output. Our policies of high wages and large volume with low profit margins per unit of product rank well up with our technical and administrative "know-how" among the immaterial aids we can offer to other countries. Production by the many for the few has no place in our society. But policies to encourage mass distribution can be carried to excess and do much damage to the economy. Just as excessive wage increases either lead to inflation or price a product and the labor producing it out of the market, tax policies which unduly emphasize consumer buying power will ignore the incentives necessary for the effective management and the capital investment which are essential for increasing productivity and higher real wages.

In our sort of dynamic economy, it must never be forgotten that it takes initiative and risk-taking to develop new products and industries. We have not reached our present level of activity under business management which waited passively for customers to send in orders. The fact that there is unutilized capacity is not a valid reason for urging that consumer income alone needs bolstering. The high level of capital investment, even in periods of recession, testifies to the vitality of our economy and the willingness of management to look ahead in spite of temporary surplus capacity. New investments come from management decisions to introduce new products or processes, to expand capacity, or to replace old equipment with more efficient items.

Our system does not depend alone on consumer demand. A tax system predicated on the false assumption that it does might so stultify the spirit of enterprise and the availability of funds for investment that our system would degenerate into something approaching stagnation.

In the next chapter, figures on the distribution of the income tax burden are given and the pattern of tax rates is analyzed. It is sufficient here to discuss in somewhat more general terms the subject of incentives and long-term growth.

It seems generally correct to say that taxation by itself represses both activity and investment. Though, as previously noted, a wise combination of government expenditure and taxation is, on balance, conducive to economic development, it is the government expenditures which provide the base for development. Taxation to finance the expenditures does not in itself lead to development. In fact the taxation must be wisely arranged lest its own repressive effects nullify the good done by useful expenditures.

Income taxation directly reduces the net reward of effort or investment. Excise taxation increases the cost of a taxed article or service. By reducing net rewards or by increasing costs, taxation is repressive. The extent of the repression will depend on the form of the taxation as well as the total tax burden. A tax on the spending of income is generally less repressive than a tax on the earning of income in the first place. But if we get less, directly or indirectly, for our efforts or risk-taking, we are less likely to push our efforts to the same degree; leisure and noneconomic activities are made relatively more attractive. There are, of course, notable exceptions to this proposition.

In a society, primitive or modern, where the customary standards of living are maintained by relatively small efforts which leave much time for leisure or indolence, taxation which reduces incomes or in-

creases living costs and thereby impinges on the traditional standard of personal consumption may stimulate enough extra effort to
maintain the ordinary way of life. Such reactions would be
analogous to the decreased activity which is often described as
occurring among a primitive people when wage scales are raised; if
three days' work a week will provide the income to live in the
customary manner, only three days' work will be done. An increase
in a basic tax, perhaps a tax on salt, in such a society would be likely
to produce extra effort out of the margin of free time to prevent a
reduction in the manner of living.

In our own society, somewhat analogous reactions may occur to
protect a customary standard of living unless the increase in taxation is so drastic as to make such attempts futile and foredoomed to
failure. Income tax rates ranging about 50 per cent would appear
seriously to discourage if not to preclude increases in efforts intended
to offset inroads made by tax increases in a personal standard of
living. The $100,000-a-year man of 1929 cannot expect by overtime
work to earn the $544,000 which he would need in 1960 to maintain
the same real income. But a person subject to tax rates which are
still short of prohibitive may work overtime or carry a second job to
maintain his standard of living. Higher taxes may make a professor
do more consulting in summer vacations or write for compensation
rather than read and meditate. They may make an investor buy
riskier securities to maintain a customary net income if he does not
retreat into riskless investment and live on his capital.

Observations on the effects of higher taxes within our own experience are of limited value. Inflation has had a much more serious
impact on people with small and medium incomes than tax increases during the past generation, and the consequences of higher
taxes are submerged by the consequences of inflation for those
whose tax rates do not go above 20 or 30 per cent. The chances of
really significant observations are further reduced by the fact that,
for most wage earners, increases in wage rates have equaled or
exceeded price increases so that there has not been a pressure of
reduced standards of living. And most retired people, who have
been hardest hit by the inflation, simply do not have the opportunity for extra gainful employment.

Adam Smith described the unusual effects of an excise tax on the
capacity of stills in increasing the efficiency of distilleries. Since the

tax was on the capacity of the contents, and not on the output, stills were made shallower and shallower as the tax increased, thus increasing the amount of liquid which could be distilled in a given period of time. But such increased efficiency is an unlikely result of taxation. Technological obsolescence is not typically created by taxation, and it is a sad reflection on the ingenuity of entrepreneurs when an improvement is made only to achieve tax reduction when it would not be thought of for its inherent cost reduction. Perhaps, however, a potential saving in taxes yields a special satisfaction and hence is a stronger stimulant than other potential economies.

In spite of such situations as those just described, it seems generally true that taxation by itself is repressive rather than stimulating. To a greater or lesser extent, both work and investment are undertaken for pecuniary rewards, and when the rewards are reduced directly or indirectly by taxation, the balance is tipped to some extent against work and investment. The speed and the extent of the reaction will vary with individuals and with all the attending circumstances. The phrase so frequently used by economists must be applied here: "All other things being equal," higher taxes will produce less economic effort and less investment.

An appraisal of the force of nonpecuniary incentives, which help to maintain activity in spite of tax increases, opens up areas as yet largely undeveloped in economic analysis. The importance of satisfactions from creative work or full application of one's abilities, power, prestige, social pressures, the avoidance of idleness, duty, participation in group activities—all these are significant to different people in different degrees. Their existence and importance make a mockery of the proverbial "economic man" who was presumed to make all his decisions among alternative employments and between additional employment and leisure on the basis of relative net monetary rewards. Though we cannot measure these other satisfactions or their strength as incentives, it is naïve to ignore them. Both introspection and observation must convince anyone of the effectiveness of rewards which are unrelated to economic gain. This is especially true for human effort and activity. To a much lesser extent it is true of individual investments. Landownership as a symbol of social status has influenced investment in various countries and even in this country, and the social acceptability of different forms of investment varies within a particular group in a manner similar to, though considerably less than, the social acceptability of different forms of employment. Even among listed stocks there are still some industries which some passive investors would not consider holding, as, for example, stocks in liquor companies, regardless of their investment caliber.

But though it is foolish to pretend that economic motives are controlling, it is equally foolish to ignore them. To varying degrees with different people and under different circumstances monetary incentives are important; in many instances they are dominant. They seem, unfortunately, to be the sole motives in some conscienceless and predatory economic activities. The fact that most people are offended by an individual who is motivated exclusively by economic gain is itself evidence that for most of us the economic motive is intuitively placed in perspective. But political action, including tax legislation, which ignores monetary incentives runs the risk of self-defeat. It is ironic that differences in net individual earnings in communist Russia are greater than they can be in our capitalist country. Such a situation reflects not only the greed of a selfish dictatorship but also the realization that, contrary to basic communist dogma, economic motives are important and must be satisfied in the interests of national development and to secure a desired allocation of human activity.

Though a high level of taxation by itself is repressive, differences in the relative tax burdens on different sorts of work or investment may actually increase the total amount of work or investment in the areas which are relatively better off. For example, if all wages were subject to a 50 per cent tax except those paid to people working on the construction of churches or highways or aluminum yard furniture, which were taxed at 10 per cent, there would doubtless be a great increase in the number of people seeking employment in the jobs subject to the much lower tax rate. Relatively lighter tax loads can lead to absolute increases in the favored pursuits.

Differential tax rates on incomes from property can also redirect the flow of capital to such an extent that the amount available in the areas subject to low taxes will be greater than it would be under generally low tax rates, even though the total capital available for all purposes is reduced. The special deductions and allowances on investment in oil and mining very likely have increased the total flow of capital to these fields over what it would have been with uniform taxation at a lower rate.

Differential tax rates or other special tax concessions can be very powerful forces, and the higher the total level of taxation, the greater is the room for differential treatment. A 50 per cent reduction or even complete tax exemption is not very significant if the general tax rate is 10 per cent, but it would be tremendously important if the general rate were 90 per cent.

The possibility of redirection of effort and investment by differential tax rates, even to the point of actually increasing the total activity in some areas by large differentials, is tempting both to lobbyists for special interests and to legislators or policy officials of the executive branch of the government concerned with fostering certain parts of the national economy. The temptation should be resisted except in the most extreme situations. Every differential rate or special deduction granted becomes a precedent for others, with a progressive reduction in the tax base and ever-higher rates necessary on "ordinary" sources of income to secure the necessary total revenue. The acceptance of the idea of tax favors for some is a long step toward the acceptance of a scheme of tax penalties for others. Such a system would be subject to drastic shifts with political changes and with changes in attitudes toward different industries and activities.

The limited application of five-year amortization of defense facilities during World War II and the Korean hostilities is a good example of differential tax treatment in this country. Within limits, this was a useful alternative to direct government construction and ownership of plants and equipment, but it was applied too broadly and continued too long. It served as a precedent for many proposals for similar concessions to induce investment for other purposes. To bring in new industries, to retain old industries, to foster adoption of antipollution equipment, to provide housing for migratory workers are but a few of the worthwhile objectives for which five-year amortization was proposed. Once it is made available for other than defense needs strictly interpreted, additional applications can be extended by a succession of logical analogies to the point where it would be regarded as discrimination against an industry not to give it special amortization.

In brief, taxation by itself is repressive, though differential tax rates favoring some activities may in those areas more than offset the generally restrictive effects of a high tax burden. However, the more broadly the advantageous rates are made available, the less effective they become until the system becomes one in which the regular rates become a penalty rate rather than a norm from which concessions are made.

It has already been noted that a judicious combination of expenditure and taxation can provide a base for economic growth—indeed is necessary to finance minimum government services which are essential for any society or economy. It is not appropriate here to discuss the variety of expenditures which, in different situations, may be beneficial. It is sufficient to note that the higher the expenditures, the higher the tax load must be if destructive inflation is to be avoided. And, to repeat a previous statement, the higher the tax load, the greater the danger that its repressive effects will begin to outweigh the benefits of expenditures.

There does not appear to be any universal point at which a total tax burden becomes destructive, as is sometimes asserted. This point was recognized briefly in the preceding section. Much depends on the structure of the tax system. A low total burden could be destructive if the taxes fell especially heavily on increases in incomes from year to year or on risk investment. A much higher burden can be carried successfully if the tax system is skillfully designed to minimize the restrictions which it inevitably imposes. The higher the total burden, the greater the need for care in the design of the tax system. At levels anything like those now prevailing, particular care is needed.

The tax system we now have is peculiarly bad in repressing economic growth. It might be made worse by conscious effort, but it is hard to see how it could have happened to become as bad as it is. Fortunately, there is fairly widespread agreement on the few major reforms which need to be made. This should mean that they can be made in the national interest and without partisan advantage or controversy. Subsequent chapters present the analysis of what should and should not be done. There remains, however, the second general issue of tax policy stated at the start of this section, the question as to whether taxes may at times be permitted to fall short of government expenditures in the interests of economic stability.

Taxes and expenditures do not have to be in balance. All government bodies may borrow within their debt limits and credit standings, and national governments may even finance their outlays by creating new money directly or indirectly through the banking system. If long continued, borrowing is the road to inflation and financial ruin. Even those most enthusiastic about large-scale government programs recognize that they should in general be financed by equivalent taxation. There are, however, differences of opinion about the extent of latitude which may be permitted in periods of economic recession.

Attitudes toward deficits have changed greatly during the past thirty years. Until the 1930s, all deficits were quite generally regarded as signs of irresponsible government finance. In many countries deficits have been associated with and presumably were the cause of declines in and eventual destruction of the value of a currency. Common sense reinforced the record of history with the belief that a spendthrift nation, like a spendthrift family, would end up in financial ruin. In 1932, even Roosevelt made budget balancing a principal issue of his campaign. Nor were there at that time any theories of antidepression deficit spending or compensatory fiscal policy to give a semblance of intellectual respectability to deficits.

By the middle 1930s, new ideas had been advanced to rationalize the continuing deficits of the depression period. Since inadequate spending was a phenomenon of a depression, government action to inject new spending into the economy was proposed to induce expansion. Deficit spending was considered preferable to expenditures financed by taxation because the deficits presumably mobilized otherwise idle funds or, better yet as it was thought, led to the creation of new money. The ultimate rationalization came in the concept of the mature or stagnant economy—the economic fallacy which has been responsible for more unsound policies than any other during the past generation.

A mature economy was thought of as one in which there was a deficiency of potential investments or an excess of savings. Thus savings, to the extent that they exceeded the demand for new capital funds of all sorts, were deemed to be uneconomic and antisocial. This idea in turn gave an economic justification for highly progressive and even confiscatory income tax rates, because savings were thought to be proportionately larger in higher incomes. If excess savings could be taxed away and spent by the government, it was thought that the process would simply put otherwise idle funds back into circulation. It would not only not be repressive; it would actually offset the stagnation that would otherwise occur because of the lack of use for the desired savings. This theoretical justification for confiscatory tax rates reinforced the bias of many economists to use high taxes to redistribute income on social or noneconomic grounds and gave a basis for political attacks on wealth and business.

In spite of large and continuing deficits, unemployment persisted through the 1930s and was finally relieved only by the many military and civilian demands which arose in World War II. In the opinion of many observers, the policies which grew out of the mistaken idea that Western civilizations were economically mature was to a considerable extent responsible for the long continuation of the depression in the United States. A temporary condition of excess savings and deficient investment might better have been overcome by attempting to encourage investment rather than to repress savings or artificially foster consumption.

During World War II there was universal agreement that deficits should be kept to a minimum under the great inflationary pressures arising from war demands and shortages. But those who had previously been under the spell of the mature-economy fallacy expected that the postwar period would need recurring, if not continuous, deficits along with tax policies designed to reduce the potentiality for savings. However, a new aspect of the theory of deficit financing arose with emphasis on tax reduction, instead of increased expenditures, to produce deficits. The high level of taxation and the system of withholding for income taxes also made a temporary tax reduction a feasible method of creating a deficit. The tax reductions to increase consumption were thought to be quicker in their effect than expenditure programs. Perhaps there was also some belated recognition that the "make-work" projects of the 1930s were inherently wasteful and that spending programs once undertaken were hard to reverse and might carry deficits on for too long into a recovery period.

The theory of "compensatory fiscal policy" received wide attention in the decade following the end of the war. In brief, it advocated budget surpluses in boom times and deficits in recessions.

Under it, the government would, on balance, withdraw funds from the private sector of the economy in periods of high activity and thus exercise a restraining influence. In slack periods, by deficit spending, it would inject new funds into the system and thus provide an expansionary influence. Some of the supporters of the theory thought that it should take the place of traditional central bank operations to influence the supply of credit. Others regarded it as a logical and necessary complement to monetary policy.

Consistent with the emphasis on tax reduction as a means to create a deficit during a recession, a tax system which by its nature produces large swings in revenues between boom and recession periods is considered desirable as part of a compensatory fiscal policy. Large and rapid reductions in tax receipts during a recession and large and rapid increases in boom periods are thought of as adding to the so-called "built-in stabilizers." From this standpoint, the most desirable tax system would appear to be the one whose yield fluctuates to the greatest possible extent between periods of boom and recession. This sort of tax system is likely to place undue emphasis on progressive aspects of the income tax which is especially bad from the standpoint of economic development. There is thus a conflict between short-run and long-run economic objectives. Even more immediately, a large reduction in tax receipts in a recession is likely to mean that the deficit created thereby will be too large and continue too long into the subsequent recovery period.

The experience of 1958–1959 demonstrated this unmistakably. A deficit of over 12 billion dollars, the major part of which arose from a decline in receipts, made many of the proponents of compensatory fiscal policy realize that it can be carried too far. The lag in the recovery of receipts meant that the deficit ran through the fiscal year beginning two months and ending fourteen months after the turn around in economic activity in April, 1958. A deficit lasting so long was taken as evidence of irresponsible, rather than compensatory, fiscal policy, with consequent international repercussions and difficulties in the management of the national debt. A balanced budget for the fiscal year 1960 was particularly important to overcome the damage to confidence from a too long continuation of the deficit arising from the 1957–1958 recession.

The dangers of excesses in deficit spending from the application of compensatory fiscal policy were dramatically shown by attempts continuing as late as May, 1958, to reduce taxes by up to 6 billion dollars—when a deficit of 8 billion to 10 billion dollars was already projected for the next fiscal year and, as later became apparent, *after* the economy had started its recovery. The persistence and undue emphasis on deficit spending in a recession probably come to a considerable extent from continuing vestiges of the mature-economy concept. This notion gave an economic basis to those who favored large increases in government activity and were at best skeptical of the vitality of the private segment of the economy. Each successive recession since the war has perhaps been regarded by some critics of existing policies as at last providing evidence that their belief in an inherently stagnant economy would be vindicated and massive government intervention justified. There have, to be sure, been universal disavowals of any desire for recession, but there has also been an eager advocacy of government action on a scale which indicated little confidence in the potential for a resumption of growth in the private sector of the country's economy.

The postwar period has demonstrated the error of the mature-economy idea of the 1930s. It is especially ironic that England, where the concept originated, has been most persistently plagued by a shortage of savings to meet the demands for new capital. The needs of countries in all stages of economic development for additional capital have fairly conclusively demonstrated that the apparent excess of savings in the 1930s was a phenomenon of the depression.

The direct impact of a deficit of even 2 billion or 3 billion dollars in an economy with a gross national product of 500 odd billion dollars is relatively small compared with some of the other variables in the economy. Ordinary fluctuations in purchases of durable consumer goods, in business investment in plant and equipment and in inventories, in construction, and in state and local expenditures may be substantially larger. Even changes in the composition of the Federal debt, under a balanced budget, as in a shift, for example, between savings bonds and Treasury bills held by banks, may have a greater direct impact on the supply of money and the use of funds than a 2-billion- or 3-billion-dollar budget deficit. But the Federal budget has a symbolic value with indirect consequences far more important than its direct effects. It is a symbol of sound and responsible government finance. Deficits at a time of high-level activity call to mind inflation and depreciation of the currency. They suggest that government expenditures are out of control and that small deficits will be followed by larger deficits with greater inflationary consequences. Balanced budgets in good times are a necessary and important objective of policy.

But balanced budgets do not assure a sound currency. In the past decade we have been confronted with what is so aptly called the "cost-push" type of inflation. The wage-price spiral can operate under a balanced budget, and even a moderate budget surplus cannot overcome it; only a credit policy so restrictive as to create substantial unemployment can nullify the inflationary effects of wage increases which are not justified by increases in productivity. A discussion of the variety of inflationary forces goes far beyond the subject of tax reform and will not be developed further here. It is enough to recognize that balanced budgets, important though they are in times of reasonably full economic activity to prevent an inflationary force which a deficit would create under those conditions, are not enough to prevent inflation arising from other forces. In this sense, undue emphasis on a balanced budget may distract attention from the other causes of inflation and give a false sense of assurance. Fortunately, budget deficits and surpluses have come to be seen in fairly good perspective in recent years.

The proper role of tax and budget policy to counteract recession may be summarized briefly. During a recession tax receipts inevitably decline, regardless of the structure of the tax system. The greater the reliance on the corporation income tax, on high-bracket income and capital gains taxes, and on excises on postponable durable goods, the greater will be the decline in receipts. If a budget is balanced or shows a modest surplus prior to a recession, it will thus show a deficit as economic activity declines. A balance can be restored only by increasing taxes or reducing expenditures. Neither of these actions appears to be desirable at a time of recession because either one would tend still further to reduce the total flow of spending in the economy. Increased taxes would reduce the funds available for private spending, and reduced government expenditures would directly curtail total outlays, with no expectation of offsetting increases in private spending. Expenditures in a recession are in fact likely to be increased through relief programs or the acceleration of construction or procurement activities. Thus some deficit spending appears inevitable in a time of recession.

If kept within limits and promptly stopped during the subsequent recovery and expansion, a deficit may be a corrective factor in a period of economic slack. However, a tax structure designed to give maximum fluctuation in tax receipts is likely to be especially repressive on long-term growth. Moreover, a too ready acceptance of deficits and conscious actions to increase them voluntarily are likely to produce deficits so large that they will not be promptly wiped out during recovery periods. And continued deficits will add to the other inflationary pressures which may be inherent in our economic system. Deficits have a symbolic danger even greater than their direct fiscal impact. They can undermine confidence and jeopardize a nation's currency and, with it, a nation's financial and social system. In brief, deficits are stimulants which arise automatically in recessions, but they are very dangerous stimulants and must be used with restraint. If they are too readily accepted and actively sought, they, like physical and mental stimulants used to excess by individuals, can become totally destructive.

Chapter 2 THE INDIVIDUAL INCOME TAX

Rates—Split Income—Personal Exemptions—
Dependents—Withholding—Tax Exemption

The individual income tax is by far the most important single source of revenue in the United States. Its yield rose from 30 billion dollars in fiscal 1953 to 41 billion in 1960, in spite of a reduction in rates of about 10 per cent in 1954. Its relative importance also increased from less than half of net budget receipts of the Federal government prior to fiscal 1957 to more than half in 1957 and later years. This increasing importance reflects the great increase in personal income which rose from 273 billion dollars in calendar 1952 to over 400 billion by the spring of 1960. By contrast, corporate profits, the basis for the corporation income tax which is the second largest source of revenue, fluctuated around the 40-billion-dollar level throughout the decade of the 1950s starting at 40.6 billion in 1950 and averaging 40.9 billion for the 10-year period. No other country in the world places such great reliance on income taxation.

The individual income tax is regarded by some as the ideal tax, sometimes with an enthusiasm that suggests the tax is thought of as positively good and not merely the least objectionable way to secure necessary revenue. The presumed advantages of income taxation rest principally on its greater adaptability to the varying abilities of different individuals to pay their fair share of government expenditures. Personal exemptions, allowances for dependents, itemized deductions, and progressive rates may all be varied to meet current social and economic objectives and changing ideas of equity, or so it is presumed by the most ardent advocates of income taxation.[1] Though one may be skeptical of the alleged attractions of the tax, it must be accepted on practical grounds as an effective tax already in existence.

The problem in this country with reference to income taxation now is to try to unwind some of the overrefinement and overelaboration which has developed during the years. Proposals are constantly being made for additional deductions or for ways to average one's income for a period of years, or even over a lifetime. The tax is already too complicated; many of the proposals sincerely advanced to make it fairer would make it monstrously complex. Fortunately the momentum appears to be in the direction of simplification rather than additional refinement in the tax.

This and the two following chapters are devoted to problems in individual income taxation. Rates, split income, personal exemptions, and tax-exempt income are covered in the present chapter. The next chapter deals with various problems in connection with compensation and earned income, including expense accounts, fringe benefits, pensions, deferred compensation, and retirement income. The last of the three chapters discusses the deductions allowed in computing taxable income of individuals, after first considering the discrimination between homeowners and renters and the possible ways to eliminate it.

Substantial general tax reduction, as already noted, does not seem possible in the foreseeable future, nor is it necessarily needed to remove the disincentive aspects of the present income tax. A reform which combines a revision of individual income tax rates with a closing of loopholes to prevent present inequities and abuses would restore tax morale and make the total tax burden supportable without undue damage. This is the most important single item in tax

---

[1] The flavor of affection for the income tax is revealed in a side remark in an excellent article which concludes regretfully that income taxation is not suitable as a major revenue source in newly developing countries and includes the comment that realization of the fact "will help to dispel some of the frustrations of the tax experts who accept overseas assignments, and make those who remain at home aware of the favorable environment in which they operate." David E. Shirley, "Income Taxes for Lesser Developed Nations?," *National Tax Journal*, vol. XII, p. 265, September, 1959. It is discouraging to realize that some tax experts feel frustrated if they are not constantly creating new and bigger income taxes throughout the world.

reform. This and the two following chapters present the elements of a reform package of this sort in the course of a general review of the controversial issues in the individual income tax.

Individual Income Tax Rates

The first step in the development of our present virtually confiscatory individual tax rates (50 per cent at $16,000 of taxable income, 75 per cent at $50,000, and 91 per cent at $200,000) took place in 1932 and arose out of confusion over the fairness of different forms of tax increases. The results of the initial error were reinforced and compounded by the punitive attitude toward wealth in the New Deal period. Since that time, there has been growing recognition of the perverse effects of very high tax rates, even by those who earlier had supported them as a matter of social policy. However, in spite of the change of opinion and the fact that the high rates bring in only a very small fraction of the total revenue, selective rate reduction applicable only to the upper brackets without other changes in the law does not seem feasible or appropriate. The history of our individual income tax rates is shown in Appendix A.

In 1932, the individual income tax rates ranged from 1½ per cent (or 1⅛ per cent after an earned income credit) to 25 per cent. With minor changes, this had been the level of rates since 1925, when the reductions after World War I were finally completed. It was decided in 1932 to increase taxes to reduce the deficit—an action which will probably not ever again be proposed in a depression year by any political group. But the bipartisan action was taken then by a Democratic House and a Republican administration and Senate. As is inevitable, substantial additional revenue had to come from the bottom-income brackets, because that is where the bulk of the income is. The lowest tax rate was increased from 1½ to 4 per cent, and the question immediately arose as to the appropriate increase in the top bracket, which had been 25 per cent.

This is the point in the history of our tax legislation where the fetish of progressive taxation created confusion, and the confusion led to what has thus far been an irreversible error in tax policy. It was apparently thought that, since the bottom rate was increased by about 150 per cent from 1½ to 4 per cent, the top rate should be increased by at least this same proportion. It was increased from 25 to 63 per cent, almost exactly 150 per cent. The error arose from looking at the increase in *rates* alone. Actually, this increase reduced the net income in the bottom bracket only from 98½ cents of the pretax dollar to 96 cents, or by a little over 2½ per cent. At the top, the increase in the rate reduced the net income from 75 to 37 cents, or by over 50 per cent. The pattern established in 1932 would have pushed the top rates far above 100 per cent if it had been followed in the subsequent increases which have brought the bottom rate to its present 20 per cent. The top rate would indeed have gone to 315 per cent! In practice, the need for a ceiling somewhat below 100 per cent has been recognized. The highest rate was 94 per cent in 1944–1945, acceptable and probably desirable as a temporary measure during a war when controls are general and austerity and pecuniary sacrifice should, to the extent possible, be enforced on those who might have the poor taste to seek personal gain when others are making supreme sacrifices for their country. It is the continuation of the 91 per cent rate fifteen years after the war under different economic and social circumstances, not the wartime peak, which is damaging.

The confusion in 1932 arose from the failure to distinguish between absolute and proportional increases in tax rates and between changes in taxes and changes in net incomes after taxes. Superficially it might seem that, if one accepts progressive taxation as a standard of fairness, each increase should itself be progressive and that even a proportional increase in rates would somehow be inequitable. But a very little analysis shows, as in the action in 1932, that even a *proportional* increase in rates, when applied on top of a rate structure which is already *progressive*, is itself *highly progressive* in its effects. Even a *uniform* absolute increase in rates, on top of a progressive structure, is progressive in its effects. If, for example, all rates were raised by one percentage point when rates ranged from 10 to 90 per cent, the effect would be to reduce net income from 90 to 89 cents for each dollar in the bottom bracket, or by 1.11 per cent, while at the top the net income was reduced from 10 to 9 cents, or by 10 per cent.

When a reduction of rates is considered, the reverse of the concept adopted in 1932 is likely to be advanced by some of those active in a political debate. Even a uniform reduction in rates gives progressively greater improvement at the top bracket. A reduction in the bottom tax rate from 20 to 19 per cent would increase net income from 80 to 81 cents, or by 1.25 per cent, while the same 1-cent increase in net income from 10 to 11 cents at the top bracket, with a reduction in the top rate from 90 to 89 per cent, would increase net income by 10 per cent. A proportionate reduction in rates would have an even more pronounced effect. Thus a 10 per cent reduction in rates would reduce the bottom rate from 20 to 18 per cent, increasing net income from 80 to 82 cents on each dollar of income, or by 2.5 per cent, while it would reduce the 90 per cent rate to 81 per cent, increasing net income from 10 to 19 cents, or by 90 per cent. The ultimate in demagoguery is to use an absolute increase in net income as a standard; thus for a family with $100 of taxable income after exemptions and deductions, complete exemption from tax would increase net income by only $20, and any greater increase to any other family might be criticized as unfair.

In fact and theory, changes in taxes can be analyzed from the standpoint of absolute and proportionate changes in tax rates and absolute and proportionate changes in net incomes. Each of the approaches has some significance. In a controversy, each protagonist will select the point of view which is most likely to support his own position and many will attempt to discredit their opponents as being unfair to the proverbial "little man." In the absence of full understanding of the interrelationships of the alternative approaches, what should be an objective analysis is likely to degenerate into an exercise in what may be thought of as the "political arithmetic of tax rates."

The advocates of rate revision in the middle and upper brackets must do so on the grounds that it is necessary to reverse the inequity created by confiscatory rates, to remove the perverse economic and social consequences caused by very high rates, and to arrive at a system of rates generally viewed as fair. The opponents of the rate revisions may be expected to reverse their standard of analysis and argue in terms of the effects of rate changes on net incomes after taxes—the very point of view which they ignored when the rate increases were being adopted in the first place.

The facts concerning the relative importance as sources of revenue of the different brackets of the income tax have become familiar over the years, and yet whenever repeated they are often still a source of surprise. Out of the total revenue of over 40 billion dollars from the individual income tax, approximately 6 billion, or between one-sixth and one-seventh, come from the progressive rates in the tax. The basic rate of 20 per cent produces about 85 per cent of the total revenue. As has been said many times before, the individual income tax, when called upon to yield vast amounts of revenue during World War II, became a mass tax rather than a class tax. Between 1939 and 1943, the number of taxable individual income tax returns increased tenfold, from 4 million to 40 million. When bulk revenue is required, it must come from bulk income.

The tax yield of the highest bracket rates is itself a small fraction of the small fraction produced by the entire progressive element in the tax. All rates above 50 per cent, for example, yield only about 800 million dollars, or less than 2 per cent of the total individual income tax. By contrast each percentage point of the basic 20 per cent rate yields more than twice as much, or 1.8 billion dollars. Thus, it would cost no more revenue to cut all elements of progression in half than it would to reduce the basic rate from 20 to 18 per cent. Or as much revenue would be lost by reducing the basic rate from 20 to 16 per cent as would be lost by completely eliminating all progression above the basic rate. Comparisons such as these emphasize the fact that rate relief in the middle and upper brackets to restore a sound rate structure would involve relatively minor direct revenue loss. But the same comparisons also show how expensive it would be to have general rate reductions.[2] Together they show the need for a combination involving both rate revision and the removal of special privileges to make a politically acceptable package of reform legislation. The distribution of taxable individual income and tax liability by size of income is given in Appendix B.

One other set of facts is helpful in giving the background of the

[2] The fact that the bottom rate of the income tax begins at 20 per cent does not mean that the tax is any less progressive than it would be if the bottom rate were 10 or 15 per cent. Because of personal exemptions and deductions, there is an element of untaxed income for everyone. Whether the beginning rate is 10 or 20 per cent, the range of effective rates of tax on incomes thus always begins at zero and extends up to the ceiling rate. A higher beginning rate influences the speed of progression in the effective rate as incomes increase above the tax-exempt level, but progression in the effective rate always ranges from zero to the ceiling.

individual income tax. It is often noted that taxable income is less than half of total personal income. Though this suggests widespread evasion, it really indicates generous personal exemptions and deductions. The figures for 1959, the most recent official estimate released, put the components into perspective. The detail is given in Appendix C. It can be summarized briefly as follows: The 383 billion dollars of personal income is first reduced to 337 billion by a series of adjustments to make it comparable to the concept of taxable income. The biggest single adjustment is the elimination of 27 billion dollars of transfer payments (largely social security benefits and veterans' payments); the elimination of nontaxable imputed rent, interest, food consumed by farmers, and the like; and the addition of employees' social security contributions and net capital gains. Of the 337 billion dollars remaining, 81 billion is offset by the $600 personal exemptions and 41 billion by itemized or standard deductions. This reduces personal income to 215 billion dollars; of this 20 billion is reported on nontaxable returns. Of the remaining 195 billion, 165 billion is reported taxable income. This leaves a gap of 29 billion dollars, which includes income of persons not required to file tax returns, estimating errors in personal income and sampling errors in the *Statistics of Income,* and income of tax evaders, including an estimated 4.4 billion dollars of interest and 1.2 billion of dividends not accounted for on tax returns. Significant though evasion may be, the notable conclusion from this analysis is the large and identifiable amounts of personal income eliminated from the tax base by established tax policies. Several of these eliminations will be the subject of later discussion.

The recommendation for a tax reform which will reduce rates in the middle and upper brackets does not necessarily imply approval of either the sources or uses of all large incomes. It is made in spite of a strong personal distaste for and even revulsion against many of the sources and uses. Maneuverers and manipulators stand in unpleasant contrast to those who create more efficient processes of production and new products of intrinsic worth. The large incomes of some entertainers who hold an audience for the highly paid promoters of some products of trivial inherent worth seem a travesty on economic processes. But the subjective character of judgments in this area is clear. Opinions differ as to when an entertainer degrades himself and his audience and when composers and performers combine to give great delight to millions. And ostentatious and frivolous consumption is not made less objectionable by becoming more widespread as more and more people can afford to indulge in it.

But after one has given free rein to his feelings and prejudices regarding some of the sources and uses of wealth, one is left with the question as to whether income taxation should be used to redress what may be regarded as an unpleasant social and economic spectacle. More fundamentally, we are confronted with the question of whether we can even afford to jeopardize the income tax by using it for this purpose. Under high rates, maneuvers become more important and tax advisors proliferate. The devious takes precedence over the straightforward. The worthy are punished by high taxes along with the unworthy, with the notable difference that the truly worthy will not resort to all the devices which the unworthy use to "beat the game." Even if one were disposed to support confiscatory income tax rates because of objections to the sources of many large incomes, it seems that high tax rates imposed for this reason are self-defeating because they shift the balance away from productive and creative activity to the acquisitive and parasitic.

In the previous chapter the significance of a general high level of taxation was discussed and the importance of nonpecuniary incentives was emphasized. In this section, some more specific comments may be made about income tax rates, particularly marginal rates, that is, the rates applicable to the last increment of income. The point at which income tax rates either repress or divert activity has not been and perhaps cannot be determined. It seems unlikely, however, that a reduction in the 20 per cent bottom rate would make much difference in anyone's attitude or activity. But it is also notable that even some professors, whose marginal tax rates are presumably well short of 50 per cent, assert that taxes discourage them from taking on extra activities.

It is interesting for purposes of analysis to make the extreme assumption that a tax is wholly shifted forward and then ask whether even then one might refrain from making a speech, for example, for $500 subject to a 50 per cent income tax while he would do it for $250 if there were no tax. Logically, the tax should be irrelevant, since the net income is the same in both cases. It seems probable, however, that the tax is not really irrelevant, in spite of the logic to the contrary. The real alternative is not between $500 taxable at 50 per cent and $250 tax exempt, because in the actual environment there is a tax. Unless an individual relates a particular effort to a particular item of consumption, the new enlarged gross figure of $500 will probably come to be regarded as the true worth of the effort, which is then cut in half by the tax, making the effort less attractive than it would be for $250 in the absence of a tax. To the extent that people do react in this way, the tax would have a repressive effect. A contrary result would occur if an individual did not apply his marginal tax rate to mental calculations on increments of income. In this case the $500 taxable figure may even seem more attractive economically or as a matter of prestige than the $250 figure with no tax.

The impact of marginal income tax rates on action has certainly not been explored on any experimental basis, nor is it clear how it could be. It should be the subject of more systematic thought and discussion, however. In the meantime, everyone will have to draw his own conclusions as to the effects of various marginal tax rates on his own attitudes and activities and then attempt to decide whether his reaction is typical. The example of the compensation for a speech is, of course, not a good one for generalizations because the activity was itself a marginal one which could be rejected without interfering with a principal activity, contrary to the additional compensation which goes with a promotion in a business.

On balance, it seems probable that, as noted in the last chapter, marginal income tax rates are more likely to repress or divert activity than most other forms of taxes, even a flat rate of income tax which secures the same revenue. Certainly, a person would be less likely to be discouraged or diverted by the extra tax on extra income if he were taxed at a flat 25 per cent on all his income than if he paid the same total tax on a progressive scale with a 90 per cent bracket on the last increment of income. The implications of this simple comparison between a progressive and proportional tax are worth reflection; they emphasize the damage which may be done by taxation when it takes the form of highly progressive income taxation, with the form rather than the amount of tax being critical.

One final comment may be made about highly progressive income tax rates. Those subject to the great increase in marginal rates over the past generation have not only been prevented from sharing in the increase in general economic well-being, they have actually had their real net incomes reduced. No conceivable pay increases could have kept the incomes of the higher salaried groups even, let alone permitted them to participate in the general increase in economic welfare to which their activities and investments have so significantly contributed. It would have taken an income of $531,000 in 1959, for example, to give a net real income equivalent to $100,000 in 1929. The redistribution of income through progressive taxation is made clear by such figures, as well as the strength of the inducement to seek nontaxable or lower taxed forms of income.

It has become popular in recent years to say that high-bracket rates are not really onerous because they are not applied effectively to large incomes. Statistically this is correct if one includes all capital gains with income. The reasons why true capital gains should be regarded as quite separate from ordinary income are discussed in Chapter 5. The existence of tax-exempt bonds, the income from which also reduces the statistical averages, is unfortunate. They do give high-bracket taxpayers who own them an opportunity to reduce their effective tax rates. But they are of no significance to those who do not own them. An executive with a high salary but with little capital and little opportunity to save to buy any securities because of very high tax rates gets no tax relief from the existence of tax-exempt bonds.

Whatever the statistical averages may show, there are many individuals who have only ordinary fully taxable income, and for them the tax rates are fully effective. And even for those whose average rate might be less than expected because of tax-exempt income and capital gains, the marginal rate is still high on those parts of his income which are fully taxable, and it is the high marginal rate itself which is destructive. If a married man has a taxable income from salary of $100,000, he is subject to a marginal tax rate of 75 per cent, and he continues to be subject to it even if he has $200,000 of tax-exempt interest which would bring his average effective tax rate down to 18 per cent. The reduced average is interesting and significant for many purposes, but it does not in any respect reduce the significance of the 75 per cent marginal rate, which continues to be effective in discouraging and distorting the activities of the man subject to it. Too frequently the statistical average rate has been presented and used in analysis as though it made excessive rate schedules unimportant. Their significance cannot be brushed aside.

Split Income

Since 1948, married couples have been permitted to divide their total incomes for tax purpores. Under the progressive tax this gives a substantial tax saving to couples in the middle and upper income brackets if one of the two has most of the income. A salary of $30,000 treated as two incomes of $15,000 each pays a much lower tax. For very small and very large incomes there is no saving in taxes. A taxable income of $2,000 is subject to a 20 per cent tax, as are two incomes of $1,000 each. If one's income is so large that it is subject to the over-all ceiling of 87 per cent, whether divided or not, there is again no saving in taxes. Some tax programs advocate repeal of this provision.

The present provision grew out of the community-property concept in a few of our states, including California and Texas, which derived their law from the Continental European rather than English common law. Under the community-property concept, each spouse is deemed to have an equal interest in the income earned by either spouse or derived from property acquired by either after marriage. Even more significantly for family purposes, each spouse is deemed to have a half interest in property acquired after marriage, but the equal interest in income was the important fact for the Federal income tax. The courts held that the community-property concept was to be recognized for Federal income tax purposes under existing law. This gave great advantage to married couples in the middle-income brackets in community-property states. Residents of other states suddenly developed a distaste for their traditional concepts of property law, and several legislatures adopted the community-property concept to secure Federal income tax advantages for their residents.

The discrimination in Federal income tax burdens among residents of different states was intolerable. A statutory change to ignore the local property laws for Federal income tax purposes was never seriously attempted under the threat of filibuster from the representatives of community-property states; the constitutionality of such a provision has not been tested.

Prior to 1948, the administration at various times recommended that all married couples be required to file joint returns with no splitting of income. For the sake of emphasis, it seems appropriate to say quite bluntly that it is hard to imagine a more inequitable, immoral, and antisocial tax proposal. Its adoption would have imposed an annual progressive tax on the maintenance of the legal state of marriage. The tax on a combined income of $30,000 is more than the total tax on an income of $10,000 plus the tax on an income of $20,000. When each of two spouses have separate incomes from salaries or property, the proposal of the administrations prior to 1948 would have imposed the additional annual tax. Joint returns are required in England; as a result one hears the phrase "It is too bad they can't afford to get married" when referring to pleasant and respectable couples. Perhaps if such a proposal were ever adopted here, some states would authorize divorce on the ground that a continuation of the legal state of marriage had been made incompatible with sound family management.

Fortunately the Congress did not adopt the proposals made prior to 1948. Since the Congress was unwilling to attempt to ignore the community-property concept for Federal income tax purposes, it adopted the split-income approach to give uniformity of treatment. Split income can be justified only on this pragmatic basis. It is capricious by giving relief to married couples only in the middle- and upper-income brackets. But it is so much better than the alternative of compulsory joint returns that it should not be repealed unless income in the community-property states can be taxed to the person receiving it for Federal tax purposes, as is now done under the social security law for earned income.

The Size of Personal Exemptions

Two questions of policy arise in connection with the size of personal exemptions: the relative amounts for single people, married couples, and their dependents and the absolute level of the exemption. The uniform personal exemption was first adopted in 1944 at $500 and raised to $600 by the Eightieth Congress in 1948. Prior to 1944, the exemption was not uniform. In the original modern income tax law in 1913, a single person had an exemption of $3,000 and a couple had $4,000. This continued until 1917, when the exemptions were reduced to $1,000 and $2,000, respectively, with an additional $200 for dependents. In 1921, couples for the first time were given more favored treatment with a $2,500 exemption for net incomes of $5,000 or less, while the single exemption was kept at $1,000. The discrimination in favor of couples continued until 1944, with the single exception of 1941, when the exemption for a couple was only double that for a single person.

It is apparent that the attitude of Congress has not only denied the saying that "two can live as cheaply as one" but for over twenty years proceeded on the assumption that social policy or fairness, or both, required an exemption for married couples which was more than twice that of single people. The exemption for dependents, originally adopted in 1917 at $200, was increased to $400 in 1921 and continued at that level until 1942, when it was reduced to $350, before being raised to $500 in 1944 when all personal exemptions, for taxpayers, their spouses, and their dependents, were made uniform.

The balancing of tax exemptions among single people, married couples, and families does not rest on any statistical analysis of relative living expenses any more than does the absolute size of the exemption rest on an analysis of absolute living expenses. The distribution between single people and married couples simply arises from the legislators' sense of what is fit and fair and least subject to effective objections. The uniform exemption adopted in 1944 was a triumph for convenience and simplicity. Especially under the withholding tax on salaries and wages, it was a great simplification to classify taxpayers merely by the number of exemptions, regardless of marital or family status.

Objections to the present rule come, as might be expected, from single people, who argue that a family with three children does not need five times the income of a single person to maintain the same relative standard of living. Without resorting to budget figures, it seems probable that this objection is valid and that the present exemption is somewhat unfair. And yet it is less unfair than the situation up to 1944, when married couples had more than twice the exemption of a single person. There is no doubt an element of social policy in our treatment. Since precise justice is not possible because of differences in personal desires and satisfactions, such inequity as exists should be in favor of rather than against the family status which perpetuates society. On political grounds, this group is in the majority. The foregoing comments are not intended to brush aside the inequity to the single person. It appears to be a real one, but it is less than it was at one time, and there is no objective way to determine exactly what would be equitable.

Absolute Level of Exemptions

Any presumption that the personal exemption should be sufficiently high to allow for an untaxed income to cover a basic standard of living (however it may be defined) is both financially unrealistic and theoretically unjustified. With total government receipts running at over 31 per cent of national income in each of the years 1956 to 1959 (an all-time high proportion) and the Federal income tax by far the biggest single source of revenue, it cannot be used simply as a supplemental source of revenue intended to achieve ulterior social purposes.

The figures previously referred to on the distribution of taxable income and tax revenue show the inadequacy of middle and upper incomes to provide the needed revenue. It would, for example, have taken complete confiscation of all taxable incomes in excess of $3,000 to provide the 39 billion dollars provided by income taxes in 1959. The scale of government activity is so great that its high costs can be covered only when taxes are imposed on virtually all citizens.

Even if government services could be financed by taxes imposed solely on the rich, action to do so would be an unintended application of the supposedly repugnant slogan of "from each according to his ability; to each according to his need." Any denial of universal responsibility for the support of the government, except for exemption of the truly destitute, would be rejected if it were proposed directly as an abstract policy. It should not be accepted indirectly through the idea that the personal exemption should provide untaxed income sufficient to cover a basic standard of living even if it were financially possible to give such an exemption, which it is not. Essential government services are an integral part of everyone's standard of living as soon as society has passed beyond the stage of an isolated self-sufficient agricultural or nomadic community; they are no more a luxury than food, shelter, and clothing.

Over the generations the major problem of equity in taxation has been to move away from sole reliance on regressive consumption taxes which characterized despotic societies. That has now been accomplished. The present problem is to reverse the momentum which might carry a responsible democracy to a degree of confiscatory taxation which has been formally advocated only under communism and is not even applied there.

In spite of the foregoing analysis, which might seem to argue against any personal exemption, there are at least two reasons for it in the income tax law. Historically, the income tax was regarded as a supplemental source of revenue, intended to increase the fairness of an existing tax system which was based overwhelmingly on excise and customs and therefore quite likely to be regressive in the distribution of its burdens. The income tax was not adopted as the principal source of revenue. The $3,000 exemption in 1913 excluded the vast majority of the population. The income tax with large exemptions at that time added supplemental revenue and increased the equity of the entire system. As more and more reliance has been placed on the income tax, the exemption had to be reduced to bring in the necessary revenue, but the earlier sources of taxation still exist, albeit as a very minor part of the total system. Thus income taxation has never been dispassionately viewed as a sole source of revenue for an expensive government; if it could be so regarded, the attitude toward the personal exemption would probably be quite different, in unpredictable ways, from what it is now.

A personal exemption is also desirable from an administrative standpoint. Very small collections on very large numbers of returns are costly, since there is a minimum cost of each return which may exceed the tax due. Under the ability principle, if there were no exemptions, those with modest incomes would pay very modest taxes indeed under a progressive tax system. The personal exemption when first adopted made it unnecessary to file many returns with negligible taxes. But the objectives of administrative convenience may conflict with the objective of fairness and the desirability of having all citizens conscious of a direct tax obligation to the government. To achieve this latter result, it has been proposed that there be a requirement for universal filing of individual tax returns with a minimum flat fee which would at least cover the cost of processing. This proposal has merit from the standpoint of trying to make everyone aware that "government money" comes from taxpayers and not from a munificent abstract entity. Over the years, the retention of the $600 exemption, with the filing requirement related to the income and exemption of the taxpayer and not to the combined exemptions of his family, has brought about a situation approaching universal filing of income tax returns.

After all the foregoing discussion of theories about the desirable size of the personal exemption in the individual income tax, one must conclude that it has actually been determined on the pragmatic basis of revenue needs. It will probably always be thus. The only specific issue which may be before the country in the foreseeable future regarding exemptions would be the relative desirability of increasing the exemption or reducing the bottom tax rate at a time of general tax reduction or of decreasing the exemption or increasing the bottom tax rate if much additional revenue were needed. In 1956, the Democratic platform proposed an increase in the exemption but the Democratic candidate for President reviewed in a speech the alternatives and seemed to prefer a reduction in the bottom-bracket rate because it would maintain tax consciousness (and with it more responsible citizenship) and because it would be more readily reversible if additional revenue were needed later. One can only hope that these two good reasons will prevail in the future, in spite of the greater political appeal of an increase in the exemption which can be referred to as "relieving X millions of people from all income tax liability."

Definition of Dependents

A broad definition of dependents for income tax purposes would ordinarily be regarded as fair, humane, and consistent with good social policy by giving tax recognition to those generous impulses by which someone supports people not in his immediate family. But unfortunately, too broad definitions in the past have led to gross abuses through false claims or contrived arrangements by which tax savings to an individual exceeded the actual costs of support. A review of some of the changes in the law in recent years will indicate the nature of the problems involved in developing a fair and simple provision.

The most spectacular example of abuse is the "adoption" previously noted, of a foreign orphanage by a motion-picture actress in a country where the cost of support of a child was less than the reduction in taxes arising from an additional dependent for a high-bracket taxpayer in this country. Ostensible generosity under such facts merely represented a successful tax shenanigan at the expense of all other taxpayers. This loophole was closed by denying the dependency status to most aliens.

Parents, grandparents, children, and grandchildren should and do qualify as dependents. The tax law conforms to normal family relationships in this respect. Other relatives also would seem to be qualified under most standards of fairness. But what of friends with whom the sentimental ties may be as strong as with some relations and for whom there is less moral obligation for private assistance—should not a generous action of support, which may keep the person assisted from becoming a public charge, get the same tax treatment as the more obligatory assistance to a member of the family? When the problem is stated in those terms, it will almost universally be regarded sympathetically. The definition in the law was broadened in 1954 to include anyone supported in the taxpayer's household and then in 1958 was tightened to exclude, of all things, resident mistresses who under some interpretations might be considered to have inadvertently been qualified as dependents by the 1954 liberalization. With the tax subsidy to social immorality removed, a further problem remains as to whether attempts are being made to distort payments to domestic help into the "support" of a "dependent" with a consequent tax benefit from another personal exemption. Such action must clearly be prevented in the interests of fairness, but the potential abuse requires review by tax agents of the *bona fides* of personal relationships in questionable cases.

The denial of dependency status for nonresident aliens, except for those in contiguous countries, following the orphanage incident turned out to produce harsh results in cases where American residents living abroad adopted alien children. Under the laws of citizenship, these children, though legally adopted, did not become United States citizens until they were brought to this country, and for military service personnel and others it might be a matter of several years before occasion arose for a trip home. The law was amended in 1958 to ease this result by providing that adopted alien children would qualify as dependents if they were supported in the taxpayer's home, thus still denying dependency status to people supported in institutions or farmed out to others with a probable absence of a genuine family relationship. The continued denial of dependency status to aliens, other than adopted children, even if they are supported in the homes of United States citizens residing abroad is necessary in view of the potentiality of abuse through more or less honest confusion in the distinction between servants and dependents, with the known shortage of personnel of the Internal Revenue Service for enforcement purposes putting a strain on taxpayers' integrity.

The dependency status of students presents an especially difficult problem for which there appears to be no really satisfactory solution. Prior to 1954, a student, like any other dependent, became disqualified as a dependent if he had an income of $600 or more a year. This meant that if vacation or part-time earnings reached $600, the student's parents had one less dependency exemption with an increase in their own taxes of at least $120. For families in tax brackets above the beginning tax rate of 20 per cent, the increase in tax was commensurately more; at a 50 per cent marginal tax rate the increase in tax was $300. It was a peculiarly perverse tax law which meant that an extra dollar of earnings by a child toward his self-support, if it brought him to the total level of a $600 income, meant that the parents in most cases would have their own taxes increased by $120 or more. It was especially unfortunate to have young people first become aware of the application of the income tax through such an inequitable and uneconomic provision; a first impression of that sort hardly provided a basis for respect for the income tax law generally.

In recognition of these bad consequences, the Treasury recommended and the Congress adopted an amendment in 1954 which permits a parent to continue to claim a child as a dependent even if he has an income of over $600 as long as he is a student and as long as he meets the other tests for dependency including the provision of more than half the expenses by the parents or as long as he is under nineteen even if not a student. The student or dependent under nineteen, if he has an income of his own, must file a tax return and pay tax on his taxable income, but he also gets his own $600 exemption. Thus there are two personal exemptions for such students, a dependency exemption for the parents and a personal exemption for the student himself. This seems a reasonable way to dispose of the problem under the previous law of discouraging full efforts toward self-assistance by students. But the solution in turn created a new tax discrimination between students who are self-supporting and those who still qualify as dependents of their parents by receiving more than half their support from home.

This new discrimination is especially noted by graduate students who often do support themselves alone or with the help of their wives. A young couple has, of course, only two personal exemptions, regardless of the activity of the husband as a student. If the student were supported by his parents under the new rule, they would still claim him as a dependent with a $600 personal exemption and the student would also get his own $600 exemption on his own income. But in the situation where the student does not get enough help from home to qualify him as a dependent and by his own efforts or the joint efforts of himself and his wife is self-supporting while going to school, there is no extra personal exemption.

Though this new discrimination was created by the permission to let parents claim a student as a dependent even if he earned over $600, it does not carry with it the perverse economic result or the sense of outrageous nonsense which developed under the old law. A self-supporting student does not lose his own exemption by earning over $600. There is thus no reason to stop earning income, as there was under the pre-1954 law. The present problem is entirely one of fairness.

An obvious solution to this present difference in treatment would be to extend an extra personal exemption to all self-supporting students, as is done for the blind and for people over sixty-five. This is appealing in view of the importance of education, its high cost, and the admirable efforts of those who get themselves through university work by their own efforts or, even more admirably, are helped through by the earnings and the stintings of their wives. If there were to be any more double exemptions granted, this would appear to be the most justified place for them.

On balance, however, double exemptions should not be extended. There are too many occupations and conditions which have social importance or emotional appeal, and each additional category given a double exemption makes it that much harder to resist the next drive for similar tax relief. If relief is given for students, why not for schoolteachers whose pay scales often do not permit support of a sizable family, especially if some of the children are in college, without income from extra jobs? And what of country ministers and even some country doctors where the population is sparse and fees relatively low? Scoutmasters have been suggested for additional exemptions because of the importance of their efforts. The use of additional personal exemptions can too readily accelerate and carry us too far toward the ultimate situation where everyone has exemption except the conjectural "last taxpayer."

Alternative ways of removing the favored treatment of partially self-supporting students who receive their principal support from parents all involve undue complications. One possibility would be to require the student-dependent's income to be taxed as though it were part of the family income, that is, at the top-bracket rates at which it would be taxed if it were added to the parent's income. The parents and students could then reallocate the total tax between themselves as they chose. This would be extremely complicated, however, for taxpayers to compute and for the government to audit and would be an undue refinement in the law. The present treatment seems to be the least unsatisfactory solution, and the difference between the personal exemptions for students who are supported by their parents and those who support themselves is another regrettable imperfection in the tax law.

Withholding and Estimated Taxes

Withholding of income tax on most wage and salary payments was adopted during World War II to assure collection of the tax when it was first applied on a very broad basis to help finance war expenditures. Without withholding, it was believed that too many people would have been without funds to meet even a modest tax payment due in the following year, because of either ignorance of their tax liabilities or improvidence. But though the withholding system has improved collections, it has had undesirable consequences in reducing and even destroying the consciousness of many taxpayers about their shares in the Federal tax burden. It has also led to the extremely complicated administrative burdens on both taxpayers and tax officials arising from the declarations of estimated tax which have been adopted to provide equality of treatment as regards timing between those subject to withholding and others. An extension of withholding to interest and dividends has been proposed many times. This would doubtless improve enforcement of the tax on these forms of income, but it would add greatly to administrative burdens. The subject of withholding and payments of estimated taxes presents the familiar conflict between fairness and simplicity; on balance theoretical perfection appears to have been pushed too far and made the law unduly complicated.

Withholding of tax by employers or others who make income payments gives greater assurance that taxes will be collected and improves taxpayer morale by avoiding the need to set aside or borrow substantial amounts to meet tax payments at late dates. But it is also probable that withholding decreases the sense of political responsibility and participation by citizens who know of their personal tax payments only as one among many figures used in computing their net take-home pay. The overwhelming emphasis on the net figure and the ever-increasing number of other deductions for such items as life insurance, medical insurance, social security taxes, state income taxes, union dues, and even charitable contributions make it hard to maintain an awareness of any individual deduction or even of the gross pay. Even for those who are alert on financial matters, it is the net figure which counts and the gross pay is simply a point of departure for a series of calculations. Differences in attitudes toward state and Federal income taxes, when the former are not withheld, testify to the way in which withholding may make one oblivious of the burden. A much smaller state tax is resented because "it comes out of my own money," whereas "I never got my hands on the money that went into the Federal tax."

In eighteenth-century France, it was a maxim of government finance to pluck the public goose in whatever way would give the most tax feathers with the least squawking. This was understandable when taxes were used so largely to support an extravagant court and pay for military adventures. But it should have no place in a responsible democracy. Harassment of taxpayers and administrative costs should, of course, be kept to a minimum, but this does not mean that taxpayers should be confused or kept uninformed about total government costs and, as far as they can be determined, about their individual shares of the total costs. Some local governments have experimented with itemized tax bills to show an allocation of an individual's property tax among the costs of schools, roads, police and fire protection, and the like, an excellent way to help citizens know what they are getting for their compulsory payments for government services.

Though tax consciousness has been decreased by withholding, this method of collection seems to be necessary for the great bulk of earned income. But any reasonable change to increase an individual's awareness of his personal tax burden would be desirable. At the very least, information on the Federal income tax withheld should be kept separate from all others, as should the employee's social security contributions. It has been proposed that a combined withholding of income tax and social security contributions might be adopted as a simplification in administration. Any such plan should continue to be opposed, as it has been in the Treasury, because it would blur and confuse the small remaining basis for tax consciousness.

The fact that taxes on wages and salaries are withheld means that the taxes are paid sooner than they would be on other forms of income, in the absence of some plan for current estimates and interim payments of nonwithheld taxes. The present system of estimated taxes was adopted to avoid a charge that withholding alone would be unfair. But estimates of taxes are extremely annoying to those taxpayers who must make them. The checking of interim payments against the amounts which should have been paid, when the actual tax due has been determined after the close of a year, is also burdensome to tax administrators. On balance, the gain in theoretical equity has probably not justified the increased complexity in the law and its administration.

Several alternatives are given as a basis for estimating the tax on the estimated income of the current year. The simplest basis, which was recommended by the Treasury and adopted in 1954, is to accept the previous year's tax as an estimate for the current year, but even this is not altogether clear or simple. If the amount of tax withheld on salary falls slightly, as is likely from a reduction in the number of dependents, payment of an estimated tax equal to the difference between the total tax and the tax withheld in the previous year might not meet the requirements of the law. As one further simplification, it would seem desirable to accept an estimate of current tax equal to the difference between the total tax and the tax withheld in the previous year. This would be consistent with the intent of the present law but permit the additional assumption that the tax withheld will also be the same. A desirable amendment was adopted in 1960 waiving filing of returns and payments of small amounts of estimated tax. Further liberalization of this sort may be possible.

The requirement for an estimated tax by corporations was introduced in 1954 primarily as a way out of the concentration of corporate tax payments on March 15 and June 15 which had developed out of the acceleration of payments to those dates. The first acceleration had been adopted in the late 1940s to bring receipts from a later to an earlier fiscal year and thereby improve the budget position. The result had an unfortunate impact on the money markets and complicated the problem of debt management. Since a reversal of the plan for acceleration would have had a large adverse effect on the immediate budget, the only solution was to require some payments on an estimated tax in the last two quarters of the calendar year. This was supported by an analogy with individuals who were required to make current payments. The fact that a penalty was applied only for underpayments on taxes in excess of $100,000 relieved the vast majority of corporations from the annoyance of filing returns for estimated taxes.

The extension of withholding to interest and dividends paid to individuals would improve collections substantially. The evasion of taxes is particularly high on interest, especially in small savings accounts and savings bonds. Evasion on dividends probably occurs principally for small stockholders, most of whose income is earned. Small additional sources of income, such as dividends and interest, are simply ignored in preparing tax returns in too many cases; this may be an incidental corollary of the fact that the tax is withheld on the principal source of income.

Withholding should not be adopted on dividends unless it is also applied to interest; the bulk of the revenue would apparently be found in the latter category, and withholding on one without the other would seem to condone continued laxity in the second source of income. Unfortunately, withholding on small casual payments presents difficult administrative problems because of the virtual impossibility of allowing for personal exemptions, as is done in withholding on wages. For retired people living on a modest income from investments, the amounts withheld would be excessive and make a system of prompt refunds essential. There would also be additional clerical burdens on the companies paying interest and dividends.

Withholding of tax on interest and dividends presents a clear conflict between the objectives of greater equity, through improved collection of tax on income not now paying its full share, and simplicity. Many companies paying interest and dividends gave much better information to the recipients about their tax liabilities on 1959 and 1960 income than previously. This was done with the hope that it would make it unnecessary to adopt withholding. Study of the results of such efforts at better enforcement of the present law will indicate whether the new complexities of extended withholding will be necessary to assure adequate tax collections from those who receive small amounts of interest and dividends.

Tax Exemption

Tax exemption is often suggested as fair and economically sound for forms of activity or investment which are deemed to be socially or economically desirable. Teaching, nursing, and scientific or engineering work have all been proposed for partial or complete tax exemption in recent years. The proposals sometimes come from those engaged in the work but often from others who want to foster increased interest and participation in a sort of activity which they regard as underpaid or especially important.

The appeal of tax exemption as an inducement is obvious. It is, or at least it presumably is, equivalent to a pay raise, and it is a particularly dramatic sort of reward because it confers its benefits in a way which might be thought to have prestige as well as monetary value. Perhaps its proponents think of tax exemption as creating some sort of elite status for the favored group. But in spite of its apparent attractions, tax exemption for favored activity or investment appears, on balance, to be a thoroughly bad policy for several reasons.

The extent of the monetary advantage from tax exemption is capricious, and there may in fact be no advantage where an extra reward is most needed. A poorly paid teacher with several children, for instance, would probably have his salary entirely offset by the personal exemptions of his family and his deductions, with no net taxable income and no tax. Exemption from income taxation would thus be completely meaningless and give no real advantage. By contrast, a single teacher with the same salary would get substantial benefit. Even for married teachers with very good salaries, substantial fractions, perhaps half or more, of the total income would be offset by the personal exemption of $600 for each member of the family, plus the allowable deductions. Thus, a family with four children would have $3,600 plus at least 10 per cent of the income before exemptions (or a total of $4,300 of an income of $7,000) not subject to tax in any case. In brief, the actual benefit of the tax exemption would depend on family status and size of income, with the greatest benefits going to single people or those with small families and large incomes and little or no benefit to those with small incomes and sizeable families. This perverse and unintended result should be reason enough to refute the proposals for tax exemption for forms of activity in which the pay scales may be deemed to be inadequate.

But an additional reason lies in the very fact that tax exemption, being publicized as it inevitably would be, would distract attention from the basic problem of pay scales themselves and be popularly considered as having provided whatever remedy was needed. Proposals for pay increases would be countered with the argument "But you have tax exemption!" The intended prestige value of tax exemption would seem likely to be too effective by creating resentment or at least indifference on the part of those not covered by it.

And finally, if tax exemption were once adopted for one sort of activity, there would seem to be no reasonable place to stop its extension short of those activities which might be generally regarded as actually harmful or parasitic, and even there opinions will differ. Once a single group is given a favored tax status, others with more or less similar reasons will have more or less appealing reasons to have the exemption extended to them, with a cumulative reduction in the amount of income left subject to taxation and necessarily higher rates on that diminished amount to raise the requisite revenue. Tax exemption to induce desired activity seems indeed to be a poor policy, sympathetic though one may be with its objective.

Sick-pay Exclusion. The present sick-pay exclusion, a limited form of tax exemption, represents unfinished business for the Congress. Prior to 1954, a major loophole existed in the law through complete tax exemption of payments in lieu of compensation paid through insured plans. It had been supposed, apparently, in developing the previous law that the self-interest of insurance companies would assure adequate policing of claims for insurance benefits and prevent any malingering to receive tax-exempt pay, but this supposition did not give full credit to those who create special insurance policies for their tax advantages. It was reported to the Treasury in 1954 that special policies were being prepared on a cost-plus basis which opened a new area for collusion among employers, employees, and insurance companies, all at the expense of the revenue. For a high-salaried officer in a closely controlled company, extended sick leave would represent tax-exempt income under the cost-plus policy, and for the employer, it would mean a deductible expense similar to compensation but with a much greater benefit to the employee than regular compensation because of its tax exemption to him. A year or two of sick leave before retirement could be more useful than an elaborate pension plan. It was necessary to act quickly to close this newly developing abuse.

The second inequity in the pre-1954 law was the preference it gave to insured plans. Large corporations, which could run the risks of self-insurance and preferred to do so to avoid having to pay the additional costs to an insurance company, were nonetheless forced to use insurance to give their employees the benefits of tax exemption. This favoritism to insurance companies was unjustified.

The law was changed in 1954 to put a ceiling of $100 a week on tax-exempt benefits and to remove the discrimination against benefits from self-insured plans. The $100 ceiling would prevent extreme abuses, but it left a tax incentive for malingering under sick-pay plans which gave full pay while sick. A good deal of thought was given in 1954 to making benefits fully taxable if they exceeded some stated percentage of regular compensation. This would have removed the tax benefit from malingering. The problem of selecting the percentage for a cutoff seemed insuperable, however. Benefit payments under existing plans ranged from less than half of normal compensation to full pay, with most plans for wage earners in the 50 to 65 per cent range. The use of a low figure in the range would have led to strong protests from those whose benefits were just above that level, with perhaps some pressure on employers to reduce benefits and substitute a smaller tax-exempt benefit for a larger taxable one. The selection of a high figure in the range would have been regarded as setting government approval on it as a norm, with pressure on employers to raise benefits to that level.

It was recognized in 1954 that full taxation of benefits would be fair. The Senate Finance Committee tentatively dropped the exclusion for payments in lieu of wages but later reversed its position because of protests. The medical-expense deduction gives what relief is deemed appropriate in the tax law for expenses of sickness. Various restrictions have become necessary to limit abuses in the sick-pay exclusion. The present restricted exemption is complicated for taxpayers, their employers, and the government. It is not required to produce equity, and even as now limited it puts some premium on malingering and provides another way to try to "beat the taxes." Repeal of the remaining part of the sick-pay exclusion is an item of unfinished business. It would make the law fairer and simpler and remove the tax inducement to idleness with a pretense of sickness.

Tax-exempt Prizes and Scholarships. The law now includes in taxable income all prizes except those received in recognition of religious, charitable, scientific, educational, artistic, literary, or civic achievement, and even for those the prize is exempt only if the recipient took no action to enter a contest or submit his work and is not required to render any substantial future service. The intent is to exempt only such prizes as the Nobel and Pulitzer prizes.

This provision was adopted in 1954 to give certainty. Under the previous law the tax status of the prize depended on whether services were required, and this was at times difficult to determine. The shout of joy heard over a telephone and included in a television program which gives prizes to names picked at random from a telephone book adds to the appeal of the program. Does the housewife render services by providing the happy noise? This was the sort of problem which had to be resolved under the prior law. From the standpoint of equity, prizes seem to be peculiarly suitable for taxation, since they are windfalls and a tax on them does not impinge on a customary or planned standard of living. The exemption of the public-recognition prizes can be justified on the ground that they are purely gifts and that it is sound social policy to refrain from reducing them by taxes.

The fact that ordinary prizes are taxable made the general public well aware of the repressive effects of high taxes rates during the period when television quiz shows were popular. Those who watched the major program came to know that carrying the final $32,000 question to the $64,000 level would increase net income by only about $9,000 while a failure to answer it would mean a loss of about $18,000, since this was the net receipt from all the questions through $32,000. The larger apparent prize at the top turned out to be minor because of taxation. It is doubtful if any planned program of education could have been so effective in demonstrating the impact of excessive tax rates.

Scholarships have been nontaxable as gifts for many years. Fellowships present a problem because they may be abused. A young university instructor may be given a fellowship which, incidentally, requires him to teach classes. Ordinary salary should not escape taxation by being designated as a fellowship. To the extent that services are rendered, the going rate of pay for the services is included in the taxable income of the holder of a fellowship. But a danger still exists that a regular salary might be designated as a fellowship during a period when teaching is not required. When the present rules was adopted in 1954, it was thought that tax-exempt fellowships should be confined to candidates for advanced degrees, but this limitation was set aside when it was pointed out that postdoctoral fellowships were common in medical schools for research. It was then thought that a fellowship should not be entitled to tax exemption unless it was substantially less than a person's previous regular income. This would have prevented established professional people from trying to convert their regular taxable salaries into tax-exempt fellowships. But again the medical fellowships presented a problem because, though they were quite small, they were larger than the nominal earnings of interns, and young doctors would increase their incomes when they received even modest fellowships. It was finally decided to limit tax-exempt fellowships to $300 a month for recipients who are not candidates for a degree. It was felt that this would be sound social policy and not leave enough of a loophole open to encourage abuse. Unfortunately it has been proposed in many places that regular salaries paid during sabbatical leaves should be designated as fellowships and thereby become tax-exempt up to $300 a month. If this practice becomes common, the law should be tightened to remove the opportunity.

Tax-exempt State and Municipal Securities. Exemption of the interest on state and municipal securities from the Federal income tax is the most familiar and controversial form of tax exemption in the country. No attempt is made here to add any new points to previous discussions. The issues may be summarized briefly.

It is sometimes argued that reciprocal tax exemption between the Federal government and the state governments and the municipalities which they create is required by the constitution or is at least necessary to maintain the autonomy of the separate governments in our Federal system. This does not appear to be a valid argument as long as the income taxes imposed are general and nondiscriminatory. The Supreme Court settled the analogous issue on wages and salaries of municipal employees over twenty years ago, and there is no more reason to give exemption to interest of bondholders then to wages and salaries of employees.

Emotions on the subject are strong. In 1954, the House Ways and Means Committee acted to prevent what was widely recognized as an abuse of tax exemption by denying it to bonds which were issued by municipalities to build factories for lease to private industry when the bonds were backed by the rents on the factories with no guarantee or obligation by the municipality itself. The organized outcry was so great that the action was rescinded in less than a week and before the bill containing it was reported by the Committee. Some of the states which were not able or willing to misuse tax-exempt bonds to lure industries into their areas then proposed that all factories built through state or municipal industrial development boards should be given, in effect, five-year amortization. This was rejected in the Senate. Extensions of the normal functions of government to spread the benefits of tax exemption are a continuing problem.

But peripheral abuses only add to the main objection to tax-exempt bonds. They are criticized as unfair and uneconomic. They are unfair because they create a privileged category of income. Even those of us who consider the tax rates themselves as unfairly high for middle and upper incomes resent the sort of selective relief given by tax-exempt bonds.

The benefits to high-bracket investors are much greater than the savings in interest to borrowers. If there were only a small amount of tax-exempt bonds outstanding, perhaps 10 million dollars, one would expect them to be bid up in price to the point where the net yield after tax for the purchaser would be the same from comparable taxable and tax-exempt bonds. If taxable bonds yielded 4 per cent, an investor in a 90 per cent tax bracket would be as well off with a tax-exempt bond which yielded only $\frac{4}{10}$ of 1 per cent. With a very small amount available, those who can benefit most could be expected to bid a high enough price for the bonds to make the savings in interest to the borrower about equal to the loss in revenue to the Federal government. But by 1960, there were about 60 billion dollars of bonds outstanding, and in 1959 the yield on AAA state and municipal tax-exempt bonds was 3.35, and 4.38 per cent on AAA corporate bonds. The amount outstanding was so great that all high-bracket investors had all the tax-exempt bonds they wanted, as did all corporate investors subject to the regular rate of corporate taxation. The differential in yield was only 1.03 per cent, or enough to give a comparable after-tax yield to an investor in the 23 per cent bracket. For the highest bracket individual investors, it would have required a 37.2 per cent bond to give the same yield as tax-exempt bonds at 3.35 per cent. For corporations, a 3.35 per cent tax-exempt gave the same yield as a 6.98 per cent taxable bond. It is clear that many holders receive tax benefits much greater than the savings in interest to the issuers.

Not only does tax exemption of state and local bond interest make the Federal income less fair by giving its greatest benefits to high-bracket investors; it also tends to divert into loans to governments the funds which can best afford to take the risks of loss from investments in business enterprise. The principal argument in favor of continued tax exemption, other than the emotional one, is that the state and local governments are in more need financially than the Federal government and tax exemption for their bonds is an established form of assistance which should not be withdrawn. Without accepting the merits of this contention, one must recognize its persuasive appeal when proposing a reform in this area.

After the abortive attempt to limit a real abuse without even touching the fundamental problem in 1954, it is apparent that reform can come only if borrowers are given some financial compensation. This could be done by providing for Federal payments to borrowing states and municipalities in some relation to the interest on new issues of taxable securities.

It would, of course, be unfair to change the tax status of outstanding bonds. Earlier attempts to remove tax exemption in the 1930s and 1940s did not distinguish between outstanding and future issues. The inequity of such a retroactive change probably helped to crystallize the opposition and now makes it more difficult to get a fair change accepted.

The amount of Federal subsidy to states and municipalities to compensate for the higher interest costs arising from removal of tax exemption on future issues could be fixed either in relation to the total interest paid or as some absolute percentage of the principal amount. The former would appear to be preferable because it would be more likely to give a reasonable result regardless of the absolute level of interest rates. The plan might first be set up on an optional basis to test what differential rate would be appropriate and to prove that it would not undermine the Federal system of government. As a first estimate, one might give a payment determined by the regular corporate income tax rate at the time of issue of a bond. If the rate of interest on issue was 4 per cent and the corporate tax rate was 52 per cent, the Federal government would reimburse the issuer annually at the rate of 2.08 per cent of the principal amount outstanding. This would put the Federal government in a break-even position with respect to the tax received and payment made to issuers on bonds held by corporations. For high-bracket individuals, the Federal government would gain revenue on balance and the issuers would not lose. On the basis of the differentials in the market between taxable and comparable tax-exempt bonds in recent years, the combined effect should be to give a net increase in Federal revenue and a decrease in net interest cost to state and municipal borrowers. This apparent paradox is explained by the fact that many holders now receive tax benefits greatly in excess of the savings in interest by the issuers.

The new taxable state and local securities would have to develop their own position in the financial markets and would have a different place in investment portfolios from tax-exempt bonds. Since the new taxable status would apply only to new issues, the transition would be a gradual one without significant disturbance. When the optional feature of the plan is dropped and all subsequent issues of state and local bonds are finally made taxable, the tax exemption of future issues of Federal bonds from general state income taxes should also be waived.

The problem of tax exemption of state and local bonds has resisted solution for almost forty years. Successive administrations have attempted to find ways to remove tax exemption. This reform is not an essential part of a general reform; it should not even be included in a comprehensive reform bill because of the sentiments which it can apparently be made to raise with possible danger to the more important reforms. The proposal made here is far from ideal, but it would appear to improve the Federal tax system substantially and improve the financial standing of both Federal and state governments. Though no system of payments from the Federal government to states and localities is desirable, a new one for this purpose is less bad than continued tax exemption of state and local bonds and its adoption would seem to be the only possible way to eliminate tax exemption on future issues.

Chapter 3 THE BREADTH OF THE INCOME CONCEPT

Expense Accounts—Pensions—
Annuities—Retirement Income—
Deferred Compensation—Gifts

In the previous chapter, reference was made to the fact that taxable income is somewhat less than half of the total personal income in the country because of personal exemptions, allowable deductions, and various forms of transfer payments and imputed income which are not included in taxable income. The broader the base of taxable income, the lower the tax rates which will be necessary to produce any given amount of revenue. It has already been noted that high marginal tax rates repress and divert activity even though the total tax burden may not be excessive. It thus seems to follow that a broader tax base, by permitting lower rates of tax, is desirable to keep the damage done by our tax system at a minimum.

Numerous proposals have been made to broaden the tax base. Existing deductions in computing taxable income might be removed or curtailed. Various forms of income in kind not now included in the tax base might be brought into it, and items of income now taxed only on a delayed basis might be made taxable at earlier times when they typically would be taxable at higher rates and produce more revenue. This chapter deals primarily with proposals to broaden the tax base or to accelerate the taxability of items of income. It covers expense accounts, retirement income, annuities, and deferred compensation. A discussion of education expenses and the tax treatment of owner-occupied houses is left to the next chapter, which deals with the general subject of deductions. Stock options, often considered as a form of income in kind, are covered in the chapter on capital gains.

Much of the theoretical literature on tax policy is devoted to suggestions to broaden the tax base and make it as all-inclusive as possible. The existence of any untaxed income in kind or imputed income seems to be regarded by some not only as unfair but as a challenge to a writer's ingenuity to devise some way to measure the noncash income. But too broad a concept of taxable income is complicated and at times unreal. If one includes as part of taxable income the farm produce raised and eaten on the farm, as has been proposed, what about the farmer's satisfaction of country living which some city dwellers pay to enjoy on vacations? If one includes the annual rental value of a home occupied by its owner, as is done in England and as is urged here by many enthusiasts for a more inclusive income concept, what about the recurring satisfaction from a work of art which is owned and kept in the house or even the rental value of one's furniture in his house? And if one includes the value of the free or below-cost lunches in an executive dining room, what about the value of the psychological satisfaction of titles, multiple telephones, corner offices, and other symbols of success? [1]

There seems to be a need for a pragmatic approach and a rule of reason in this area. It may be theoretically sound and intellectually satisfying to the purist to cast a wide tax net to include forms of income in kind which exist in the ordinary course of events and have little or no tax motivation, but this approach would make the tax law fantastically complicated and would not even appeal to most people's sense of fairness. On the other hand, to include in income only cash payments would be an open invitation to gross abuse. Fringe benefits and payments of income in kind would proliferate at a tremendous rate if they were available as nontaxable

---

[1] The problem of imputed income is of long standing. A German tax philosopher in the last century meditated at length on the proper amount of imputed income to be deemed as taxable to the young aide to the Emperor who attended his sovereign at the opera in the Imperial box. The prestige was enormous, the opportunity for hearing and seeing the opera was incomparable, but the theorist finally gave up when he realized that the aide might thoroughly dislike opera and would not go except as part of his duties.

substitutes for taxable cash compensation. Thus, it is necessary to cast the tax net wide enough to include those forms of income which are tax-motivated substitutes for what would ordinarily be regular taxable income. This must be done to prevent abuse and to maintain the integrity of the tax system and taxpayer morale, though it inevitably complicates the law and the tax forms and imposes annoying burdens of compliance on those who must value and report their income in kind or justify its noninclusion. Judgment is required in striking the right balance. The three criteria of fairness, simplicity, and minimum adverse economic consequences are all relevant to the decision.

Before specific issues of income in kind are dealt with in this and the next chapter, the differing positions of employees and self-employed business and professional people should be recognized. The problems in tax legislation and administration are quite different for those two groups. For employees the question is whether the value of services and benefits provided for employees, but with no transfer of cash to them, should be currently taxed as imputed income or income in kind. Self-employed people are in a different position. For them, the problem is whether they shall be allowed deductions in computing their own taxable incomes for the sorts of services or benefits which are provided to employees by their employers. In terms of fairness, it is argued that self-employed people must be given deductions for certain of their own cash outlays to match the noncash benefits which some employees receive from some employers. A comparative analysis must thus shift back and forth between the imputation of noncash income to employees and allowable deductions of the self-employed.

From the standpoint of administrative feasibility and simplicity, both the inclusion of imputed income and the allowance of deductions are complications. Simplicity alone would thus leave employees untaxed on imputed income while denying deductions to the self-employed. A clear conflict between the objectives of fairness and simplicity thus exists in many aspects of this general problem. Closely controlled corporations present special problems because owner-managers, who may be like self-employed people in most practical respects, can have great tax advantages if they use their corporate entities to provide imputed income or hide personal expenses.

Expense Accounts

High individual income tax rates are an inducement to abuses of expense accounts. Personal expenses paid directly by an employer or charged to or reimbursed by an employer, if nontaxable, are preferable to a taxable salary to the extent of the marginal tax rate applicable to the employee. For a person in a 75 per cent tax bracket, it would take a $4,000 salary payment to net $1,000 for personal expenses; if the expenses are covered directly by the employer in a manner that is nontaxable to the employee, there is a saving to everyone except the national revenue. In the foregoing example, the employer could cover $2,000 of personal expenses at half the cost of a $4,000 salary, the employee would be twice as well off, and the national Treasury would be poorer by the amount of tax avoided. A loss in the national revenue means, of course, that in one way or another everyone else will have to pay more to make up the deficiency.

Under the law, personal expenses paid directly by an employer or charged to or reimbursed by an employer are taxable to the employee as income in kind. This rules out the family groceries and the children's clothes and other purely personal items. But with personal and business life as closely intertwined as they are, a great number of things which are desirable personally have business implications or uses. Company cars, travel, club dues and expenses, and entertainment which if given in the home may include some of the family groceries are all provided to varying extents. In flagrant cases, usually in closely controlled companies, a personal residence of an owner-manager may even be provided by the company under the pretense that his personal preference is to dwell in his simple country cottage and that he and his family live in a place accessible to his work only for "the convenience of his employer."

The problem in this area is that of balancing stringent enforcement, with its inevitable harassment of the many taxpayers who are not guilty of abuse, against the prevention of gross abuse and unfair practices by what is probably a distinct minority.

It appears that most large, widely owned corporations have relatively strict rules on expense accounts and direct payments of personal expenses, though abuses doubtless occur. But the opportunity for collusion is especially great in companies with owner-managements. None of the penalties, in the absence of fraud, are sufficiently rigorous to prevent attempts at abuse by those who are disposed to such practices.

The mildest penalty is a disallowance of the expense to the company on the ground that it is not a business expense. This still makes cheap living for the employee benefiting from the expense. The second level of penalty is taxation to the employee as income in kind, with a corollary deduction allowed to the company as a payment of compensation in kind. This produces a tax result no more stringent than would have existed under a forthright salary payment, except for the interest on the employee's tax deficiency. As long as the personal expenses are no more than would have been incurred anyway, this is not a real penalty. To be sure, if the costs of a company yacht or hunting lodge are all attributed as compensation in kind to the owner-manager who uses it and he could not have afforded the yacht or lodge on any after-tax salary, the effect of the attribution may be catastrophic to him; for a high-bracket man the additional tax could amount to much more than his existing net income after taxes.

The third level of tax penalty is to treat the expenses as a distribution of corporate income to stockholders; this means a disallowance of the deduction to the company and the taxation of the expenses to the individual as a dividend in kind. This is the proper treatment if salary plus expenses exceeds reasonable compensation or the expenses are in some other way akin to a distribution of profits. Here again, the net tax effect is no worse than if a dividend had in fact been paid to the owner-manager unless the scale of the expense covered by the company and taxed to the individual is beyond the possibility of being covered by after-tax dividends, as may well be the case.

The present practice of the Internal Revenue Service is to have simultaneous audits of owner-managers and the closely controlled corporations with which they work. This is a sound and necessary practice. But since direct payments of personal expenses are likely to be scattered among numerous company accounts, and since the personal use of company property would never appear anywhere in regular books of accounts, tighter controls and some supplementary records for tax purposes are necessary. This is an annoyance and expense both to companies and to employees as individuals, and it is here that a difficult balance should be maintained.

On the one hand, there is the need to prevent gross abuse which brings the tax law into disrepute by those who flaunt their evasion in front of others, conversationally and in practice, until taxpayer morale is undermined and fraud becomes socially acceptable. On the other hand, there is the need to avoid excessive prying into personal affairs and elaborate record keeping in instances where abuse is not a threat or a fact.

Tax regulations adopted in 1958 concerning reimbursed and directly charged expenses attempted to strike a balance in one aspect of this problem. A line added to the 1957 individual tax form went too far in requiring a report of all amounts of expenses reimbursed by employers. For those who report in detail to employers and whose employers have strict standards, this was unnecessary harassment. The protests were so great that it was announced that this line did not have to be used. The rule then adopted in 1958 exempted from an employee's individual tax return all reimbursed expenses for which an employee accounted to his employer in some detail and required the inclusion only of lump-sum expense allowances or reimbursed expense for which no report was made to the employer. This seemed a reasonable compromise at the time, but it was by no means certain that it would be adequate to control abuses. The spectacular growth of Diner's Club and other charge accounts and their use in such places as the camera shop in the airport at Shannon, Ireland, and Rue St. Honoré dress shops in Paris suggested that stricter controls would be necessary.

In 1959 a further step was taken to restrict tax abuses of expense accounts. Companies were required to collect into a single account, available for inspection, all accounts of the twenty-five highest paid officers and employees. This was intended to prevent questionable charges from being scattered among various areas of business expenses; by being brought together in one place an unusually large total will itself raise doubts, and the information necessary for inquiry will be at hand. Also, companies which maintain yachts, hunting lodges, and other vacation appurtenances must so indicate on their tax returns, with a presumption that questions will be asked to determine whether there are abuses.

As additional restrictions for the future, consideration may well be given to disallowance by statute of certain types of expenses. Resorts, yachts, and theater tickets come to mind most readily. In closely controlled companies, the cost of maintaining yachts and resorts might regularly be imputed to owner-managers. There also have been many proposals for complete disallowance of entertainment expenses.

Personal or family uses of company cars, employees, and supplies are especially hard to detect in closely controlled companies. (They are sometimes revealed privately when the owners of a company want to adjust its income to reveal the "true income" during negotiations for sale or merger.) Such costs might always be disallowed to the company, even within the limits of reasonable compensation, and taxed to the owner-managers. As noted above, this would be an effective penalty against attempts to convert taxable compensation into hidden income in kind, but it would not impose any greater tax than would be due if corporate income were paid out as a dividend. To secure a really effective penalty, it might be further provided that tax deficiencies arising from attempted abuses of this sort should always be increased by some stated percentage, perhaps 50 per cent.

The problem is as pervasive as income taxation itself. Tax officials in other countries tell of the same sorts of problems on the same items of expenditure—in fact, the exchange of views and discussions of methods to restrict abuses is a frequent subject of conversation among them. For some years, England was reputed to be relatively lax or sympathetic to the problems of executives who were absolutely precluded by excessive tax rates from maintaining a standard of living deemed appropriate to their business positions except by liberal expense accounts and the use of company apartments and cars, but the rules have been tightened there also in recent years.

Dress and gift shops and interior-decorating establishments may serve as "fronts" for tax-deductible travel, especially by women or retired couples. The question here is how much business is necessary to justify annual trips to European fashion showings or tours of Asia and South America in search of exotic gift items or decorative motifs? These businesses are variants of the "hobby" farms and ranches which received publicity in the 1940s and led to the very minor restriction now in the law. It is provided that if deductions exceed gross income of an individual's business by more than

$50,000 in each of five consecutive years, the taxable income is recomputed, with deductions limited to $50,000 plus gross income. This restricts tremendous losses from a major publication or a very large and unsuccessful farm but is ineffective to prevent substantial tax deductions for hobby businesses and farms. There must, of course, be some actual business conducted, and the expense must bear some reasonable relationship to the scale of activity, but the area is one requiring strict audits to prevent deductions for the expenses of personal hobbies and travel.

In spite of the strong arguments in favor of strict control of expense accounts to maintain general taxpayer morale (and morals), there may be conditions in which extreme liberality might be a useful feature to encourage economic development. In other countries, where business activity has been traditionally scorned and where entrepreneurship is notably deficient, a public acceptance of untaxed expense allowances and fringe benefits of executive employment might help to shift attention toward business careers. This would be especially the case if high income tax rates were imposed. A policy of high income taxation seems almost foolhardy in a country especially concerned with starting its industrial growth, but if it is adopted as a matter of social policy, its adverse economic effects might be substantially alleviated by forthrightly permitting active businessmen to receive untaxed residences, cars, and living allowances. If this were done, the high income tax might be a positive inducement to activity.

In the late 1940s, several members of a group of English graduate students preparing for business careers, during a discussion concerning the reasons for selecting business, said that they had done so because of high income and inheritance taxes. Only as active businessmen with liberal "perks," as untaxed perquisites are popularly called in England, could they hope to maintain the standard of living to which they had become accustomed; the inherited wealth on which their parents were living would not survive to another generation. This incident should not be the basis for any generalization that high taxes are on balance a stimulus to entrepreneurship, and even this event occurred under a more liberal rule toward "perks" than exists now. But it does suggest the validity of the idea that where a country is particularly short of entrepreneurs, as in some places in Asia, it might be desirable on balance to adopt an intentionally liberal policy in the tax laws that govern expense accounts in order to make entrepreneurship more attractive, in spite of the general objection to tax exemption discussed in the previous chapter.

Business and Professional Expenses of Self-employed

Similar problems of potential abuse in connection with personal expenses exist for self-employed people, especially among professional groups. The opportunity for abuse is probably less than in closely controlled corporations, because to a much greater extent the expenses must be claimed as deductions and hence are available for audit on an individual's own return, but it is greater than that for employees of corporations with strict standards for expense allowances.

Travel, entertainment, and expenses allegedly helpful in maintaining professional knowledge and in establishing contacts are particularly susceptible to abuse. How much time and how much work at a meeting of a professional association are necessary to legitimatize the deduction of travel expenses which take one to a resort area for a vacation? The meeting of the American Bar Association in London in 1957 provided much discussion, a good deal of soul-searching, and probably a good deal of abuse by those who used the fact of a few days' attendance at the meeting as a justification for a travel-expense deduction to Europe for a long-planned vacation trip. The entire expenses of a cruise to Hawaii, advertised as designed to follow a medical association meeting in San Francisco, were ostensibly made deductible by brief professional meetings on shipboard and available but not compulsory visits to hospitals and a leper colony in Hawaii. The advertisement was made the basis for a Treasury ruling that such expenses would not be deductible. But the fact that it was organized and advertised indicates the attitudes which have developed.

Considerable ingenuity is used to justify a wife's presence, either for secretarial work or for social contacts. A reputed example of rather petty but nonetheless offensive shenanigans occurred when a major hotel in San Francisco substituted rate cards in its rooms during a bar association meeting in the city showing that the rate for single occupancy was the same as that for double occupancy instead of being lower, as was normal. This presumably was done to provide evidence that the entire room expense was attributable to the lawyer and none to his wife. The report did not state whether the collusion in tax evasion extended to a special menu which showed nothing but steak dinners for two.

The roster of the professions can be continued with the example of a professor in a major university who requested from an administrative official a statement that two studies, one upstairs and one downstairs, were necessary in the professor's eight-room house to enable him to conduct his university duties successfully. The request, which was, of course, denied, apparently arose from the fact that the professor had the effrontery to claim one-quarter of his house expenses as professional expenses. Somewhat less flagrantly, conversations indicate that professors who do consulting work on the side may often claim the fraction of a house expense represented by one study as a professional expense, though they had private university studies available at all times.

The fact that members of such professions, where honorable conduct is thought to be the general rule, will not uncommonly descend to such tax shenanigans is depressing. The righteous indignation of those who object to the practice is met by the indignation, perhaps equally righteous, of those who want to get away with whatever they can, short of fraud, under the letter of the law or inadequate audits, and as long as the facts are stated, there is no basis for fraud and only an interest penalty on a tax deficiency for an unsuccessful claim for a deduction.

Here again, the level of rates has been largely responsible for the attitudes which are developing, but the attitudes are extending to those whose rates are far short of confiscatory.

To attempt to reverse this trend and to make laws fairer in their application there might be consideration, along with a reduction in tax rates, of a specific disallowance of the following deductions, with a strong Congressional indication that the whole area is one which calls for strict audits:

1. Any part of the expense of a home unless one's trade or business is conducted exclusively from his home.

2. All travel expenses of wives or other members of the family except under extremely rare and unusual circumstances justifying it. (This is no attack on family travel but is merely to secure equality

with the vast majority of citizens who pay family travel expenses with after-tax dollars.)

3. That part of travel expense for professional purposes which is in proportion to time spent for vacation purposes. This means that if most of the time in a resort or vacation area is spent on vacation, most of the expense of getting there will be nondeductible. (At present, all the expense is deductible as long as the vacation aspects are not a primary purpose.)

Pensions

The tax treatment of pensions and other forms of retirement income raises many problems. Their analysis presents a fine example of the conflict among the objectives of simplicity, fairness, and minimum distortion of economic development.

Under the present law, pension plans which are fairly broad in coverage and do not discriminate in favor of owner-management or key employees get very favorable tax treatment. Payments by an employer to the trustee of a pension fund or to an insurance company are deductible in computing the employer's taxable income. There is no tax on the employees, however, until they actually receive their pensions, perhaps thirty or forty years later. The income of the pension fund itself is tax exempt, which means that the investment income can accumulate in full to increase the pension or decrease the cost of the plan to the employer.

In contrast to pension plans for employees, an individual has to build up his own retirement income out of savings from his net income after taxes, and the income from his own investments is currently taxable. Thus, if an individual is in a 75 per cent bracket, he would have to receive $4,000 of salary to have $1,000 available to save, and the $1,000 invested at 4 per cent would accumulate, after the tax on the income, only at $10 a year. But if the company paid the $4,000 to a pension trust, the full amount would be available for later distribution and in the meantime could be invested at the same 4 per cent rate to provide $160 a year for additional accumulation.

The tax advantage of deferral and tax-free accumulation employment is partially offset by the fact that a pension provided entirely by an employer is fully taxable to the individual as he receives it whereas, if he is living on his accumulated savings, there is no tax on anything except the current income on the dwindling savings. Since people are generally in a lower tax bracket after they retire than while they are employed, the full taxability of the pension is a small disadvantage compared with the advantage of nontaxability during the period of accumulation. The difference between an individual's tax rates before and after retirement is one measure of the advantage to him of securing retirement income through a pension plan qualified for favorable tax treatment. The higher his tax rate while he is actively employed, the greater the chance for a large difference between the two rates.

Total employer deductions for corporate contributions to pension plans amounted to 3,999 million dollars in 1958; there were over 47,000 qualified plans. By 1960 the number had risen to over 59,000. These are all large figures, and they have been increasing rapidly year by year. Taxability of the employers' contributions in 1958 would have produced a significant amount of revenue, 800 million dollars, if one assumes an average applicable tax rate of 20 per cent. The present treatment is understandably criticized on grounds of fairness; those who are covered by qualified pension plans clearly have a tax advantage over those who are not.

However, the fact that the concept of taxable income of employees has not been broadened to include allocated parts of an employer's current contribution to a general pension plan reflects simplicity from all standpoints and fairness from at least one point of view. It is clearly simpler not to try to apportion an employer's contribution to a typical pension plan among the various employees, taking account of their varying ages, family statuses, and prospects for continued employment for a long enough period to secure vested rights under the plan.

The present treatment is also fair from the standpoint of the very considerable proportion of employees who will get no actual benefits from a plan because they change employment before securing vested rights. They would resent and resist being taxed on imputed income consisting of a presumed cost of a prospective pension which they have no expectation of ever receiving. The failure to include employers' contributions to pension plans in the current income of the employees is also consistent with a broad social and economic policy of encouraging private provision for retirement income. Since pensions are fully taxable as received, the favorable tax treatment is a postponement of taxation, not an exemption from taxation.

But those not covered by pension plans resent the tax advantages of those who are. Various groups of self-employed professional people have been especially articulate in requesting legislation to give them tax deductions for some part of their own earned incomes which they set aside to purchase annuities or provide their own retirement income in other ways, with their annuities or other forms of retirement income then being made fully taxable as received. These proposals are not simple; they would, in fact, complicate the tax law considerably. Though they seem fair from some standpoints, they are not from others. Their economic and social consequences would probably be good, on balance. They can be analyzed and compared with employee pension plans on the basis of the three criteria.

From the standpoint of simplicity, the comparison is clear. Whereas it would complicate the law and the tax forms to require the inclusion in an employee's taxable income of a share of an employer's contribution to a pension fund, it would also complicate the law and the forms to attempt to give equality by permitting self-employed people a current deduction and then to make sure that the amounts set aside were later converted into taxable retirement income and taxed.

From the standpoint of equity, self-employed people frequently do not retire and do not want to retire; they can continue their professional activities on a reduced scale and are happier doing so. Thus, they have an advantage over employees who face forced retirement and the complete termination of compensation. This distinction was made rather emphatically when the representatives of one of the professional groups advocating a deduction for funds set aside for retirement income were once asked if the eligible self-employed should not be confined to those covered by social security as self-employed. They said, "Oh no, because doctors don't retire and wouldn't get any social security benefits; what they need is a retirement income deduction." The contradiction was thus stated before it became apparent that it largely destroyed the equity argument for a deduction for funds set aside privately for retirement incomes. There are many other tax differences between the status of employees and self-employed people in terms, for example, of the availability of tax deductions for professional or self-employment expenses, which mean that full tax equality in each and every respect is not really possible.

A second main point in the comparison of the equities in the tax treatment of retirement income of employees and self-employed turns around the income levels of those who benefit from such tax postponement as may be available. Under a general pension plan, by definition, employees at all income levels have to be covered. That is a requirement if a pension plan is to qualify for favorable tax treatment. As noted before, the extent of the advantage of postponement varies with the difference between preretirement and postretirement tax rates; the higher the current salary, the greater the probable advantage. But some tax advantage exists for everyone who gets a pension as long as he does get a pension and his marginal tax rate after retirement is less than that during employment. For many wage earners, the double personal exemption and the retirement income credit after sixty-five will make their pensions nontaxable, making the tax postponement in effect an exemption.

Under the proposals for self-employed people, the plan by its nature must be a voluntary one and will be used by those who can best afford to use it and who find it most advantageous. In most instances, these will be people with larger incomes subject to the higher tax brackets. To be sure, these are the very incomes for which tax reduction may be appropriate as part of a general reform, but a selective and elaborate mechanism for retirement income is an involved way to give relief from excessive rates.

From the standpoint of economic and social results, it is argued that the present availability of pensions for employees makes it hard to get young people to go into self-employment. It seems unlikely that this is a critical factor in many instances. The way of life and the satisfactions and dissatisfactions of employment and self-employment differ in many ways; it is a matter of taste and temperament as to which line of work will be most attractive to an individual. But though it is probably slight in its total economic effect, the removal of a tax discrimination against self-employment would be desirable to the extent that it would be significant. This judgment reflects a bias in favor of maintaining as many autonomous "centers of initiative" as possible. At least, all other things being equal, it is undesirable to discriminate against self-employment or small economic entities; if there is to be any discrimination, it should be favorable rather than adverse to them.

A balance among the arguments under the three criteria seems by a small margin to be against the creation of a new complication in the law to give a deduction for amounts set aside for retirement income for the self-employed. The equities in the case are not clear cut nor are the economic and social consequences. The nontaxability to employees of employers' contributions under general pension plans merely avoids an artificial broadening of the concept of taxable income to include a fringe benefit of uncertain current value, the use of which developed and spread for nontax reasons, though it does confer varying tax advantages on different individuals. It was not adopted to give a tax advantage or to discriminate in favor of employees. The deductions for individual contributions by self-employed people for their own retirement incomes would create an artificial and complicated deduction which has meaning only for the tax advantages which it confers.

Legislation which would have given deductions to self-employed people for limited contributions to provide their own retirement income passed the House and, in a substantially modified form, was reported favorably by the Senate Finance Committee in 1960. Many of the changes made by the Finance Committee were recommended by the Treasury; if legislation is ever to be adopted in this area, it should contain at least three restrictions. Since the avowed purpose is to give similar treatment to those available to employers, it was and should be provided that self-employed people who themselves have employees must provide pensions for their employees if they are to take advantage of the deductions for themselves. This restriction is in line with the requirement in company pension plans that they must not discriminate in favor of stockholder or key employees. It was further provided that withdrawals could not be made as capital gain. This would be a desirable change for all pension plans and will be discussed in the chapter on capital gains. It is particularly important for amounts set aside by self-employed people who could readily "terminate their plans" and would do so if they could thereby receive an especially favorable tax treatment.

A final condition, which has been in all recent versions of proposed legislation, is that amounts set aside must in fact be converted into annuities with taxable withdrawals started at some reasonable age, perhaps not later than seventy. It may come as a surprise to those not versed in the ingenuity of tax maneuvers that annuities beginning at an age of ninety have been proposed and supposedly offered by some insurance companies in another connection as tax gimmicks. The use of such "annuities" would permit a deduction for an individual with an accumulation of a capital sum in an insurance company to pass on to his heirs without ever constituting taxable income to anyone.

Two problems exist under the present treatment of pension plans: one involves an unintended discrimination against small business, and the other an unintended discrimination in favor of selected employees of tax-exempt organizations. Both discriminations should be removed to the extent possible.

The conditions for qualification of a pension plan are not simple. Various limitations and restrictions have been imposed to prevent it from being used for the exclusive or primary benefit of owner-managers or key employees in closely controlled corporations. These have been regarded as necessary to limit the inherent tax advantages to genuine plans which are presumably established for other than tax reasons. They have, however, had the effect of discouraging some small companies from adopting plans because of the effort or expense involved in meeting the tests for qualification. To the extent that this discouragement does occur, it is an unintended and undesirable discrimination against small businesses, which will find it harder to compete for good employees. In 1954, an attempt was made to provide more liberal rules for qualification, but it appeared that the methods under consideration would open the door to abuse, and the attempt was dropped. In the meantime, trustee banks and insurance agents have become increasingly active in working out pension plans for small companies as part of their efforts to sell their own services. This free advice may simplify the problem of qualification for small businesses. If the conditions still significantly discourage small businesses, another attempt should be made to liberalize the requirements for qualification.

The second problem, and it is both current and substantial, arises because pension plans for employees of tax-exempt organizations do not have to meet the tests of nondiscrimination applicable to pension plans in general. Such a requirement apparently was thought to be unnecessary because of the unlikelihood of tax shenanigans between such employers and employees, and in the interests of simplicity, qualification was not required. However, a request was made for a ruling by a university which proposed to pay some of its law school professors (whose principal income came from outside the university) entirely by buying them annuities payable after retirement. This was a clear tax maneuver to shift income into postretirement years for the benefit of active professional people and indicated that any presumption that any group is above tax manipulation is a naïve one. The ruling was not given, but because of possible uncertainty in litigation if such a plan had been adopted, the law was changed in 1958 to limit to 20 per cent the fraction of total compensation which could be used to purchase annuities for employees of tax-exempt organizations.

This restriction was an alternative to the extension of the general requirements for qualification of pension plans. It was again desired by the Treasury and the Congress to avoid imposing any unnecessary complications on tax-exempt organizations if that could be done without permitting their employees to get an unfair tax advantage over other employees.

It now appears that the 1958 legislation may have been inadequate to prevent abuse. Various insurance companies seized on the 20 per cent rule and proposed that salaries be reduced for individual employees, with the amount of the reduction put into retirement annuities. Any such individual arrangements could not, of course, be made under qualified pension plans, and there was no intent in the law to give professors, doctors, and hospital clerks any special advantages. Some universities have agreed to such special arrangements; others have refused to make special deals with faculty members. Unless the substitution of individual annuities for salaries is held to be illegal, the law should be amended to put employees of tax-exempt institutions in the same position as all other employees. This is not an uncommon situation where companies too eager for business find a loophole which is used by enough people to force a change in the law which will complicate the affairs of many who would not engage in the practice.

Annuities

Annuities purchased by an individual have been taxed under three different approaches under the tax law. No one of the three, including the present treatment, is altogether satisfactory. A review of the changes reveals a continuing conflict between the objectives of equity and simplicity.

An annuity consists of periodic payments, usually starting at a specified age and continuing for the duration of a person's life, which returns to an individual the amount of his investment in the annuity contract plus some assumed rate of interest on the capital sum and less the expenses and profits of the insurance company which issues the contract. The contract may be purchased by a single payment of capital or by periodic payments into the company extending over many years. The annuity from the company may be for one person or be continued to surviving beneficiaries. An early death may absolve the insurance company from any payment, or the contract may provide for a guaranteed return to an estate of at least the investment in the contract. The actuarial calculations which fix the costs and benefits of annuity contracts are based on assumptions of life expectancy, the probable rate of earnings on capital sums, and expenses and profit margins. In the aggregate, after adequate margins for safety have been allowed for, annuity benefits are established which will pay out to annuitants as a whole, over their lifetimes or other specified periods, the capital sums and the net earnings on those sums. The problem in tax policy is to determine how much net income is involved in a series of annuity payments and when to tax it.

The simplest approach is to assume that all benefit payments are a return of the capital invested in the annuity policy until the cost is fully recovered while all subsequent payments constitute net income. Thus if a policy costing $10,000 pays an annual annuity of $1,000, the receipts of the first ten years would be nontaxable and all subsequent payments would be fully taxable. This rule was adopted in the tax law prior to 1942. It had the advantage of simplicity, and it was fair in the sense that a person would not be taxed on any income until his capital was fully recovered. But the law was criticized on the ground that elderly people after living for many years on a nontaxable annuity were suddenly subjected to taxation on the full amount, perhaps at a time when their expenses were becoming greater and their chances for modest outside earnings were less. The sudden taxability of a previously tax-exempt receipt was hard to explain and led to understandable resentment.

In 1942, the law was changed to provide that 3 per cent of the cost of an annuity would be deemed to be income and the rest a return of capital until the tax-free payments had equaled the cost of the policy, after which time all payments would be deemed to be income. The 3 per cent figure approximated the rate of earnings assumed in the actuarial calculations of insurance companies. This method avoided change from complete tax exemption to full taxation, but it involved an oversimplification which under some annuity contracts made it very unlikely that the capital investment could ever be recovered tax-free. In an annuity purchased for a lump sum, with the benefits starting immediately, the capital sum on which the insurance company could earn income would be depleted by the successive payments. A tax presumption that each payment contained income equal to 3 per cent of the original cost would overstate the income element, and a person would have to live long beyond his expectancy to recover his capital investment tax-free. By contrast, in an annuity purchased by periodic payments between the ages of twenty-five and sixty-five and then paid out over a ten-year period, the interest on the capital sum would have compounded over many years and the true net income above cost might amount to more than three per cent of the cost.

Because of complaints about the lack of refinement in the 3 per cent rule, the law was changed in 1954 to the present rule, which seems theoretically correct but is more complicated. It is now provided that when benefit payments begin, the cost of an annuity must be divided by the beneficiary's life expectancy and this amount will be allowed as a tax-free return of capital in each benefit payment, with the balance of each payment treated as taxable income. This division of the benefit into tax-exempt and taxable parts continues forever. If the beneficiary dies before his life expectancy, he will not have recovered the cost of his capital tax-free, even though he has been taxed on part of his receipts. If he lives beyond his life expectancy, he will recover more than his cost tax-free. On the average, annuitants will recover their investments if the life-expectancy assumptions are correct, but most individual annuitants will either fall short of a full tax-free recovery of capital or receive more than their cost tax-free.

The three methods described seem to cover the range of possible tax rules. Clearly no one is ideal. The present rule is the most complicated, especially when necessary adjustments are made for more than one beneficiary and for policies which guarantee a full recovery of cost or a specified number of payments, as ten years certain, even if a beneficiary dies before that time. The present rule, however, appears to make the tax law conform to the essence of an annuity contract under which a person may risk losing part of his capital if he dies too soon in return for the assurance of greater annual payments if he lives beyond his expectancy. It was on this theory that the Treasury and the Congress accepted the proposals to change the 3 per cent rule in 1954. The present law is administratively feasible only with the cooperation of the insurance companies, which notify their policyholders of the taxable part of the annuities under standard assumptions authorized by the Treasury. Since it was the insurance companies which urged the change in the law to this more complicated method, it is reasonable that they should assist in its administration; with a few minor exceptions at the start, they have done so effectively.

Resentment now comes because of complexity and because there may be a tax on some part of benefits, even though capital is never fully recovered. On balance the present law, however, seems the most acceptable of the three possible methods. The foregoing description of the evolution of the law to its present stage gives another example of the conflicts among objectives and the seeming impossibility of establishing a perfect rule to cover a moderately complicated situation.

Retirement-income Credit

The retirement-income credit is quite complicated. Under it, a retired person may get a credit against his income tax substantially equivalent to the savings in tax which a bottom-bracket taxpayer gets from his social security benefits. The retirement-income credit was introduced in 1954 to remove a discrimination between those receiving tax-exempt social security benefits and those with other sorts of taxable retirement income, including state and municipal pensions. Much of the complication comes from the fact that the retirement-income credit was designed to be an alternative for, not an addition to, the exemption of social security benefits. If the retirement-income credit had not been so designed, the result would not have been equitable because the law would have continued to discriminate in favor of those with social security benefits instead of moving toward a more equal tax treatment of all retired people regardless of their source of income. Over the years, as social security benefits come to be virtually universal, the retirement-income credit as such will become of less importance and it may be possible to eliminate it in the interests of simplicity.

The exemption of social security old-age benefits, which provided the precedent for the retirement-income credit, was the result of a ruling, which may not have been well reasoned, given shortly after the social security system was established. With the double exemption for people over sixty-five, the tax exemption of old-age benefits is not, in fact, significant for people dependent primarily on them because, typically, the personal exemptions exceed the benefits. The exemption of benefits is of value to those with other sources of income, and the greater the income, the greater the value of the exemption. One of the complications in the retirement-income credit is intended to remove this greater tax advantage to people with larger incomes. It is achieved by the use of a tax credit instead of a deduction of the retirement income in computing taxable income.

On balance, it would have been preferable to make the old-age benefits taxable when received and avoid the retirement-income credit. This would be fair in that it would eliminate the present complete tax exemption of the bulk of the old-age benefits which are attributable to the employer's contributions and to interest, neither of which are taxable at any time to employees. For greater equity but with some complications, the employees' own contributions could be regarded as the cost of the benefit payments and allowed as a tax-free return, preferably by a statutory rule which would establish an average investment for all employees and a standard period of tax-free benefits to recover this investment which would be applicable to everyone. With this change there would be no precedent or need for the retirement-income credit.

The taxation of old-age social security benefits should have been adopted at the time the double personal exemption was granted in 1948. This was recommended in the report of the Staff of the Joint Committee on Internal Revenue Taxation, but it was not done apparently because the double exemption was sufficiently generous to make most social security benefits nontaxable anyway. This was the very fact which would have made it reasonable and equitable to remove the tax exemption of the benefits and forestall the complications of the retirement-income credit. It might still be considered as a belated offset to the double exemption for people over sixty-five. It would certainly be a reform in the interests of simplification through the elimination of the retirement-income credit which would then be fair.

Deferred-compensation Contracts

Deferred-compensation contracts also raise major problems involving fairness, simplicity, and possible adverse economic consequences. Such contracts are used fairly frequently for key executives, especially those who change employers and forego their rights under nonvested pension plans. They are, in fact, often necessary to prevent a high-salaried man from actually losing financially when he changes jobs. This is true because it is virtually impossible to save enough from any conceivable increase in salary to make up for the pension rights foregone by a change of employer, and the pension to be built up in the remaining years of new employment will be far short of the pension foregone, because of the shorter period of time. A bad consequence of pensions, from the standpoint of the country, is the effect that the usual plans, with limited and delayed vesting, have in freezing executives into their existing positions. Deferred-compensation contracts serve to offset this freezing effect; they can also be used with existing key employees to freeze them more tightly and as outright tax gimmicks to spread income.

There is no specific reference to deferred-compensation contracts in the Internal Revenue Code or the Regulations issued under it, and for many years prior to 1960 there were no rulings on the subject in spite of numerous requests for them. They were used fairly extensively, though in many cases they were not used, partly because of uncertainty as to their tax consequences. When written, they usually included various conditions and contingencies to strengthen the case for postponing the taxability of income until the time of its receipt, in spite of the fact that the primary services, for which the compensation was paid, terminated at retirement.

A forthright clarification of the law on deferred-compensation contracts was needed. It was given in a Treasury ruling early in 1960. It accorded with the prevailing legal opinion that the existing law did permit a spreading of compensation over a longer period of time than actual employment, even for taxpayers on a cash basis, as long as the contract was initially drawn on that basis and was not a subterfuge to reallocate income already earned under an existing arrangement. Arrangements for spreading of income also can be made in advance for payments in connection with services or royalties when there is no employer-employee relationship.

Arguments to the contrary had urged that the doctrine of constructive receipt or some modification of it should be applied to attempts to tax currently, or at least no later than at the time of retirement, compensation which is really based on present services. Under this approach, requirements to give consulting services and refrain from employment with competitors after retirement would have been subject to a skeptical review and usually ignored. Even cash-basis taxpayers thus would be deemed to have earned currently income which they would receive in the future, when the future services were nominal or unlikely to be significant.

The fact that the 1960 ruling was issued has removed uncertainty and put all taxpayers in a position to take advantage of deferred-compensation contracts where appropriate. From the standpoint of simplicity, the argument is all on the side of permitting deferral of income by contract. The fact of payment provides a simple, objective test of the receipt of income; to many people, this fact should be controlling. The complexities and prospective litigation which would arise from any attempt to tax income prior to receipt are so great in the minds of many people as to rule out of consideration any attempt to secure legislation to change the law on the taxability of deferred-compensation contracts.

From the combined standpoints of fairness and economic consequences, however, there is much to be said for making the attempt. To many laymen the distinction between contracts drawn just before and just after the occurrence of the event which fixes the right to receive income seems an artificial one. A deferred-compensation arrangement made by a boxer with his employer on the way to the ring would assure favorable tax treatment; the same arrangement made on the way back to the dressing room would not. On the basis of the familiar proposition that a given sum always has more value presently than at a later date simply because it can be invested in risk-free securities and produce income immediately, there seems no real reason for a recipient of income to defer a given sum except for the tax advantage. Arguments about improvident recipients who defer the receipt of income to avoid squandering it seem invalid; a recipient who is provident enough to arrange for deferred receipt would be provident enough to put his lump-sum payment into trust and secure extra income from interest in the meantime. Deferred-compensation contracts seem to be created so overwhelmingly for tax purposes that on grounds of fairness they should be regarded skeptically and form should not be allowed to triumph over substance.

The extensive use of deferred-compensation contracts, which may be presumed to develop in the future, will create new sets of discriminations. Self-employed people will be discriminated against as compared with employees, thereby accentuating the pension problem discussed previously. This will be true because an employee, especially with a large company, will be more confident of the value of a deferred-compensation contract than would a brain surgeon or a lawyer dealing with an individual client. This presents a further problem concerning the fairness of the law.

From the standpoint of economic consequences, the large and established company will have an advantage over small and new ones in its relations with its employees and other individuals to whom it pays compensation. An author will be ready to take the small risk of default on a deferred payment of royalties from a well-established publisher to gain the tax advantage of spreading over many years the income from a prospective short-run best seller, but he would not run the risk with a new publisher who had only a small amount of capital. An employee would be happy with a deferred-compensation contract with a large solid company, but dubious about one with a doubtful company. The tax advantage of spreading a large sum over a long period is great; the risks which would discourage the use of such contracts exist to the extent that there is uncertainty about the payment. The risk would be small in comparison with the advantages in the case of well-established employers or other contractors.

The Treasury ruling on deferred-compensation contracts has removed uncertainty, a necessary first step in establishing a workable law. The arguments of administrative simplicity are so strongly in favor of the position taken that it is probably desirable to wait for some time to determine the extent to which feelings of unfairness develop and the importance of the advantages given to well-established companies over their less secure competitors. Hopefully, the problems will not become so great as to require new complications in the tax law, but it is by no means certain that changes will not be necessary. Reduction in the middle and upper tax brackets would, of course, reduce the tax advantages of deferred-compensation contracts and restrict their use; thus, reform in rates might make unnecessary a complicated reform in the definition of income.

Compensation and Gifts

A final problem in the taxation of compensation arises from three divided Supreme Court decisions in 1960 which held that the question of whether a payment to retired employees or their heirs constituted compensation or a gift must be decided in each situation on the basis of all the relevant facts. To most laymen, it must seem unlikely that a company would, or even should, give funds away to individuals as distinct from charities without some actuality or expectation of services, past, present, or future. Certainly the court decisions invite the use of a great deal of ingenuity in contriving to make compensation look like gifts. Much litigation will doubtless result. The Court, in fact, noted that the Congress might want to establish standards by singling out certain factors which would be determinative. This should be done forthwith. The basic concept would seem to be that where a payment is made to anyone or the heirs of anyone who has rendered services as an employee or otherwise or who may be likely to render services, the payment will be presumed to be compensation. It should further be provided that deductibility to the payer as an expense clearly establishes taxability to the payee. Either of these two tests would seem to accord with common expectations and prevent those who are tempted to resort to ingenious subterfuges from getting a tax advantage over those who proceed in a straightforward manner.

Chapter 4 DEDUCTIONS FOR INDIVIDUALS

All the deductions allowed in computing the taxable incomes of individuals are designed to give relief to the taxpayers benefiting from them and thereby make the law fairer. Each one of them, however, makes the law more complicated. Each deduction may also make the law seem unfair to those who do not benefit from it; those not benefiting may think that a deduction gives a special advantage, rather than relief, to someone else.

On balance, the law has gone too far in allowing deductions. In some instances the intended increase in fairness to the taxpayers who can use the deduction is more than offset by the discrimination against those who have somewhat comparable expenses which are not deductible. Each deduction by itself adds a complication to the law, and further complications are often necessary to prevent abuses from contrived transactions which may come within the letter but violate the spirit of the intended relief. Once a deduction is adopted, however, those who benefit from it will resent any proposal for its elimination, even as part of a general reform to decrease rates and simplify the law. This chapter will, nonetheless, analyze the non-business deductions allowed in computing individual taxable income and consider what limitations might be imposed on them. The authorized deductions are reviewed to show the problems in tax policy which they present. At the end of the chapter a rather ambitious plan is proposed for a simpler and fairer law.

Before the specific deductions for taxes, interest, contributions, medical expenses, casualty losses, child care, and educational expenses are dealt with successively, the special problem of discrimination between homeowners and renters is reviewed. An appraisal of this discrimination and the alternative methods to reduce it cuts across various subjects and requires consideration of the two existing deductions for interest and taxes, a possible new deduction for rent, and a possible taxation of imputed rental income from homeownership.

Discrimination between Homeowners and Renters

A person renting a house must pay the rent from his net income, after taxes, with no deduction of any sort. If the income is subject to a marginal tax rate of only 20 per cent, a rent of $160 a month requires $200 of pretax income a month. A rent of $400 a month requires $800 of pretax income a month if subject to a marginal tax rate of 50 per cent. To a considerable extent, the rent goes to pay property taxes on the house and to provide a return on the capital invested in it by the landlord (or pay the interest on the mortgage carried by the landlord).

In contrast to renters, people who own their own houses can deduct their property taxes in computing their taxable income. The interest on their own mortgages is also deductible, or if they buy their homes outright, the income in kind received from the capital tied up in the house is not taxable. Thus, homeowners have a tax advantage over tenants to the extent of the tax saving arising from the deductibility of property taxes and interest paid (or exemption of the income in kind from capital invested in a residence). At a 75 per cent tax rate, it is almost prohibitively expensive to rent a home or apartment and thereby fail to secure the advantages of tax deductions for that part of the cost which is attributable to property taxes and the return on (or cost of) capital investment in a house. The rapid growth of cooperative apartments reflects the tax advantages of homeownership; advertisements for them regularly indicate the deductible amount of the monthly maintenance or carrying charge.

This differential tax treatment of tenants and homeowners has been the subject of frequent criticism from the standpoint of fairness, although its implications are usually approved as a matter of social policy. Homeownership is generally regarded as good; it helps to foster a sense of stability and identity with a community. Because of the reliance of municipalities on property taxes, direct payments of property taxes by homeowners are likely to make them more responsible citizens and better judges of the proper scale of local expenditures. Certainly if there is to be a differential treatment under the Federal income tax, it should be in favor of and not against homeownership. But there is nonetheless a real discrimination between homeowners and renters.

If the present tax advantage of homeownership is thought to be so unfair as to require some change in the law, it could be made in any one of three ways. Two of the possibilities seem bad; one of them has a good deal of merit, and though it may be unacceptable politically, it is nevertheless proposed as part of a general tax reform.

The proposal most frequently advanced is to make homeowners include in their taxable incomes the imputed rental value of their homes and pay an income tax on it. Though this might make for theoretical perfection, it generally would be regarded as a sign of an unreasonably grasping tax law.

The taxation of income in kind from property could be extended endlessly. If the rental value of a home could be taxed as imputed income, what about income in kind from an investment in the furniture in the house or the car in the garage? Those, too, give continuing use and pleasure; they can, in fact, also be rented, and owners have a tax advantage, in a sense, over renters. It is hard to imagine anyone seriously advocating taxing a car owner on what he might have had to pay in rent to get a similar car or the owner of furniture on what it would have cost him to rent similar furniture or, as the ultimate extreme, the owner of a dinner jacket on what he would have had to pay if he had rented his dress clothes from a clothing store. One might also contend that do-it-yourself activities produce income in kind from labor, just as ownership of property yields income in kind from capital. One would then argue that a man who paints his own house or repairs his own light fixture should be taxed on the value of his own services to himself, that is, for the amount he would have had to pay a painter or an electrician to do the same job. These analogies are not logically farfetched; they show the extremes to which a theoretical notion may carry us.

Administratively, the problem of fixing imputed rental values for homes would be great; there would be endless controversy and deep resentment by taxpayers about decisions by tax agents. Imputed rentals would be especially hard to fix on older houses or on large places with expensive features which seemed worthwhile to the person who built the place but which would not be paid for by anyone else, either a tenant or a subsequent purchaser. The apparent Congressional disinterest in proposals to include imputed rent in taxable income indicates that they need not, fortunately, be given serious practical consideration, though they will doubtless remain a favorite of some tax reformers.

Interestingly enough, England does include the rental value of owner-occupied homes in taxable income; this fact is cited by those who favor such a change in this country as evidence that their proposal is both politically acceptable and administratively feasible. There are two reasons why the British precedent is not relevant. It was first adopted when rates were low, and the inclusion or exclusion was not of great monetary importance to taxpayers. Also, it was administratively feasible for income tax purposes there because local property taxes are also based on the annual or rental value of properties instead of on capital values as in this country. The idea of "annual value" of real estate is thus firmly implanted in national thinking. Once adopted, a proposal to drop this item of income in England would have been objected to as giving a favored treatment to homeowners.

Virtually, any differential treatment may logically be appraised as constituting a discrimination in favor of one group or against another group or both. When a change from an existing situation removes a long-established advantage of one group which has come to be regarded as representing the natural order of things, it is likely to be regarded as imposing a penalty on them rather than removing an unfair advantage from them. The difference in attitude depends on the position from which one starts. It is quite understandable that in England a move from their traditional treatment to ours would be regarded as giving a favored treatment to homeowners.

A second method of securing greater equality of treatment between those who rent and those who own their homes would be to allow renters to deduct a part of their rent in computing their taxable incomes. Fortunately, this is seldom proposed. Politically it would be vastly more appealing than the taxation of imputed rent. Any new deduction or increase in an existing deduction affecting those with lower income is attractive, it seems generous, those who benefit are pleased, and those who have to pay more to make up for the lost revenue are likely to be oblivious of that fact or inarticulate.

But it would be very hard administratively to determine what part of rental payments should be allowed as a deduction to produce equality with homeowners. The deductible proportion should be the amount which covers property taxes and a normal return on capital, but with the great variations in property tax rates any standard fraction of rent would be quite imperfect. A new deduction on the scale that would be involved for partial deductions for rent would also significantly reduce the tax base, making higher taxes necessary on the remaining part of taxable income. And if deductions are once allowed for actual cash expenditures for this part of normal personal living expenses, even though it was intended to remove a discrimination, the chance for progressive deterioration of the tax base would be strengthened. If part of rent is deductible, why not outlays for food or clothing?

Neither the inclusion in taxable income of the rental value of an owner-occupied home nor the deduction of part of the rent paid by tenants is feasible or desirable. There is a tax advantage in homeownership, but the advantage is at least in the right direction and either of these two ways of removing it would unduly complicate the law and its administration.

The third method of removing the discrimination against those who rent their homes would be to disallow the deductions for property taxes and mortgage interest on homes occupied by their owners. Administratively, this would be the simplest of the three methods. It would not require the calculation of any new deductions or the determination of any imputed income. In fact, it would make the law even simpler for taxpayers because they would not have to compute two present deductions.

From the standpoint of fairness, the elimination of the property tax deduction would produce equality between homeowners and renters as regards that part of the cost of home use. The elimination of the interest deduction would also produce equality between owners and renters on income in kind from capital to the extent that the capital involved was borrowed. It would not, however, produce equality to the extent of an owner's equity in his home. One's own capital investment in a home would still yield untaxed income in kind. This seems to be the only theoretical argument against the change, but a partial solution which is practical is a good deal better than a full solution which is impractical.

From the standpoint of political acceptability, this change would probably stand some place between the taxation of imputed rental income and the allowance of a deduction for rent. The elimination of a deduction is probably more acceptable than the inclusion of a new item of income but certainly less acceptable than the granting of a new deduction. For high-bracket people with large property taxes on their residences, the additional tax burden could be substantial. People in very high income tax brackets have been much less concerned about the property taxes on their residences because of the traditional deductibility; the elimination of the deduction would increase manyfold the impact of property taxes on residences and in some instances make them seem prohibitively expensive. This change should be adopted only as part of a general reform which would give reductions to the excessive income tax rates, which have had the incidental effect of making those subject to them somewhat indifferent to those expenses which are deductible. As part of a reform, it would make the law fairer and simpler. From an economic standpoint it might tend to shift consumption from housing which now receives a tax advantage to other items, but not to any significant extent.

Taxes

The preceding analysis of the differential treatment of home-owners and home renters introduced the subject of the deductibility of state and local taxes. It is questionable whether, if the Federal income tax were being established anew, this deduction would be allowed.

Total deductions for taxes amounted to 7.5 billion dollars in 1958, the last year for which figures are available. As shown in Appendix D, a truly amazing feature of the distribution of the deduction for taxes over the various levels of taxable income is that they correspond almost exactly to the distribution of adjusted gross income from which they are deducted. Incomes of $3,000 and under $5,000 represented 15.3 per cent of total income and had 15.8 per cent of total tax deductions; incomes of $5,000 and under $10,000 had 45.4 per cent of total income and 45.7 per cent of tax deductions, and income of $10,000 and under $20,000 had 17.2 per cent of total income and 16.9 per cent of total taxes. It is notable that the deduction for taxes is distributed substantially in proportion to income; the reductions which it makes in taxable income do not vary to any appreciable extent with the size of incomes.

As with all deductions, the saving in income tax from any given amount of deduction depends on a person's marginal tax rate and hence is greatest for those with the largest incomes. Thus, the deduction of $100 of taxes for a person with $2,000 of taxable income saves $20 in tax at the 20 per cent marginal tax rate. For a person with $200,000 of taxable income the same $100 would save $90 at the 90 per cent marginal tax rate, while if deductible taxes amounted to 5 per cent of income, as it was for the man with the $2,000 income, state and local taxes would amount to $10,000 and its deductibility would save $9,000 of Federal income tax.

There are many arguments in favor of a deduction for taxes paid to states and municipalities in computing taxable income for the Federal income tax, but they are not altogether persuasive. One may contend that a deduction for state and local taxes is necessary to prevent encroachment by the Federal government on state governments and their subordinate agencies. This would be more appealing if the state governments were required to or always did recognize the Federal tax as a deduction in computing taxable incomes for state income taxes. But they are not required to do so. In fact some do and some do not, and at least one state, Massachusetts, allows a deduction only in part and in a way which is peculiarly unfair.

One may defend the deductibility of state taxes with a slogan; a removal of the deduction would impose "a tax on a tax." This would be more appealing if all taxes were included in the deduction. This was the case prior to 1942, except for Federal income and estate taxes, but in that year the deductibility of Federal taxes was repealed. The principal reaction seems to have been one of relief that it was no longer necessary to keep records or make estimates of deductible Federal taxes. Since the Federal income tax thus imposes "a tax on its own taxes," there seems no reason why it should give preferential treatment to taxes of other jurisdictions for the sake of whatever real meaning the slogan may have.

The one strong argument in favor of deductibility of state and local taxes is that it is necessary to keep combined taxes from exceeding total income in the upper brackets. This is true and the argument is conclusive as long as top-bracket rates are as high as they are. A 10 per cent state income tax and a 91 per cent Federal tax would obviously add up to 101 per cent of income if the state tax were not deductible; with deductibility of the state tax they add up to 91.9 per cent. There are also all the other state and local taxes which, without deductibility, would push the combined rates still higher. Rates have gone to their present levels on the basis of deductibility, and it would be grossly unfair to remove it unless income tax rates were substantially reduced. But with such a reduction, that is, as part of a general reform in which rate adjustments would be significant, the elimination of the deduction would seem reasonable. It would be somewhat of a simplification, though not a great one because the major deductible taxes are easily recorded with no difficult problems of allocation, except for property taxes on property which changes hands during a year. For residents of those states with sales taxes and for everyone with an automobile, the elimination of the temptation to overestimate sales and state gasoline taxes by just a little would probably improve integrity and taxpayer morale by just a little.

It is urged by some that only state and local income taxes be allowed as deductions in computing taxable income for the Federal tax. This would eliminate the deduction for property taxes on owner-occupied residences and thereby partially remove the discrimination against renters, and it would eliminate the deduction for sales and excise taxes, which are most subject to errors of estimate. However, this partial elimination of the state and local tax deduction would be unfair because it would discriminate against residents of states which have no income taxes or low income taxes, and it would be an improper use of Federal power because it would put strong pressures to shift revenue sources from nondeductible property and sales taxes to deductible income taxes. This inducement to greater use of income taxation may be one reason for support of the proposal by those who regard the income tax as the ideal tax.

Actually with the total revenue requirements as high as they are, even a perfect tax would be under an undue strain to provide all the funds needed, and the income tax is, to say the least, far from perfect. Many taxes are needed to prevent excessive rates in any one tax and are used with the hope that the inevitable inequities in each one will somewhat balance out against each other. A state which does not use income taxation should not be put under duress by the Federal government to adopt it.

In summary, the deduction for state and local taxes appears to be one which, in the interests of some simplification, might be eliminated as part of a general tax reform which included substantial rate revision. The deduction for taxes contains no element of relief for catastrophes, as in the medical expense and casualty deductions, nor any matter of social policy, as in the charitable deduction to encourage philanthropy. The deduction for taxes is one without any really good reason; the simplification started by repeal of the deduction for Federal excises in 1942 might be completed by repeal of the remaining deduction as part of a general reform.

In spite of the foregoing proposal, one final point may be made, almost as an aside. The one tax which unfortunately is not allowed as a deduction, in our practical political world, is the Federal income tax itself. It is allowed as a deduction in Denmark and perhaps in a few other countries and was in this country until 1917. With the tax paid each year on the prior year's income deductible, those who want confiscatory rates for political or social purposes can have them, and a country can avoid many of their adverse effects. The net result of deductibility is, of course, to make a 99 per cent rate tend to be the actual equivalent of a 49½ per cent rate after a series of fluctuations of lessening size extending over several years. It may be regarded as a major misfortune in our tax legislation that this deduction in the original tax was not continued here.

Interest

Total deductions for interest paid amounted to 6.3 billion dollars in 1958. The deduction, as shown in Appendix D, was distributed substantially in proportion to the adjusted gross income from which it was deducted, but with a somewhat higher peak at the place where the bulk of the income existed, $5,000 and under $10,000

(45.4 per cent of the total income and 54.4 per cent of the total interest deductions), and somewhat smaller proportions in both the larger incomes and the smaller ones under $3,000. As with the deduction for taxes, there is no notable preponderance for either smaller or larger incomes, though the point should be repeated that, as with all deductions, the tax saving for any given deduction depends on an individual marginal income bracket and hence is greatest for those with the largest incomes.

The interest deduction has led to many abuses, contrary to the situation regarding the deduction for taxes. This is especially the case in connection with some artificial sorts of life insurance policies which apparently have been created solely to take advantage of a current interest deduction offset only in part by a later capital gains tax. Abuses also occur in various sorts of security transactions. Restrictions on deductible interest have had to be imposed to limit abuses, and the restrictions have not been able to keep up with the ingenuity of those who contrive new sorts of insurance schemes and transactions.

Interest incurred in business operations must, of course, be treated as an expense to give a proper measure of net income. But interest on installment purchases or personal loans has no relation to business activities, and there seems no more justification to allow it as a deduction than any other personal expenses. The deduction was probably originally allowed because interest was thought of as primarily arising in business activities, and it was simpler to avoid any need to distinguish business from personal indebtedness. But it is necessary now to rule out some forms of interest to prevent abuses, and in many installment payment plans it is so hard for the debtor to determine the interest involved that the tax law has set up a presumptive interest deduction.

It seems likely that if we could start afresh on income tax legislation, with simplicity as a conscious objective, the arguments for a deduction of interest on personal debts on grounds of fairness would not be persuasive. Certainly the deduction for interest on mortgages on owner-occupied homes would be rejected as unfair to renters. Elimination of the deduction for interest on personal indebtedness should be considered as part of a general tax reform.

Such a change would require a new set of definitions to distinguish personal from business indebtedness. Interest on personal loans, installment purchases, and mortgages on owner-occupied houses would be easy to classify. Interest on a mortgage on a summer home which is sometimes rented to others would be more difficult, but the problem of allocating depreciation and maintenance expenses on such properties already exists, and the allocation of interest would be made on the same formula. Interest on loans to purchase securities would present the most difficult problem, but this is also the area of the greatest existing abuses.

At present, interest on loans to carry tax-exempt securities is not allowed as a deduction in computing taxable income. This is necessary to prevent a compounding of the advantage of tax exemption which would otherwise be possible. If one could reduce the cost of borrowing money to buy tax-exempt bonds to a nominal level by deducting it from his salary or other investment income, he could receive a very high return on his own funds. One could, for example, afford to pay 4 per cent interest for a loan to buy 3 per cent tax-exempt bonds and still make 13.4 per cent on his investment if he put up 20 per cent of the purchase price himself and was subject to a 90 per cent marginal tax.[1] But the enforcement of the disallowance of interest on loans to carry tax-exempt securities is difficult because it is often impossible to trace funds or associate a particular source with a particular use. As long as tax-exempt securities are not pledged for a loan, it is hard to prove the relationship.

Reference has already been made to peculiar "insurance policies" which seem to have little basis of existence except for tax maneuvers. Loans are secured to cover the full amounts of premiums either from the insurance companies themselves or from cooperating banks. The deductibility of interest makes the actual cost of carrying the policy negligible to a high-bracket taxpayer. The increase in cash surrender value is geared to the premium payments, relieving him from any personal liability and making the loan good regardless of the net worth of the policyholder. If the net value of the policy is ultimately realized as a capital gain, the full circle of tax advantages has been completed. The Treasury in 1957 and 1958, with the support of many insurance agents, attempted to secure

---

[1] Total interest received on $100,000 of bonds, $3,000. Total interest paid, $3,200 (4 per cent of $80,000). Net cost of interest paid after tax deduction, $320. Net interest received ($2,680 ($3,000 − $320). Net investment, $20,000. Rate of return, 13.4 per cent.

legislation to deny the interest deductions on loans where it was apparent at the time the policy was issued that it was to be financed primarily by loans, but others in the industry managed to block it with cries of simulated outrage and talk of increased tax burdens on desperate people taking out policy loans to meet family emergencies. The Treasury proposal was not intended to deny interest deductions for ordinary policy loans, nor would it have done so. This area of abuse should be corrected as a minimum to maintain the integrity of the tax system, and as already indicated, further reflection may lead to the conclusion that the entire deduction for interest on personal loans should be dropped.[2]

If a major change is made when middle and upper bracket rates are reduced, it would appear desirable to draw the line of demarcation on loans connected with an active trade or business rather than loans for transactions entered into for a profit. This is a point, however, on which extensive consideration of the implications would be required.

Contributions

The United States is notable among nations for the extent of private philanthropy. Our tax laws are also notable in giving liberal deductions for charitable contributions.

Our tradition is one which should not be weakened. Private philanthropy assures greater diversity in many aspects of our life, as in education. It is a substitute for larger government expenditures in many areas, as in hospitals, and thereby reduces the general tax burden. It provides important types of public services which might not otherwise exist, as children's camps, Christmas dinners and gifts for the indigent, and assistance in special cases above the level of welfare payments. It is not necessary to elaborate on the advantages of philanthropy and the pride we should take in it. And yet it must not be allowed to become a tax racket as it now is in some respects.

[2] The Supreme Court in November, 1960, in a divided opinion, upheld the Internal Revenue Service in disallowing "interest" on loans to pay premiums on a 4-million-dollar "policy," which required a net investment of $4,000. It did so on the ground that there was no economic project and no real indebtedness, only "sham borrowing." This was about as extreme a situation as one might find. Unless the disallowance can be extended fairly broadly, legislation will still be required (*Knetsch v. United States*, Nov. 14, 1960).

A person should not be able to give away his discarded furniture to a charity and claim a deduction for its original purchase price in computing his taxable income. He cannot legally do so under the present law because deductions are limited to the fair market value at the time of gift, but the government cannot check all values, and a friendly charity may acknowledge receipt of a gift at a stated value. A person should not be able to buy a painting for $1,000 and after a polite interval and a cooperative appraisal at $5,000 give it to a museum at that figure and, if he is in the 90 per cent bracket, make $3,500 tax profit on his original outlay of $1,000. Of course, he cannot under the law unless the painting has really gone up in value to $5,000, but the Internal Revenue Service is not well equipped with art appraisers and should not have to be.

The essential problem to prevent abuse is to avoid overvaluation of gifts. Money presents no problem, nor do listed or actively traded securities. On most other forms of property there is room for substantial differences, even among honest opinions, on value. The problem is emphasized because there is no conflict of interest between donors and donees which might serve to protect the interest of the government. The higher the valuation, the greater the tax reduction to the donor. A donee who is acquiescent in a valuation is more likely to get a gift and perhaps increase its own prestige by meeting a higher quota for contributions.

Several restrictions might be imposed to maintain and in some respects restore the integrity of tax deductions for charitable contributions. Before they are considered, the extent of gifts may be briefly noted. As shown in Appendix D, total deductions in 1958 were 5.7 billion dollars, amounting to slightly less than 4 per cent of adjusted gross income. Thus, total contributions are far below the traditional 10 per cent and the allowable 20 or 30 per cent under the tax law. Contrary to the situations involving taxes and interest, contributions are larger in comparison with income at the extremes of the income scale. Contributions were 9.0 per cent of adjusted gross incomes of $600 and under $1,000 and 9.6 per cent of those above $100,000, while they were only 3.5 per cent of adjusted gross incomes of $5,000 and under $10,000. The notably greater proportionate generosity of those with the largest and the smallest incomes is repeated in other years.

It is sometimes suggested that the amount of a charitable deduction should be limited to the actual purchase price of property contributed. This is intended to prevent overvaluations of appreciated property, though it would do nothing to prevent overvaluation of worn-out furniture, appliances, and clothing given to rummage sales. Though this change is appealing, the maintenance of the objectives of private charities is even more appealing, and the importance to them of gifts of appreciated securities is great. A first step to restrict abuse without significant restrictions on general philanthropy would be to limit the deduction to original cost to the donor in the case of art objects, where the opportunity for abuse is greatest. The next most serious problem probably comes in the overvaluation of investment property where valuations are subject to a considerable difference of opinion, as in a good deal of real estate. Some of the more scrupulous recipients of gifts of real estate decline to give a receipt for a specific value and notify the donor of the value received on a subsequent sale. Because of the lack of any adverse interest or conflict of interest to protect the revenue against an overvaluation confirmed by an acquiescent donee, audits in this area should be rigorous.

On the matter of overvaluations of used personal possessions, no simple remedy is available. To prevent petty abuses, a minimum figure of $25 or $50 might be established for individual items of furniture and clothing, but this would be a discrimination against those who send cloth coats and in favor of those who give mink coats to rummage sales. It would also not deal with the problem of an interior decorator who in his enthusiasm in redecorating a client's room or house appraises the old furniture at something in line with its replacement value rather than its secondhand sales price and thereby provides evidence which if unchallenged will greatly reduce the net cost to his client of the refurnishing. Perhaps abuses in this area are, in the aggregate, too petty to justify the rather drastic change of disallowing deductions for gifts of used furniture and clothing. It is doubtful, however, if this disallowance would significantly restrict philanthropy. It would improve the tax atmosphere by removing a temptation for many taxpayers and by preventing abuse by a few. Conversations indicate that the majority of taxpayers do not yet use this particular part of the charitable deduction, and its disallowance would be a matter of indifference. It might well be included in a general tax reform.

It is sometimes said that one gains more by giving property away to a charity than by selling it. This is true if the property has appreciated greatly and if it will either be sold or given away. But the familiar saying overstates the case because it ignores the third and most obvious possibility which is to keep the property, and unless one expects a fall in its value, one is better off to keep property than to either sell it or give it away.

If property purchased for $10 is sold for $100, there is a capital gains tax of up to $22.50, reducing the net receipt to $77.50. For a taxpayer in the 90 per cent bracket, the gift of the property worth $100 saves $90 in taxes on his current income, giving a true net gain of $90 from the disposition by a gift. It is in this sense that the gift is worth $12.50 more than a sale. But if the taxpayer neither sells nor gives the property, he will retain it and its value of $100 as part of his capital. It is only if there is an expectation of a fall in value that he is better off to either sell it or give it to a charity; only then is there an absolute advantage in making a deductible gift.

The idea that there is an absolute gain from giving property away has been so firmly established in the minds of many people that honest mistakes have doubtless been made both by solicitors for charities and by donors. It is less excusable to find the publisher of a popular annual tax book putting out a pamphlet for distribution by colleges and other prospective recipients with a table showing a "profit" from gifts of appreciated securities by high-bracket taxpayers. At no point in the description or table is there any indication that the table is valid only on the implicit assumption that the alternative is between a gift of the securities and a sale of the securities with a gift of the proceeds. The much more likely possibility that securities would be retained and the gift, if any, would be made from regular cash sources is completely ignored. Such a publication is thoroughly misleading. If the facts were as they are represented to be, tax reform would be required; as it is, the reform seems to be needed to stop misrepresentation by those who overstate the tax advantages of making gifts of appreciated property.

One rather unusual form of maneuver was developed prior to 1960 which did give a real gain from a gift. This plan, which has been so much advertised by one college that it bears its name, involves the gift of appreciated property to the college with the understanding that it will be converted into tax-exempt securities with the income paid to the donor and perhaps to surviving members of his family for life. Since the sale is made by the college or other tax-exempt organization, the profit is attributable to that organization and is nontaxable; hence the entire proceeds can be invested in tax-exempt securities without diminution by a capital gains tax which the donor would have had to pay if he had shifted his own investments. But since the donor has reserved an interest in income from "the property," which has now become tax-exempt bonds, the subsequent income to him is tax exempt.

The objectionable feature of this gift with a reserved life interest arises from the inconsistency of avoiding the capital gains tax on the grounds that the property belongs to the organization but claiming tax exemption on the income on the grounds that a right has been reserved in the specific property, even after a tax-exempt transmutation of form. The donor, to be sure, has disposed of the property, and gets a charitable deduction for the future value of the capital sum, which the tax-exempt organization will have the right to use for its own benefit after the death of the last-named person having the right to the income. But the net effect is to permit a sum one-third greater to be invested in tax-exempt bonds than would have been possible if an individual had sold stock with negligible cost and himself invested the net proceeds after a 25 per cent capital gains tax—and one-third more property yields one-third more income which over a good many years can more than offset the eventual right of the tax-exempt organization to use the income for its own purpose. To maintain the integrity of charitable contributions of appreciated property and even of gifts with reserved life interests, the compounding of tax advantages of the sort just described needs to be removed, especially since it seems to rest on a juxtaposition of concepts which are not even logically consistent. In December, 1960, the Treasury issued a ruling against this practice. If necessary, the ruling should be supported by legislation.

One final problem concerning charitable contributions may be mentioned here, though it concerns gifts of merchandise by businesses, corporate or proprietary, rather than individual contributions. The question is whether they should be allowed at fair market value or at cost. There have also been instances in which a company got double deductions by first taking a deduction for the cost of producing an item as a business expense and then taking a deduction for its cost or value as a charitable contribution. This is supposedly not possible under the present law; if it were found to be possible, it should be prevented by a prompt change in the law.

On the issue of cost or market value, the use of market value does not appear to involve any abuse so long as there is no overvaluation. Obsolete high-style clothing, spoiled food, or drugs kept on hand too long must not be allowed as deductions at the price that might have been received if the products could have been sold when fresh, but only on the actual value at the time of donation. In more normal circumstances, the alternatives can be seen in the example of an electronic computer to be given by its manufacturer to a university. Should the amount of the deduction be the selling price of the computer or its cost of manufacture? The former is clearly the more generous allowance. There is no basis for a net gain by making contributions as long as profit margins are no more than typical; the tax saving of 52 per cent of the market value of the gift is a good deal less than the outlays to manufacture the product. In industries where profit margins are very high, there is room for some abuse, and if it became at all frequent, for example, for toilet articles costing 20 cents to be given away with charitable deductions taken at a market value of $1, the rule would doubtless have to be changed. Liberality in the tax law toward charitable contributions should stop short of any point where a taxpayer could actually make money by making a gift. A reduction in the net cost of a gift by a tax saving seems to be sound social policy; a net gain from a gift would mean that the Treasury is not only bearing the full cost of the gift but actually paying a taxpayer to give away public money.

Medical Expenses

The medical-expense deduction is a relatively new one in the tax law, introduced in 1943. It is intended to give relief in case of abnormally high medical expenses. As such it is limited to expenses in excess of 3 per cent of income, plus expenses over 1 per cent for drugs, except for those over sixty-five, where all expenses are deductible. There is also a ceiling on the deduction of $2,500 per exemption, but not over $5,000 for single persons or $10,000 for married couples, again with an exception for those over sixty-five and disabled, where the ceiling is $15,000.

In 1958, as shown in Appendix D, total medical-expense deductions came to just under 4.3 billion dollars. Of this total 3.6 billion was taken on taxable returns. These deductions give the largest proportionate reductions in the smaller incomes, with 4.8 per cent of adjusted gross incomes under $1,000 on taxable returns, rising to 6.5 per cent for adjusted gross income of $1,000 and under $3,000 and then decreasing steadily to only 0.4 per cent for incomes of $100,000 and over. They were also by far the largest category of deductions on nontaxable returns, descending from 20.5 per cent of adjusted gross income under $1,000 to 11.4 per cent of the nontaxable returns with adjusted gross income of $3,000 and over. No other form of deduction has its benefits so concentrated in lower incomes, nor does any other deduction bulk so large in completely eliminating the taxability of smaller incomes. As a relief measure, it is obviously successful. The relief is given where personal distress can lead to financial catastrophe and where maximum personal responsibility is desirable.

The medical-expense deduction raises two issues: the definition of medical expenses and the fraction of income which they must exceed to qualify for a deduction. There are no thoroughly satisfactory ways of dealing with either of these problems. They are discussed here to indicate the continuing difficulties that arise under the medical-expense deduction.

In 1954, the definition of deductible expense was tightened to exclude such ordinary drugstore items as tooth paste, the percentage limitation was reduced from 5 to 3, and the allowance of expenses for drugs in excess of 1 per cent of income was added. As expected, these two changes substantially canceled each other, with total deductions rising from 2.9 per cent of adjusted gross income in 1952 to 3.2 per cent in 1954 and falling back to 2.9 per cent in 1958. The tighter definition was intended to rule out ordinary family expenses which were not associated with sickness or emergency and to remove a temptation to convert the entire drugstore bill into a deduction. The intent of the change was desirable, but the line of distinction is not altogether clear to ordinary taxpayers; unfortunately, no really good line has been proposed. A limitation to prescription drugs would be too restrictive and discourage the use of standard items which may be equally good, but hair rinses and tooth-cleaning chewing gum should have no place in a deduction

intended to give relief for unusually costly medical requirements.

Travel which is ostensibly for medical reasons has been another
source of dispute and abuse. No one quarrels with the expense of
travel necessary for treatment, but travel and long visits to improve
one's health by securing relief from winter cold or summer heat are
hardly the sort of outlay that deserves tax relief, especially when the
expense of living away from home is added onto the cost of travel.
Travel-expense allowances have been successively tightened to
limit them to the cost of travel itself and care in an establishment
primarily giving medical care, not simply in a resort with medical
care available. Here again the line of distinction is not so clear as
would be desirable and opportunities for collusion exist; the temptation is increased by very high tax rates. The consensus of opinion
would certainly be against any provision of the tax law which would
permit those who move about to get deductions for their travel
and living expenses for several months a year in a more equable
climate.

At the other end of the scale, it does seem equitable that all the
institutional charge for the care of a dependent, for example a
retarded child, should be considered as medical expenses, not just
that part which is attributed to medical services themselves. The
rule in this regard was broadened in 1957 by a more liberal position
in the Treasury regulations. The example given was for the costs of
a special school for blind children, a cost due entirely to a physical
condition but one in which a strict interpretation of medical expenses would have allowed only a minor fraction of the total cost.

The general intent of the medical deduction has been to permit
tax relief only where expenses are unusually high. The 3 per cent
of adjusted gross income taken as the norm in 1954, beyond which
expenses would be deductible, is perhaps too low in that it complicates tax calculations for many people for only small amounts of
tax relief and in situations where the expenses are in no sense a
financial catastrophe. The 3 per cent figure was selected because
it was thought to be an average figure, and the intent was to give
relief for expenses above the average. The problem here is to balance fairness against simplicity. Record keeping and extra calculations are resented even when they lead to deductions and a saving
in taxes. The law would probably be better if the 3 per cent base

figure were somewhat higher. Since, however, it has been reduced to that low point, resentment of an increase by those who would lose a deduction would more than offset the advantages of simplification. Regretfully, one must conclude that the 3 per cent figure should be maintained unless there were to be a major overhaul of the law, in which case a return to a figure that indicates financial distress rather than above-average expenditures would seem fair and simpler.

The ceilings on the medical-expense deduction were added to limit abuses of the sort previously described in resort living. With a proper definition of allowable expenses, the ceiling is unfair, especially when it is less than the amount required for full-time nursing care in a nursing home. The ceiling was increased to $15,000 in 1958 for people over sixty-five. It should be increased and perhaps removed regardless of age. If the principle of a medical-expense deduction is fair, its benefits should be available even to those who can efford private nursing attention.

Casualty Losses

The deduction for casualty losses is a long-standing one of relatively minor importance. In 1956, the latest year for which data are available, total deductions were 348 million dollars. This was almost exactly one-tenth of the medical-expense deduction, which in turn is considerably smaller than the deduction for taxes, contributions, and interest. The casualty losses were more important proportionately in smaller than in larger incomes, amounting to 0.4 per cent of adjusted gross incomes of $1,000 and under $3,000 but only 0.1 per cent of those of $50,000 and over.

The deductibility of casualty losses, however, are of particular significance to high-bracket taxpayers because they make self-insurance attractive. The opportunity to deduct a theft or fire loss against a 90 per cent tax bracket makes it cheaper to run the risk of absorbing the net cost of the loss than to carry insurance in view of the loading charges and high sales expenses which must also be covered by insurance premiums. High-bracket people who are thoroughly sophisticated on tax matters are, in fact, self-insurers on many items except for those involving liability to others where there are nonpecuniary advantages of insurance protection. This attitude gives a useful balance against the enticements of insurance salesmen for overinsurance.

A casualty-loss deduction is certainly not a necessary feature of an equitable income tax. Losses are an ordinary risk of life, and there is no inherent reason why they should be partially recouped by reductions in income taxes for those who are liable to tax. A casualty loss is not a cost of securing income and hence does not need to be deductible to give a fair measure of net income; it must be regarded as a relief provision in the law. Since it has been in the law for a great many years and does not create any major inequities or abuses, it may be expected that it will be continued.

The problems under the casualty-loss deduction involve the definition and the measurement of the loss. On the whole, the definition must be strict. If a house is blown down by a windstorm, it is clearly a casualty. If a house falls down because the wood rots away from a lack of paint and maintenance, it just as clearly is not a casualty. Damage in an automobile collision is a casualty, but if the fender of an automobile rusts away by the action of salt spread on the road to reduce icing, it is not a casualty, even though it may be regarded as a misfortune to live in a place where such damage to automobiles is a normal fact of life. Termite damage has been the most controversial item in the casualty deduction. Is it like the tornado or the lack of paint and maintenance? The position taken by the Internal Revenue Service and upheld by the courts follows the idea back of this distinction. If the damage can be proved to be from a sudden onslaught of termites, it is deductible; if not, it is just another form of deterioration which can be prevented by proper care. Even this allowance seems a generous one in view of available preventive measures, but disallowance of termite damage has been a source of much resentment—another example of the proposition that the resentment of those who fail to receive a tax benefit may outweigh the satisfactions of those who do, with a net loss in total taxpayer morale from the very existence of a relief provision.

The other problem under the casualty loss is the measurement of the loss. One may first think of the cost of replacement, but this turns out to be unreasonable if one considers the fantastic expense of replacing a mature tree blown down in a windstorm. The difference in value of property before and after damage gives a somewhat more reasonable basis, with the property defined as the land on which the tree was located, not just the tree itself. Also, there is a question as to whether one should be able to claim as a casualty more than the cost of property to him. Here opinions differ as to what is fair. The loss in value is unrelated to cost, and hence many argue that cost is irrelevant. But since the rise in value over cost does not represent any outlay and has not led to any taxable income or gain, should one be entitled to partial reimbursement of the loss in excess of cost through a deduction in computing taxable income? For example, if a house purchased for $10,000 is destroyed by fire after it has risen in value to $20,000 because of inflation, should one get a deduction for the full $20,000? The law limits the loss to the cost of property. This seems a reasonable limitation, but there is by no means full agreement on the subject.

Child-care Expenses

A deduction for the expenses of child care for a woman who is the sole support of her family or for a widower or for a working wife if the combined family income is small is the newest and smallest of the deductions. It was adopted in 1954 to give relief in those unusual situations where a woman by the force of circumstances had to provide the family income or where she was unable to give ordinary care to her children and the husband had to incur special expenses for care of the children in order to be able to leave his home to earn his income. Total deductions for child care in 1956, the latest year for which data are available, were 110 million dollars and they occurred almost entirely in families with relatively small incomes.

The limitations on the deduction as it was finally adopted are a fine example of the consensus of opinion which can be developed under the democratic process. Congressional discussion reflected differences of opinion based on urban and rural attitudes and occupations and on religious and philosophical aproaches to the role and proper places of mothers. The final result gave relief where it was felt to be needed, but the intent was to prevent giving any tax inducement to a mother "to leave her children at home while she went out to earn money for a fur coat."

Once adopted, this deduction is peculiarly susceptible to pressure for extension to somewhat comparable but less needy situations. It is to be hoped that the attitudes of those who originally introduced it will be continued and that it will not be brought into disrepute by unreasonable broadening to the point of giving tax relief where both parents work simply because the wife prefers to be out of the home. There should be no tax advantage to influence a choice in favor of a career out of the home.

Education Expenses of Employees and Self-employed

In the preceding chapter, the discussion of the scope of taxable income covered various fringe benefits and recognized that in some instances a problem of fairness was raised unless an untaxed fringe benefit of an employee could be matched by a deduction for self-employed people. Pensions and retirement income were considered at that time. Another area of possible differential treatment involves education expenses; that subject was left to this chapter because even in the case of employees it is usually the individual who pays the expenses rather than the employer who provides a tax-free fringe benefit. In the less common situations where advanced education is provided by an employer, it is usually held that it is for the advantage of the employer, and the employee will not have the costs imputed to him as part of his income. Employees do benefit in these situations and have an advantage over the self-employed, for whom there is no one to provide such fringe benefits.

In the more frequent situations where individuals pay for the education expenses themselves, however, the self-employed until recently had an advantage over employees. The problem is to secure reasonable uniformity in the standards for deductions for educational expenses for these two broad groups.

Among the professional or business expenses which self-employed people are permitted to take in computing their individual incomes are the costs of refresher courses to maintain their skills. Doctors, lawyers, accountants, and others can decide for themselves what courses or training programs they need and where they should take them. The costs are allowable deductions as long as the work undertaken merely maintains skill and does not lead to a specialist rating qualifying for a different and presumably higher scale of fees. In the latter case, the educational expenses are deemed to be personal, similar to general education expenses and basic professional training, and as such are not deductible.

Until 1958, the rules for deductions for educational expenses of employees were stricter than for the self-employed, because the former were permitted to deduct such expenses only if the courses were required to be taken by employers as a condition for keeping a position and only if they did not qualify the person taking them for a higher position. These strict rules were regarded by teachers and other employees as discriminating against them in comparison with self-employed professional people whose individual decisions to take courses were sufficient to justify an expense deduction.

On the basis of numerous protests against a tentative regulation embodying the previous practice and in view of some court decisions adverse to that position, the final regulations were liberalized. They base the deductibility of expenses on the customs and practice in a profession instead of on the requirements of an employer and specifically recognize that the mere fact that courses taken qualify for an in-grade increase in salary or lead to a graduate degree will not disqualify the deductibility of the expenses, as would have been true previously. Courses taken primarily to qualify for advancement, as from teacher to administrator, or to secure basic qualifications as a full-fledged member of the teaching profession will still be disallowed.

The new regulations removed a discrimination and were generally regarded as fair and reasonable, but it will take several years to develop clear lines of demarcation. On the basis of hypothetical questions posed by teachers' groups there will be possibilities and temptations for abuse in this, as in all other deductions. A major difficulty will come in connection with short summer courses in foreign universities which will be alleged to legitimatize travel expenses abroad, with most of the time spent on vacation travel. And some universities will probably be ingenious in developing travel seminars which will purport to be primarily educational but will include the major tourist attractions. And so teachers will be tempted by tax shenanigans, along with other professional groups, and will resent the disallowance of the more flagrant ones.[3] The alternative

[3] The chairman of the department of economics in a major university in a newsletter in May, 1958, referred with apparent approval to an opinion given

to the present rule would be to disallow all deductions for educational expenses for both employees and self-employed. From the standpoint of simplification of the tax law this would be desirable; it would not be particularly unfair, but it would be so contrary to public policy as to be unsuitable at present. But the allowance of the expenses will lead to abuse and to complications from the attempts to restrict the abuses.

Basic Educational Expenses

The present deductibility of educational expenses for both employees and self-employed people when the education maintains their skills and professional standing appears to discriminate in favor of people who are established in their work and against those who are still trying to get the basic training to secure their first jobs in their chosen activity. From the standpoint of both fairness and social policy this seems undesirable. But a general allowance for a deduction of all educational expenses of an individual and his dependents, as is often proposed, is also undesirable because it would add a new and costly deduction to the tax law for a social purpose without really getting at the heart of the economic handicaps to education which do need attention.

A deduction for education expenses would give the greatest relief to those in the highest income brackets and no relief to those with so many dependents that there is no taxable income anyway. To prevent disproportionate relief to those in the highest brackets, where presumably education expenses will be covered whether they are deductible or not, the proposals for tax relief for education have been modified. They usually take the form of a credit against taxes for some specific percentage of the expense; a common proposal is 30 per cent of expenses up to some specified maximum. This assures equal dollar relief to the extent that there will be sufficient tax to absorb the credit. But this still does not deal with the problems of

---

in the *Bulletin* of the American Association of University Professors that travel expenses of faculty members on sabbatical leave for research could be made deductible if the universities required a written report on any research which was done. While hoping that the opinion is incorrect, one may wonder whether, if valid here, an attempt would be made to extend the idea to vacation travel.

the able student who does not go on to college because, presumably at least, of economic handicaps.

A report of the President's Commission on Education beyond the High School noted that a child in the bottom half of his high school class was more likely to go to college if his family income was above $9,000 than a child in the top quarter of his class with a family income below $5,000. The family with an income below $5,000 is not likely to have enough taxable income to absorb a tax credit if one were authorized. Thus, though the credit would be welcome relief to those who would benefit from it and would be consistent with an important social purpose, it would not give assistance where it is most needed, though its cost in revenue foregone would be large (estimated at 250 million dollars a year for a 30 per cent credit up to a maximum credit of $500). If such an amount were to be spent, it would appear that a better way could be devised to have the money go where it would do the most good.

The Standard Deduction

The standard deduction was introduced in the tax law in 1942 as an alternative to itemized deductions for taxes, interest, contributions, and casualty losses. The later deductions for medical expenses and child care have also been made alternative to the use of the standard deduction. The standard deduction was a tremendous simplification, greatly reducing the calculations and paper work involved in the introduction of the withholding tax. By allowing a presumptive 10 per cent as an alternative to itemized deductions, it was unnecessary for those taxpayers whose deductions were less than the 10 per cent presumption to keep records and list deductions. Less desirably, it gave tax relief to those whose deductions were less than 10 per cent. One might even note that it gave a miser the same tax relief that went to a person contributing the traditional tithe to charity. In this respect at least, simplification triumphed over fairness.

The standard deduction presents several problems in tax policy at present. The first is whether it should be extended to higher incomes. At present, the ceiling is 10 per cent of adjusted gross income or $1,000, whichever is smaller. This means that anyone with an adjusted gross income over $10,000, whose actual deductions exceed 10 per cent, must itemize them to get his appropriate tax reduction. In the interests of simplification, it is urged that the ceiling be raised to $2,000 or even a higher figure. Opposition to an increase comes from the representatives of organized charities, who argue that the availability of the standard deduction at higher incomes would reduce the willingness of people in the higher tax brackets to make contributions. They are doubtless correct in this argument, since it is only for those whose total deductions exceed the presumptive 10 per cent that an actual deduction involves a tax saving. We are confronted here with a conflict between simplification benefiting both taxpayers and the government and a desire to encourage philanthropy. In substance, while giving tax relief for charitable deductions, the law imposes an administrative burden to make the relief effective.

But there is another argument against the proposal to increase the optional standard deduction which seems conclusive. Its existence would, as does the present one, give relief to those whose actual deductions are less than the presumptive 10 per cent. For those with larger deductions, the effort of making the calculations is worth the saving in taxes. The simplification itself would thus benefit only those whose deductions are exactly 10 per cent; those with smaller deductions would get a tax reduction from an extension of the standard deduction; those with larger deductions would get no simplification. Since there is no great preponderance of deductions just at that figure, the case for extension does not seem persuasive.

As homeownership has increased over the years and deductible interest and taxes have become important to more people, the optional standard deduction has been less widely used. The proportion of returns using it has dropped from 83 per cent in 1948 to 64.8 per cent in 1958. This reduction in use has been reinforced by the introduction of the medical-expense deduction. Thus the optional standard deduction is coming to be less of a simplification than it was originally. Even for many taxpayers who use it, it is not the simplification that it appears to be because they use it only after computing taxes both ways to decide which method gives the minimum tax. In this sense, the apparent simplification is really a complication to the taxpayer, though the final tax return is simpler.

There is not a clear case as to what, if any, change should be made in the optional standard deduction to restore it to its former importance. An increase to some higher percentage would secure this result, but at the expense of giving selective relief to those whose actual deductible expenses are less than the higher presumption. This would be unfair and unjustified. Alternatively, if certain deductions were eliminated or reduced as part of a tax reform in the future, as is suggested here, the optional standard deduction should be reduced or eliminated to give equal treatment to all taxpayers. An elimination of the deduction would permit a 10 per cent reduction in rates for those using it, with no net change in tax burdens and with the advantage of a more straightforward calculation.

Possible Composite Reform of Deductions

From the combined point of view of simplification and fairness, the following combination of changes might be developed on individual deductions and rates. Elimination of the deduction for taxes and interest would be equitable in removing a discrimination against renters. An increase in the percentage of income which medical expense must exceed to qualify as a deduction would seem to be consistent with its basic objective of giving relief only in distress situations. These three changes would eliminate the most frequent deductions, except that for charitable contributions, and approach a point where it would be fair to eliminate the optional standard deduction if it were balanced by a rate reduction.

The final step necessary to secure real simplification would be to restrict the charitable deduction to the excess over some specified percentage of income, comparable to the medical-expense deduction. It would seem reasonable to relate the deduction to unusual generosity rather than to the sort of gifts which normally go with being a decent member of a community. Solicitors for charities might even be expected to develop a slogan to "give more and save taxes." Casualty losses might also be limited to the excess over some specified percentage of income. If these two additional changes were made, most taxpayers would not have any deductions, though with lower rates their tax burdens would be about the same.

Under such a plan, taxpayers with child-care expenses and with unusually high contributions, medical expenses, and casualty losses would be the only ones to have specified deductions. For all others, withholding taxes at lower rates could be applied on the basis of the number of exemptions as is done now, but with no need for adjustments for either presumptive or actual deductions.

The plan proposed above would very likely seem more appealing than our present law if it could have been proposed as an alternative before the present rules were adopted. As an alternative to an existing law, its general advantages of simplicity and fairness to most taxpayers would be less appealing politically than its disadvantages to some of those who would stand to lose certain existing privileges. It is nonetheless worth consideration as the sort of reform which might be made. It would certainly make the law simpler, and it would seem to make it fairer.

Chapter 5 CAPITAL GAINS AND LOSSES

A discussion of the tax treatment of capital gains and losses logically
begins with a consideration of just what they are. Are capital gains
simply another form of income, slightly differing in origin but substantially similar to salaries, interest, rent, and trading profits? If
they are, then they might reasonably be included in taxable income,
with deductions for capital losses, unless there are overriding reasons on grounds of economic policy to exclude them or give them
differential rates. Or are capital gains and losses so completely
different from what is ordinarily regarded as income that they
should be completely ignored? This is the accepted concept and
policy in Great Britain and many of the Commonwealth countries;
it is a point of view urged by many for adoption in this country.
Or should capital gains be regarded as having a definite taxpaying
capacity, somewhat analogous to but quite different from income,
and hence reasonably subject to some taxation as long as general
taxation of income prevails but presumably taxable on different
terms and rates? This third concept seems to be the most acceptable.

This chapter first develops the three concepts of capital gains
and losses listed in the preceding paragraph and considers some
pragmatic arguments for special treatment of capital gains. It then
turns to the present definition of capital gains in the tax law and
describes some of the many ways in which the concept has been
brought into disrepute by the inclusion of items of income which
by no stretch of the imagination can logically be thought of as

capital gains. Even those who advocate more liberal tax treatment of genuine capital gains object to the present tax relief given to various forms of ordinary income under the pretence that they constitute capital gains. Holding periods and tax rates will be considered in the next two sections of this chapter. Capital losses are given separate analysis; they may be given special treatment in the law to secure desired economic results. The final section proposes a fundamental change in the treatment of capital gains, permitting tax-free exchanges of investment securities, as is now possible for residences, but imposing full income taxation of realized gains when they are spent for consumption. This approach seems equitable and would have desirable economic results.

The basic facts concerning the present taxation of capital gains to individuals are simple and presumably well known. Fifty per cent of net gains from the sale or exchange of capital assets held for more than six months is a deduction from gross income, and therefore the remaining 50 per cent is in the income subject to tax. This means that the effective tax rate on long-term gains is half of the rate on ordinary income. Alternatively, one may omit the gain from the regular tax base and merely apply a 25 per cent tax to the gain. This alternative tax is preferable for those whose regular rate of tax exceeds 50 per cent, the rate reached on taxable incomes of $16,000 or $32,000 for married couples.

Capital losses must be applied against capital gains. A net loss may be deducted from ordinary income up to $1,000 and carried forward for five years. Short-term gains and losses are not subject to the alternative tax or to the 50 per cent reduction for inclusion in regular income, and a net loss on short-term gains must be applied first against net long-term gains.

The revenue from capital gains taxes is conspicuously erratic, fluctuating with stock market prices and investors' decisions on when to sell securities. The estimated yield of the capital gains tax on individuals, for example, increased from 700 million to 1.7 billion dollars from 1953 to 1955.

The Nature of Capital Gains and Losses

Many economic theorists believe that the ideal measure of income is found by adding unrealized gains and losses to what might be regarded as regular income (salaries, rent, interest, royalties, and the like).[1] Thus, a person with a salary of $10,000 and dividends of $2,000 whose investments had appreciated in market price from $50,000 to $70,000 would be deemed to have an income of $32,000; if the securities had fallen from $50,000 to $30,000, he would be deemed to have a negative income of $8,000.

In a major study of tax policy in the 1930s, this concept of income was considered so persuasive that the second recommendation for tax reform was the annual inclusion of unrealized gains and losses in measuring taxable income with a constitutional amendment to authorize this approach.[2] This is perhaps the most impractical proposal ever made in a serious study of tax reform. Quite apart from the merits of the concept of income, which is discussed below, the administrative problem of making annual valuations of unlisted securities and properties and the disruptions in the financial markets as taxpayers were forced to sell property to pay taxes, which in many cases would exceed their total cash receipts of ordinary income, would make such a plan utterly impractical. The proponents of the annual inclusion of unrealized gains and losses in taxable income have regretfully concluded that it is not feasible, even with some form of averaging of income over a period of years and a reduction in top-bracket rates. They now urge full taxation of net realized gains as the next best alternative. When gains are realized, they can at least be measured and there are funds available with which to pay a tax.

Those who argue that capital appreciation is a form of income, even though for practical reasons its taxation may have to be postponed until the gain is realized, point out that a person without capital must build up his net worth by saving some of his income after it has been fully taxed. By contrast the person with capital may have his net worth increase with no tax until the gain is realized; the postponement of taxation is itself a tax advantage. No additional advantage through a differential in rate or additional postponement by a tax-free roll-over should be allowed. This is an appealing argument from the standpoint of fairness.

[1] Technically, the ideal measure of income is stated to be net worth at the end of a period plus consumption and income taxes during the period minus net worth at the beginning of the period.

[2] Twentieth Century Fund, *Facing the Tax Problem,* 1937.

Though the concept that even unrealized capital gains and losses should be included as part of an annual income is attractive to many, it fails to recognize important distinctions. An increase in net worth from appreciation of property seems very different from the receipt of cash income from salary or from interest, dividends, or rent from property. The all-inclusive concept appears to be based simply on a point of view that whatever makes a person better off economically constitutes income. This is defensible; the eminence of many of the scholars who support it is itself evidence of its appeal. But it fails to distinguish between capital and income, which in the minds of many others is theoretically sound and corresponds to the way people actually think about their own affairs.

Capital and income are regarded by most investors as quite distinct, and fluctuations in the value of one's capital are unrelated to one's income. The flow of income may even continue while the value of capital declines, and the value of capital, if it is in a marketable form, will almost inevitably vary even though the income remains steady. Income may be well defined as what an individual can spend without believing that he has reduced his capital.

The analogy of the tree and the fruit is often used in distinguishing capital and income. The crop of apples is clearly income, but the growth in the size of the tree is not; it cannot be eaten or sold, nor can a branch be cut off to be eaten or sold, except as firewood. The growth of the tree does not seem to be income as it occurs. And to continue the analogy, if a grown apple orchard is disposed of and the proceeds reinvested in a pear orchard of equal value, there would still seem to be no final realization in the form of income. Capital, including the appreciation on it, has been changed from one form to another, but it has at all times remained as capital as distinct from income. The proposal for a tax-free roll-over of capital investments made in the last section of this chapter is consistent with this distinction between capital and income.

As a matter of equity, a capital gains tax may be resented as a special form of capital levy. If one rejects the idea that appreciation in value itself constitutes income, one thinks of his capital as consisting at any time of the total of his investments. A tax which must be paid from capital, when an investment is switched, is a selective capital levy. This also is a defensible reaction to capital gains taxation. It is widely held by investors and is not merely a rationalization against the capital gains tax.

Everyone will have his own opinion as to which of the concepts of capital gains is most appealing and what is the most equitable way to tax them. Controversy on the subject, both conceptual and political, exists in almost all countries. We are not alone in having sincere differences of opinion among experts and in popular attitudes.

It is often said that capital gains in many instances merely offset or partially offset the results of inflation. On equity grounds, it is then argued that a monetary gain which does not represent a gain in real value should not be taxed. This argument is appealing and, if inflation had no other effects, might be persuasive. But there are many other respects in which money measures and real values depart from each other because of inflation. A general revision in the law to adjust for the effects of inflation would be impossibly complicated, requiring as it would special provisions concerning bonds, insurance policies, depreciation allowances, and perhaps even salaries and wages which lag behind cost-of-living increases. Though inflation gives some additional justification for special tax treatment of capital gains, it should not be relied on as a major reason in the absence of general adjustments throughout the law to offset the inequities of inflation.

Pragmatic Arguments for Special Tax Treatment of Capital Gains

Two arguments may justify special tax treatment of capital gains regardless of one's opinion concerning their basic nature. On grounds of fairness, a gain which has developed over many years, if taxed on realization, may put a taxpayer in a much higher bracket than he would have been in if he could have been taxed on the gains as they accrued. It is thus considered equitable to give a lower rate of tax on gains developing over long periods in order to avoid the effects of having income bunched in the single year of realization. This point of equity was probably the principal argument for the original differential taxation of capital gains in this country and is still regarded by many as the most significant one.

To the extent that special treatment of capital gains is based on avoidance of unfair progression in the taxation of bunched income, three conclusions follow on the nature of the differential tax. First, it should be applied only on gains which might be subject to unfair progression because of bunching. This means that a special tax rate should be applied only to gains on property held for more than a year. On property held up to a year, there is no artificial increase in progression and hence no equitable need for relief. The present six months' holding period is too short by this standard, and the frequent proposals to reduce it are quite unjustified.

As a second conclusion, if the purpose is simply to give relief from undue progression through bunching of income in a single year, there is no reason to give a bottom rate of tax on capital gains lower than the bottom rate of the regular income tax. If taxation at regular rates does not involve any progression, bunching cannot create any artificial increase in progression requiring relief. On this basis, the present method of including only half of net long-term gains at all income levels is not justified, because this gives a 10 per cent rate at the bottom bracket against 20 per cent on regular income, and this reduction in rate is not needed to relieve progression.

Finally, it also follows that the ideal system would be to have tax relief vary with the length of time property was held, with the relief increasing as property is held for longer periods beyond one year. The inclusion of successively lower proportions of gain as the holding period increases may be thought to give the desired result of offsetting unfair bunching of income. This is correct only in a very rough way. It has already been noted that as long as the total taxable income is in the bottom bracket, there is no increase in progression and no need for relief. But it is also true that regular income may be so large that capital gains would always be taxed at the top bracket regardless of the timing of its accrual or realization; here again relief is not required to avoid the effects of bunching of income. Adjustments to avoid increased progression from the bunching of income would thus, if they were to be accurate, have to be extremely complicated and take account not only of the length of time property was held but also of the size of the gain in comparison with regular income.

Equity from this standpoint conflicts with simplicity. Accurate adjustments to offset the effect of longer holding periods on the effective rate of tax would require many gradations in the relief to be given, and this would make the tax form even more complicated than it is. The fact that full equalization would be very complicated does not mean that relief should not be attempted; as is so often true, a simple but imperfect approach to equity is preferable to no attempt to relieve a conspicuously unfair situation.

The second argument for special treatment of capital gains, regardless of one's opinion as to their true nature, is economic. Capital gains represent a reward for risk investment, and risk investment is especially important for economic growth. Capital gains also represent a form of "income" which is most likely to be saved; in fact, realized capital gains are automatically reinvested along with the rest of one's capital when one sells one security and buys another. Only the existence of the capital gains tax which reduces one's capital keeps the entire proceeds from the sale of one item of property from being reinvested in another. One incurs a capital gains tax by a voluntary act which may be postponed; the act which leads to the tax thus positively decreases one's capital.

It is often said that only when a smaller amount of capital in a new investment is more attractive than a larger capital in an existing investment will one rationally subject himself to an immediate reduction in total capital and net worth. Thus, if one has an investment which cost $1,000 and is now worth $2,000, he has two choices. He can continue to hold what he has, or he can sell it and, after a 25 per cent capital tax on his gains of $1,000, have $1,750 to invest in a new security. Only if there is a great preference for the new security over the old will one exchange $2,000 of the old for $1,750 of the new.

The second pragmatic argument for special tax treatment of capital gains is a threefold economic one. Special taxation is advocated to increase the total amount of capital, to encourage its used in more risky investments, and to prevent successful investments from being frozen into their existing form. These are all significant points.

Increased savings are needed to finance new capital investment which may increase labor productivity and national income. The high proportion of forced savings in the communist countries is often cited as a challenge which the free countries should meet.

Now that we have recognized the fallacy of the concept of the mature economy, savings have again become respectable and are recognized as important in almost all countries. Forced savings are objectionable except in so far as they occur when governments use tax revenues to build highways and other forms of public capital. Though there may be differences of opinion as to how far we should increase taxes to expand public capital, we should at least agree on avoiding taxes which deplete existing accumulations of capital.

It is also important to have capital go into new ventures and equity investment which is necessary for economic development. This is likely to be regarded as risky investment, and with so much of current savings going into the hands of institutional investors, risk capital may be inadequate even if total savings are sufficient. One may question this possibility in view of the high level of stock prices in the glamour industries in 1959 and 1960 and the ready acceptance in the market of new stock issues in these industries. But this is a peculiar phenomenon of a particular period. Among the circumstances permitting it to occur is the differential tax on capital gains. It is hard to conceive of any glamour which would offset the risk if the gain were taxable as ordinary income at rates up to 91 per cent.

Finally, there is the economic argument for fluidity in investment markets. A willingness to shift from successful ventures permits risk-minded investors to finance new ventures. More importantly, fluidity will help to prevent overvaluations in market booms. Investors who regard prices as unnecessarily high will be prevented from selling by taxes on the gains. Unless they anticipate a fall in prices sufficient to permit repurchase of investments with the net proceeds after tax of their capital, they will continue to hold existing investments. By restricting fluidity of capital funds, the taxation of capital gains thus accentuates stock market booms and the slumps which follow them.

For some or all of the foregoing three economic reasons, most economists accept differential tax treatment of capital gains as necessary as long as regular income tax rates are as high as they are now. The reform preferred by many would be a substantial reduction in the middle- and upper-bracket tax rates, with the full inclusion of capital gains and losses in taxable income. Others believe that full taxation of capital gains even at the rates to which they might be reduced would be unfair and economically unsound. This is the position taken in this book.

Because of their distinctive character capital gains are not really income, though they represent an analogous form of taxpaying capacity; because of the importance of capital investment and the need of substantial net gains to offset the prospects for loss in risky investments, even tax rates approaching 50 per cent would be prohibitive. On grounds of both equity and economic policy, true capital gains should be taxed at low rates, certainly not exceeding the present maximum of 25 per cent and preferably substantially lower. This conclusion increases the importance of a reasonable definition of capital gains. The concept has been brought into justifiable disrepute by the addition of provisions to the law which represent the triumph of lobbies over logic and equity.

Definition of Capital Assets

The most fundamental characteristic of a capital asset is that it is held for investment rather than as stock in trade or inventory. This means that the purpose and intent of the holding of an asset, rather than its form, determine whether an asset is a capital asset. A long-term government bond held until maturity by an investor is a capital asset under any definition or concept, but the same bond held by a bond dealer who purchased it in the morning with the hope of selling it in the afternoon would be part of his stock in trade. A machine tool used in a factory is part of the capital equipment and would ordinarily be regarded as a capital asset, but the same machine in the warehouse of the company which made it for sale is part of its inventory.

The law needs objective tests wherever possible to avoid the uncertainty which comes from reliance on intent, and various definitions have been developed in the statute and court decisions to distinguish dealers from investors. The six months' holding period is itself an objective test presumptively related to intent, with the longer periods presumably associated with investment while shorter holdings are associated with trading. Though there are inevitable difficulties in determining intent or establishing adequate objective tests, the basic concept of the gains to be given special tax treatment is simple and straightforward. But the tax law also gives the capital gains treatment to a miscellaneous assortment of forms of income which are unrelated to one another and to the basic concept. The definition of capital gains should be tightened.

Lump-sum Withdrawals from Pension Plans. A lump-sum withdrawal from a pension plan on termination of employment by an individual employee receives capital gain treatment. Under any concept, a pension is deferred compensation, with some element of accrued interest. The reasons for tax deferral on pensions have already been discussed; the deferral arises to a considerable extent from the difficulty of taxing nonvested rights. There is nothing which justifies treating the deferred income as anything other than regular income. Deferral is itself a major advantage which is resented by those who cannot defer their own compensation; to treat the pension as a capital gain still further discriminates against those who cannot convert their regular compensaton into deferred lump sums.

The reason, to the extent there is one, for capital gains treatment of lump-sum withdrawals from pension plans is to ease the impact of the highly progressive tax if income is artificially bunched in a single year. But capital gains treatment goes far beyond averaging and gives a basically lower rate. Relief from the effects of bunching could be given more equitably by permitting an averaging, as is done for the receipts of endowment insurance policies whose net proceeds may be taxed as though they were spread over three years. Or the recipient of a lump sum might be permitted to convert it into a regular annuity policy without immediate tax consequences. The annuities would then be taxable in full, just as the pension would have been when received periodically.

The present capital gains treatment gives a great inducement to maneuver and manipulate. It encourages early retirement by a few days to qualify for a lump-sum withdrawal. The advantage of the capital gains tax rate for high-bracket taxpayers more than offsets the disadvantage of paying the tax immediately instead of spreading it over the years when a pension would be received.

If one receives a lump sum, pays the capital gains tax on it, and immediately invests the net proceeds in a purchased annuity, a large part of the annuity which he purchases will be tax exempt because it represents the recovery of the capital invested in the policy. Thus, though the gross annuity is smaller than the pension would have been, the net annuity is larger because it is largely tax exempt while the pension would have been wholly taxable. If, for instance, a lump sum of $100,000 in a pension plan would have provided a wholly taxable pension of $8,000 to a person with a marginal tax rate of 50 per cent, the net income would have been $4,000. If the lump sum can be received and taxed at 25 per cent, $75,000 may then be used to purchase an annuity equal to three-quarters of the pension, or $6,000, and if 80 per cent of that annuity represents a return of the investment, the tax would be only $600, giving a net annuity of $5,400 compared with the $4,000 net pension.

A change in the law to permit taxpayers to average a lump-sum receipt or to purchase without immediate taxation a regular annuity which would be taxed as the pension would have been taxed will solve any existing problem of fairness from bunched income in lump-sum withdrawals. The law should be amended to give relief in one or both of those ways, and the loophole through capital gains should be withdrawn. This change will remove a tax incentive for termination of employment or of plans in ways that now give unfair tax advantages to a few people. It will also help to restore the integrity of the capital gains concept.

Stock Options. Though the present special provisions of the tax law concerning stock options give room for some manipulation and unfair tax advantages, capital gains treatment of restricted stock options is based on a sound economic policy. The law giving capital gains treatment to certain stock options should be tightened; it should not be repealed.

Stock options were used to give officers and key employees a proprietary interest in the companies for which they worked long before tax considerations were significant. An officer with little personal capital is not in a position to buy an appreciable amount of stock in his company. Stockholders typically prefer to have officers in a company make a substantial personal investment in it to give them the same interest in long-term growth which most stockholders have. Objections to nominal holdings by directors and officers are, in fact, a frequent complaint at annual meetings. Under a stock option, an officer can be given the right to buy stock over some period of time in the future at a predetermined price, usually at about the current market price when the option is given. The holder of the option is then in a position to benefit from future increases in the price of the stock and, if the growth is substantial, to build up the basis for a substantial personal net worth by exercising the option. Typically, safeguards are placed around an option to assure continued employment in the company and to prevent transfer of the option.

From the standpoint of national economic policy, it seems desirable to have officers and key employees personally interested in the long-term growth of their companies. Only if this is true can the capital gains treatment of stock options be justified. Unfortunately, the social and economic advantages of a proprietary interest by officers and key employees are not subject to proof or to disproof, and opinions on the matter inevitably differ. But the growth of individual companies goes along with national economic growth. It is primarily in individual companies, operating in a competitive economy, that improvements in production and distribution and the development of new and more attractive commodities take place.

In the past, owner-managers intuitively identified themselves with their companies. The evolution of a professional management class has been a notable feature of American business during the past fifty years, and the implications of dissociation between ownership and management are a subject of continuing study and comment. High income tax rates make it literally impossible for even the highest salaried executives to save enough to buy stock which gives them really significant holdings in their companies. The stockholdings of the current generation of top executives in long-established companies compared with those who were in a position to buy stock before income tax rates reached their present levels, as revealed by proxy statements, attest to this difference.

With management decisions as critically important as they are to a company's growth, an identity of interests between the personal and professional interests of management is desirable. Bonuses and profit-sharing plans do not necessarily achieve this identity of interest; in fact they may actually conflict with it. Bonuses and shares in profits are related to short-term profits. Research and the development of new products and processes decrease immediate profits, though they are necessary to increase profits over a decade or a generation. This is not to suggest that a management operating with a profit-sharing plan consciously builds up short-run profits at the expense of long-term growth, but the conflict of interest is there.

An identity of interests is desirable when it can be readily achieved. If all managements thought in terms of the value of their company's stock a generation in the future and had the financial interests of themselves and their families tied to that value, the enlightened self-interest of executives and the national interests would seem rather generally to coincide in a competitive economy. Stock options, properly restricted, can help to bring about this identity of interests.

The history of the law concerning stock options may be described briefly. Prior to 1945, profits on stock acquired under options were typically treated as a capital gain, with no tax consequences either on the granting of an option or on its exercise. Under a court decision in that year, the difference between the purchase price and the fair market value at the time of purchase was held to be taxable income. This substantially stopped the use of stock options until the law was later amended to give special tax treatment to restricted stock options. The most important condition for qualification as a restricted stock option is that the option price must be not less than 85 per cent of the market price when the option was granted. The purpose of this limitation is to relate gain from stock options to future increase in value. These presumably will be related to events over which the optionee has some influence. The favored tax treatment should not be available for options that give immediate gains. To qualify for capital gain treatment the stock cannot be sold sooner than two years after receipt of the option or six months after purchase of the stock.

The granting of an option to an officer or employee is clearly a part of his compensation; the directors of a company cannot justify an option to employees on any other basis. For some years after 1950, a strange legalistic distinction between compensatory and proprietary options was advanced and accepted by some of the lower courts until it finally reached the Supreme Court, where it was emphatically rejected. This decision put the restricted stock option on a firmer basis by removing the possibility of using a proprietary option to give an immediate bargain purchase.

The trouble with the present tax provision on stock options is that it permits a "grab-and-run" use of options which is not related to long-term growth. This use brings options into disrepute, and unless the law is tightened as it should be, the entire provision for capital gains treatment of options may be repealed. The present six-month holding of stock, even if it follows an eighteen-month holding of the option, should not justify a capital gains treatment of the profit on the stock. Optioned stock can be and in some instances is bought and sold in these brief intervals, and in at least one major company the management proposed another option plan a few years later with the assertion that it was to give the management a proprietary interest. When a stockholder inquired what had happened to the stock under the previous option plan, it was stated almost as a matter of course that the stock had been sold and so a new plan was needed. Under these conditions, one would think that a management would be ashamed to ask for a second option and the stockholders would refuse to approve it, but the request was made and the authorization granted. Unless the tax law is tightened, options will degenerate into gimmicks for extra executive pay. This is how they are regarded by their critics; unfortunately more than a few executives are coming to regard them and use them in this way.

The only effective way to prevent present abuses is to require a long holding period for stock after purchase. Ten years would appear to be a reasonable minimum. The only argument against a long holding period is that executives frequently do not have enough money to buy a significant amount of stock without borrowing. The only feasible way, it is said, to purchase optioned stock is to wait until there is a substantial potential profit in it, then borrow enough to buy all available stock, wait and worry for six months, and then sell enough stock, perhaps half or more of the total, to reduce the debt to a level where personal worry will not detract from one's effectiveness as an executive. There is enough merit in this argument to justify consideration of a limited authorization for early sale of some optional stock to reduce debt.

Without the right to sell for a capital gain after a short period, options may not be so effective as they now are. But their present abuse cannot be condoned. And after all, the proposed longer holding period does not prevent one from selling; an individual can always sell optioned stock at any time. If he sells without waiting for the longer holding period, he will simply fail to get capital gains treatment. If there is a profit, the net gain will be much less but it will not be turned into a loss. As part of the tax reform on stock options, it might be possible to permit rather long periods before any option has to be exercised to allow a substantial build-up in value. But the essential reform is a long holding period of the stock itself, with one's own capital at risk. Only in this way can the use of stock options be made consistent with the national economic objective which justifies their special tax treatment.

As further limitations, it might be appropriate to tighten the law to prevent changes in option prices or the substitution of new options, at lower prices, for old ones which have not turned out favorably. It might be provided that a person would not be eligible to receive a restricted stock option, from the same or another employer, within some specified time, perhaps five years, after the lapse or cancellation of any previous unexercised option. Such a limitation would discourage much of the manipulation of options which is so properly criticized.

Two other aspects of stock options may require amendments to the law. Under some current litigation, it is claimed that if stock purchased under an option is so tied up with limitations on its sale that it has no determinable market value, no tax can be imposed on either the granting or exercise of the option. If this contention is upheld, it will undermine the restricted stock option provision in the law and permit options to be granted at large discounts from the existing market price. Limitations requiring it to be resold to the company, if it is sold within a specified period, would prevent immediate taxation. Though the limitations would probably not, in fact, ever come into effect, they do distinguish the stock from other shares and make valuation legally uncertain. Since favorable treatment of stock options is justified only as it relates to future increases in value during a period when an executive renders services to the company, he should not be able to get a tax advantage for an immediate bargain purchase. The law should be amended to close a loophole if one develops in this area.

The second possible change in the law concerns the use of stock options by small closely controlled corporations, where options are frequently desirable to induce a successor management group to join a company. Unless the option price is at least 85 per cent of the market price when the option is granted, the option will fail to meet the tests of the restricted stock option and the entire profit at the time the stock is purchased will be taxable as ordinary income.

The present problem arises because of uncertainty as to valuation of stock if there is little or no trading in it. Even with the best of faith there may be honest differences of opinion, and with hindsight it may be held that the market price was above what it was sincerely believed to be. This uncertainty prevents the use of options in many small businesses. Because of the importance of securing new management to make possible the continued independent existence of small businesses, some relief should be given.

One possibility is to require the Internal Revenue Service to give rulings on valuation, but this is a formidable administrative task and should be avoided if at all possible. A more limited change would provide that if it is later held that the fair market value was above that which was used in setting the option price, rather than disqualifying the entire transaction as is done under the present law, only the profit up to that higher figure or something moderately above it would be taxed as ordinary income. Thus, if an option is given at $90 when stock is said to be worth $100 and it is later sold at $200 at which time it is held that it was worth $125 rather than $100 when the option was granted, $35 would be taxed as ordinary income and the remaining $75 as capital gain. Under the present law the entire $110 would be taxed as ordinary income.

To prevent intentional undervaluation to give both a bargain purchase and an option for future growth, some additional fraction of the future gain should be thrown in the ordinary income category. If this fraction were one-fifth, then, in the above illustration, $35 plus $15 ($\frac{1}{5}$ of $75) would be taxed as ordinary income and $60 as capital gain. The extra tax on part of the bona fide gain would discourage undervaluation. This change in the law would appear to make options fully usable in small corporations.[3]

Coal Royalties. There seems to be no good reason, except successful lobbying, why recipients of coal royalties should have their royalty income taxed as capital gains. Apparently there was some rationalization for the favored tax treatment in terms of distress in the coal industry and the existence of long-term contracts in which lower royalties had been fixed than might have been obtained at a later date. Neither of these is adequate to justify the tax advantage to this one form of mining income. The nearest approach to a logical

[3] This plan was developed effectively in a student report in my course on taxation; inadequate records prevent identification of the individual.

justification is that a royalty represents a return for piecemeal sale of property which, if sold in a single transaction, would receive capital gains treatment. This is correct, but the tax law consistently distinguishes operating income from the proceeds of outright sales of property, and there is nothing about coal royalties to distinguish them from all other mining, oil, and gas royalties.

The precedent of coal royalties was not overlooked, and in 1954 the Senate voted to give capital gains treatment to iron-ore royalties with no reason for selection other than a concerted drive by representatives of royalty owners of this industry. This extension of selective relief was stopped only by the most strenuous objections from the Treasury supported by the members of the House Ways and Means Committee. Bills to give this special relief to iron-ore royalties continue to be introduced in the Congress. Property owners in other extractive industries may be expected to contend, with equal lack of justification, that they are entitled to capital gains treatment. Some people in the oil industry have already done so.

The capital gains treatment is much more important to individual royalty holders than corporations. The percentage depletion at 50 per cent of net income authorized for all extractive industries gives an effective tax rate of 26 per cent (the 52 per cent regular tax applied to income after it is reduced by the 50 per cent depletion allowances). This is about the same as the corporate capital gains tax of 25 per cent. For individuals, the depletion deduction can still leave the effective marginal tax rate of 45½ per cent. (The significance of percentage depletion at 50 per cent of net income will be discussed in Chapter 9, where it is compared with the more familiar percentages of 27½, 15, 10, and 5 per cent of gross income. Taxpayers are limited to the lesser of the two; the net income limitation frequently is the controlling one.)

An outright repeal of the capital gains treatment of coal royalties is needed in the interests of fairness. There are no arguments respecting simplicity or economic policy to justify a continuation of this tax favoritism.

Timber. Capital gains treatment is also provided for timber operations to the extent of the increase in value of standing timber. The intent is to tax as ordinary income the profit attributable to cutting and merchandising timber but to tax as a capital gain the profit attributable to growth or to fluctuations in the market value of standing timber. This policy is not justified from the standpoint of fairness, and it certainly complicates rather than simplifies the law. It may, however, be justified as a matter of economic policy to encourage forest conservation.

With reference to fairness, there seems no reason why the tax rate should vary with the length of the production period in business operations. If capital has to be tied up in inventory, whether it is goods in process or finished goods, for an unusually long time, that fact is an element of the cost of doing business which should be reflected in prices along with other cost differences.

If a grower and harvester of timber should get a lower rate of tax than a farmer because his crop cycle is twenty years instead of one, then it would seem that a retail jeweler with an annual turnover of his inventory should get a lower rate of tax than the fruit or dairy store with a weekly turnover. And on the same line of reasoning, a distiller who ages his whisky should have a lower rate of tax than the distiller with brief aging or the soft-drink producer with no aging. One might also contend that profits from sugar cane should have a lower tax rate where it is a two-year crop than where it is a one-year crop. The argument that income from timber operations should be taxed at lower rates because of the length of the crop cycle does not stand up under analysis.

Nor is the capital gains treatment of part of the profits of timber operations a simplification. Rather it is a complication because it means that the total profit must be divided into two parts, with room for controversy on the basis of allocation.

Though fairness and simplicity would be best achieved by removal of the capital gains treatment of part of the profit of timber operations, there may be an overriding economic justification for it. The owner of a tract of timber may sell it outright at a price approximating its value as standing timber. If he does so, his entire profit is a capital gain. The buyer of the timber then allocates the cost of the tract to the amount of standing timber and recovers it through cost depletion; he must do this to get a true measure of income. The operator has a net income only from the cutting and merchandising of timber. Thus, if the tract is sold before cutting, the profit attributable to the growth of timber will receive capital gains treatment anyway.

In the absence of a special rule in the law, there would be a strong inducement to sell tracts for capital gains before cutting and then for the new owner to cut them over completely and promptly. The owner of the tract, again in the absence of a special rule, would have the profit attributable to growth taxed as ordinary income if he cut the growth which occurred while he owned the land. The fact that taxes are minimized if timber growers do not cut and timber cutters do not grow puts a premium on purchases and sales of timber tracts. Purchases and sales are likely to be inconsistent with sound forestry management, which in many instances is based on selective rather than general cutting.

Various timber states found it necessary many years ago to exempt timberland from annual property taxes and substitute a severance tax on timber as it was cut. The annual property tax so increased the costs of owning timberland that it was more profitable to cut off the timber completely and then abandon the land than to have continued ownership with prudent forest management. To a lesser extent, the absence of a special rule in the Federal income tax might tend to produce the same effect, but the situation has not been systematically analyzed from this standpoint and the case for continued capital gains treatment on economic grounds has not yet been established.

If it were concluded that the present rule is not justified, the tendency for successive sales and complete cutting of timber could be stopped by also denying capital gains treatment to the increase in value of timberland to the extent that it is based on the growth of timber. This would appear to be not unfair, since the growing of timber is simply the growing of a crop and the period of growth is not really relevant to the tax rate to be applied.

In the meantime, we may hope that there will not be continuing pressure to shorten the cutoff period. The distinction between nursery stock, which has not yet been proposed for capital gains treatment, and lumbering is an arbitrary one. For many years, the Treasury held the line at genuine timber. In 1954, the Congress amended the law to bring Christmas trees into the category of capital gains under the obscure phrase "evergreen trees which are more than six years old at the time severed from the roots and are sold for ornamental purposes." If the amendment had not been by its nature associated with Santa Claus, it might have been resisted more effectively. Perhaps this is as good a place as any to hold the line. The fortunate fact that mistletoe grows slowly may help to protect the six-year cutoff from another sentimental reduction in the period of growth of qualified vegetation.

Patents. The present law gives capital gains treatment to inventors and those who buy an interest in an invention "prior to [its] actual reduction to practice" on the proceeds of the sale of patents, whether received as a lump sum or by periodic payments, even if the payments are related to its use or productivity. This provision was adopted in 1954 to give certainty in an area which had become very uncertain under existing litigation. Court cases had made a legal distinction between professional and amateur inventors, which was difficult to make in practice and to justify in theory. A distinction was also made between payments of a definite predetermined amount and payments related to use. This meant that the inventor of a patent of proved worth would be taxed on a capital gain while the inventor of a patent of uncertain value, if he secured a royalty based on use, would be taxed on ordinary income. To secure a capital gain, he would be tempted to sell for a lesser fixed amount, shifting the benefit from himself to the purchaser. It seemed unreasonable and unfair for the tax law to put the inventor of a patent of uncertain value at this sort of a disadvantage.

The importance of inventions, both for defense and for industrial progress, unquestionably influenced the adoption of the present rule. In a sense the proceeds from patents are a form of compensation for personal efforts; as such they logically constitute regular income. If the litigation had not led to the opportunities for some inventors to secure capital gains on the sales of some patents prior to 1954, it is doubtful if the present liberal rule would have been established then. But the attitude at the time was that the existing distinctions among different inventors and inventions were unreasonable, and inventions were regarded as of such great importance that the pecuniary rewards of inventors should not be singled out for increased taxation by making all receipts from patents ordinary income. This attitude would probably still prevail if the same situation were presented again.

Literary and artistic royalties and the proceeds from an outright sale of a copyright are taxed as ordinary income. The contrast to the taxation of patents has been pointed out many times, often with the query as to whether the more generous treatment of inventors indicates that the country has a materialistic bias. The difference in treatment is a puzzling and somewhat embarrassing one and is not defensible on any principle of equity or national policy. The difference developed from the differing responses to basically similar problems which arose some years apart and under different circumstances. The popular and Congressional reactions led to the present difference in rules. In the case of patents, the need for legislation developed from court cases which set up seemingly artificial distinctions among inventors; some were prevented from getting the favorable capital gains treatment which others received as a matter of course. It was understandable that the sentiment was to give relief to those who were felt to be discriminated against. In the case of literary royalties, the common rule was to tax all proceeds as ordinary income. In the case of a few authors whose works were almost sure to be best sellers, it was held that an outright sale of a copyright owned for more than six months led to a capital gain. It was understandable here that the sentiment would be in favor of closing an apparent loophole in order to prevent a few from getting more favorable treatment than was generally available.

The inconsistency between the two approaches was recognized in 1954 when the patent rule was put into the law, and it remains as a real anomaly. A removal of capital gains for patent royalties is not consistent with public attitudes toward inventions; a granting of capital gains treatment to all other royalties is not consistent with a desire to prevent the creation of still more special privileges. If the tax law could be redrafted completely anew, the present distinction among types of royalties would certainly not be adopted; it could hardly be seriously proposed. But it seems likely that a continuation of the discrimination is less bad than either of the changes which could remove it. One may hope that increased use of deferred-compensation contracts for authors will give relief to them by spreading the receipt of income. Perhaps deferred-compensation contracts may become so prevalent that, in conjunction with a decrease in the higher income tax rates, they will provide a reasonable alternative to the capital gains rule for patent royalties, and it may ultimately be dropped.[4]

[4] The difference in treatment here is at least much less than it is in Great Britain, where the sale of a copyright is completely tax exempt as a capital gain if the author is an amateur but taxable as ordinary income if he writes as a

Profits on Sale of Depreciated Property. Though our tax law is unduly strict on annual depreciation allowances, discussed in the next chapter, it is unduly liberal in permitting all profits on the sale of depreciated property to be taxed as capital gains. In other countries, a profit up to the original purchase price is taxed as ordinary income on the ground that it really represents a recovery of what turned out to be excessive depreciation. Provisions to tax these "recoveries of depreciation" exist generally abroad, whether the countries tax capital gains or not.

The absence of such a provision here makes it necessary for the Treasury to be rather strict on depreciation allowances to prevent taxpayers from whipsawing the Treasury by playing the rates against each other. With depreciation deductions saving a corporation 52 cents on the dollar and with offsetting gains taxable at 25 cents on the dollar, each dollar of excess depreciation gives a net profit of 27 cents on the dollar. If a company could write down depreciable property to a figure below resale value and then replace it with new depreciable property and repeat the process, the differential tax rates might be a principal source of net income. It has been asserted that this was the basis of profitability of some of the rent-a-car companies. In the summer of 1960, the Supreme Court upheld the Treasury in preventing a maneuver to accentuate this tax manipulation, but the basic problem remains and requires constant attention.

The tax treatment of gains and losses on the sale of depreciable assets has been changed several times in the past to meet changing economic situations; it should be changed once more to meet the present need for more liberal annual depreciation allowances. Prior to 1938, depreciable property was defined as a capital asset, conforming to business practice. In 1934, however, deductions of capital losses had been limited and allowed only as offsets to capital gains. Since in the prevailing depression situation there were few capital gains, losses realized on the sale of depreciable property could not be used and did not lead to a reduction in taxes. It was thus better

professional. The status of various prominent public figures who have written one or more widely read books as an adjunct to their principal careers has never been made public; the determination on this matter by tax officials, under British tax rates, may spell the difference between a substantial fortune and negligible returns.

for a company to continue to keep machinery which it might otherwise have replaced and to take depreciation deductions on it than to sell it and take a capital loss. The tax law thus discouraged the replacement of capital equipment at a time when replacement was most needed to stimulate the capital goods industries. The law was changed in 1938 by removing depreciable property from the category of capital assets; this meant that losses on its sale were deductible in full and profits taxable in full.

During World War II the economic situation was reversed. It was desirable to have all capital equipment fully utilized, and sales of any surplus machinery were in the national interest. But the market for secondhand machinery was high, and most sales would result in gains. The full taxation of gains under the excess profits tax meant that there was little net advantage to a company in selling its property; it was better to keep it if there was any chance at all that it might be useful or even to keep it idle to sell after the war, when the excess profits tax would have expired. To meet this situation, the tax law was changed again in 1942 to permit net gains on the sale of depreciable property to be taxed as though they were capital gains. Depreciable property was still excluded from the definition of capital assets, and any losses could still be deducted in full. This unsymmetrical treatment has continued to the present time. The law has been changed twice in the past to meet urgent economic problems; it should be changed again now as part of a package reform to prevent abuse and make possible more liberal depreciation deductions in ordinary business situations.

In the Budget Message of January, 1960, the repeal of the capital gains treatment of net gains up to original purchase price was recommended with the statement that with this repeal, "the taxpayer's judgment as to the useful life of his property could more readily be accepted." This recommendation was not adopted by the Congress, principally because it had not been made clear just how depreciation allowances were to be liberalized. This rejection was understandable and probably fortunate because liberalization by itself would be less acceptable than when it is presented as part of a reform which also includes a tightening of the law to prevent abuse. Tightening should await basic liberalization of depreciation.

Gains and Losses on Sales of Bonds by Banks. Banks receive the same sort of unsymmetrical tax treatment on gains and losses from the sales of bonds which business generally secures from sales of depreciable assets. Gains are taxable as capital gains; losses are deductible in full. This provision cannot be justified on grounds of either equity or simplicity. Its only defense is in terms of economic policy.

The argument in favor of the existing law is that it increases the fluidity of bank investments. In boom periods, when interest rates move up and bond prices move down, banks would be less willing to sell bonds and thereby secure funds to meet business demands for loans if they could not get full deductions for losses on bonds. And at all times, it is said, they would be less willing to buy longer term bonds if they could not get capital gains treatment on any profits from later sales. In view of the difficulties of government debt management and the importance of facilitating longer term debt issues, it is urged that the existing law should not be changed.

More thorough analysis than has yet been given is necessary to determine the justification for continuing the present treatment of gains and losses on bond sales by banks. There is evidence that individual banks tend to bunch their gains and losses in different years. This is understandable, since losses which are applied against gains offset only 25 cents in taxes for a dollar of loss as compared with 52 cents when they are realized in years with a balance of losses. This practice, however, suggests that the law is being used for tax maneuvers rather than to facilitate ordinary transactions.

This provision of the law is another one which would probably not be adopted if a law were being written on a clean slate. The consequences of repeal on the government bond market require thorough analysis, however. Especially when the Congress keeps those responsible for debt management in a strait jacket through a ceiling on the interest rate, it may have to give artificial support through a special tax rule. If the law were to be changed, each bank might be given an option to elect irrevocably to treat all gains and losses on bonds either as capital gains and losses or as ordinary income and losses.

If there were to be a mandatory rule for a single one of the alternatives, the treatment as ordinary gain and loss seems preferable on first analysis. This would avoid a tax penalty on dispositions at a loss, similar to that which developed on the sale of depreciable property in the 1930s. It might be, however, that just such a penalty would strengthen the influence of the Federal Reserve System in boom times, when flexible monetary policy involves some increase in interest rates with consequent decreases in bond prices. Limitations on increases in bank loans are needed to limit inflationary pressures, and limitations on the deductibility of losses would discourage banks from shifting their portfolios from bonds to loans and thus reinforce credit policy. The effect of the limitation on loss deductions might be more subtle, however, and if the banks wish to be in a position to meet customers' demands in boom periods, they would avoid commitments in longer term securities in prior periods of credit ease. It is uncertainties of this sort about the consequences of a change in the present law which may justify its continuation.

Gains on Sale of Livestock Held for Breeding Purposes. A special provision in the statute gives capital gains treatment to profits on the sale of livestock held for breeding purposes. This treatment is closely analogous to the treatment of gain on the sale of depreciated property used in a trade or business. There seems no more logical reason for one than for the other. Logically the livestock provision should be repealed along with the section on machinery and business buildings. Though its revenue cost may be relatively small, this provision of the tax law is highly selective, going only to livestock breeders with negligible benefits for small family farmers. Surely a better form of relief, to the extent that relief is appropriate, could be devised than this anomaly in the tax law.

The present tax rule on breeding livestock is not justified whether the breeding livestock has been purchased or raised on the farm. If purchased, it has presumably been depreciated, and the case is exactly parallel with machinery. Any profit above original sale price might be taxed as a capital gain, as in the case of machinery. If the livestock has been raised on the farm, the expenses have been merged in with other expenses and taken as current deductions under the cash system of accounting permitted to farmers; the costs will not have been capitalized or offset by a growing value of inventory as would be required in other forms of business. Thus, to the extent of previously deducted expenses, a profit taxed at the capital gains rate also permits the tax rates to be played against each other as in the case of depreciated property. But indefensible though the present capital gains treatment of profit from sale of breeding livestock may be, a change in it is not sufficiently important to run the risk of endangering a package reform of the capital gains provisions by bringing into the opposition the influential lobby group which would oppose repeal.

Two other special provisions affecting farmers are reasonable and should not be removed from the law. A profit on the sale of livestock may be ignored for tax purposes if the sale is made because of drought or disease as long as the proceeds are reinvested in similar livestock within a specified period. This relief amendment was adopted in 1956 with the support of the Treasury; it is analogous to the general relief measure permitting postponement of tax for such involuntary conversions as a cash payment from insurance after a fire or for property condemned for a road. If the amounts received exceed the tax basis, a tax on the profit would prevent a reinvestment of the full proceeds to continue the same scale of business. By requiring the basis of the old property to be carried forward, the tax is not waived; it is simply postponed. The extension of the concept of involuntary conversion to farmers is a proper recognition of the vagaries of nature which add to the problems of farming.

Another special relief provision for farmers permits them to file their returns on a cash basis. This gives them an advantage over other businessmen who, if they have an inventory, can treat their current outlays as deductions only to the extent that they do not represent increased inventories. It is a great advantage to be able to deduct all expenses on a cash basis. It is justified for farmers to simplify their tax returns and records, but it should be appreciated as a favored and illogical treatment and should not be compounded by giving capital gains treatment to part of the profit.[5]

Holding Periods

After the foregoing long discussion of some of the problems in the definition of capital gains and losses, the remaining problems con-

[5] For many years the Treasury did not permit taxpayers to change from the accrual to the cash basis of accounting to get the further benefit of the capital gains on the sale of breeding livestock. Since, however, it seemed clearly the intent of Congress to permit this combination of benefits, the barrier to a change of accounting method was removed in 1953. It is not proposed to reverse this relaxation by administrative action.

cerning them can be described briefly. The selection of any specific holding period is arbitrary. Originally, the holding period was two years. This was consistent with the original purpose to prevent an unfair bunching of income in a single year. A holding period of a year or less cannot be justified for this purpose.

Nor can a holding period as short as the present six months be justified on any basis of fairness or simplicity. Its sole justification is to increase the liquidity of security and commodity markets. It doubtless increases the willingness of speculators and short-term investors to "make a market" and reduces interim price fluctuations. But the shorter the holding period, the more likely it is that trading profits, which are ordinary income and should be taxed as such, will get the benefit of the capital gains rate. Short holding periods are thus likely to bring the general concept of capital gains into disrepute. An increase in the holding period would be a reasonable part of a general tax reform which included a reduction in the tax rate on true capital gains.

There is nonetheless continual agitation to reduce the holding period and a good deal of ingenuity in proposing special periods for special types of property. It has been suggested, for instance, that since contracts for commodity futures have a total life of less than a year, compared with perpetual life for corporate stock, the six-month period is unreasonably long and that they should have a special two- or three-month period, since this would still be a considerable fraction of a lifetime. Though this suggestion was not accepted by the Treasury, it deserves some sort of a prize for resourcefulness.

Rates of Tax on Capital Gains

An ideal difference in tax rates applied to capital gains and ordinary income cannot be prescribed by any theoretical formula. The present 25 per cent maximum is probably the highest which could be imposed without serious curtailment of investment in new ventures and other high-risk fields. This is not subject to proof a priori, but a chance to retain three-quarters of a profit sounds a good deal more attractive than a chance to retain, say, only two-thirds of a profit.

Various proposals have been made to reduce the regular top-bracket tax rates, adopt a general system of year-to-year averaging of income, and then tax all capital gains as ordinary income. It is hard to imagine any single change in the tax law which would do as much damage to economic development as the full taxation of capital gains, even if the maximum rate were reduced to 50 per cent. The risk of loss is so great in so many important areas of investment that anything like a half-and-half sharing with the government would seriously curtail investment. It must be remembered that there are no nonpecuniary incentives for investment, as there are for personal activity, to keep the economy active in spite of high taxes. With the exception of certain forms of landholding, investments do not give direct personal satisfaction. Cash and risk-free securities are an ever-present outlet for available funds. The riskier commitments are made after balancing the chance of gain against the risk of loss, and a tax on the gain reduces the attraction of the gain commensurately. For emphasis it may be repeated that a tax on capital gains is a more serious barrier to investment than the ordinary income tax is to activity because there are no nonpecuniary incentives for investment.

Though the present 25 per cent maximum tax probably does not significantly deter investment, it does discourage the sale of property on which a large gain has developed. The fact that the capital gains tax is an avoidable capital levy on a shift of investments was noted at the beginning of this chapter. The principal reason for a reduction in the tax rate would be to thaw frozen investments and permit those who have made successful investments in the past to make more funds available for other ventures. A lower tax would also help to prevent excessive stock market fluctuations by reducing the tax barrier which now discourages many people from selling stock when they are convinced that prices are too high.

It is not clear how much lower the tax would have to be to "unfreeze" existing investments. In the late 1920s, the 12½ per cent capital gains tax froze many investments during the 1929 stock market boom. A small reduction in the maximum tax to 22 or 23 or even to 20 per cent would probably not have any very great effect in liquidating investments. A reduction to 12½ or 15 per cent probably would. A reduction which was highly controversial with a reasonable expectation that it might be reversed would perhaps be the most effective of all but is not to be preferred for that reason.

A substantial reduction in the tax rate would probably bring in more revenue than the present tax, at least for a good many years while investment portfolios which have been frozen over the past generation were being realigned. This is a matter of opinion, but it is one which is widely held.

The timing of a change in the capital gains tax rate is important. The first impact of the change would be to induce very large immediate sales if the market was thought to be unusually high. The proceeds of these sales would probably be kept liquid in anticipation of lower prices. Thus, if the lower tax rate were adopted when the market was regarded as high, the immediate selling might break the market. It would be better to make the change at a time when there would be no general desire for temporary liquidation of investments. This timing would encourage an orderly change of portfolios from the present abnormal situation to one where artificial tax influences are reduced.

It is often proposed that a scale of rates be established with a lower rate for each additional year that an investment is held. This would be desirable to avoid any recurring freezing of investments as an investor's holding period approached a major change in rates at, say, five or ten years. The problem here is to balance simplicity against economic advantages. Each additional rate requires at least one additional line on the tax return and makes for another chance for error in a taxpayer's own records and computations. Appealing though a smooth gradation is from an economic standpoint, the complication it involves does not seem justified by the advantages.

As a combined reform of rates and holding periods, an increase in the minimum holding period to one year with a 37½ per cent maximum rate on holdings of one to three years, 25 per cent on holdings of four to ten years, and 12½ per cent on holdings of over ten years would make the law fairer, very little more complicated, and preferable on economic grounds. It would be fairer because it would give the lower rates to the longer term gains which are more likely to be embodied in capital and not regarded or used as ordinary income. It would be preferable economically because it would reduce the tax discouragement to risky investment, though this discouragement is not too serious with the 25 per cent maximum. It would thaw many frozen investments, which is a major problem. This change would somewhat reduce the liquidity provided in the financial markets by speculators and short-term investors, but it would increase liquidity by thawing long-term portfolios. This reform package would also probably increase revenues.

A final point on the capital gains rate may be mentioned here simply by way of cross reference. The case for a differential tax rate on the capital gains of corporations is by no means as strong as it is for individuals; a change to eliminate it would greatly simplify the law without serious adverse economic effects. This suggestion is included in Chapter 7 on the taxation of corporations.

Prevention of Step-up in Basis at Death

Many proposals have been made for a change in the law by which it would be presumed that all gains on capital assets would be realized at death and taxed. It is argued that the present law, which establishes the value of property at death as the basis for computing subsequent gain or loss on sales by an estate and heirs, is unfair and adds to the freezing effect of the capital gains tax.

The equity argument for taxation of unrealized gains at death is consistent with the all-inclusive concept of income and is usually advanced by those who regret their inability, for political or administrative reasons, to tax unrealized gains during an owner's life. The reasons for rejecting this income concept have already been given. To those who believe that estate tax rates are already excessive, the idea of an additional tax imposed at death seems unfair, regardless of its name or logical justification. It seems not unfair to let heirs get a fresh start in the computation of future capital gains. After all, a step-up in basis at death can occur only once in a generation; it is available to all; and the event which brings it about is sufficiently drastic to make an additional death tax imposed on successful investors seem more vindictive than equitable.

From the economic standpoint, the prospect of a step-up in basis at death undoubtedly does add to the freezing effect of the capital gains tax. Especially where property is to go to immediate descendants and where property is thought of as belonging to the family group, the chance to avoid the capital gains tax is attractive and will influence investment decisions for many years before one expects to die. But though a tax at death on unrealized gains would increase the fluidity of capital, it would also, by its full amount, decrease the amount of capital. It is questionable whether the net economic result would be desirable.

Death taxes and the capital gains tax on large gains are distinctive in reducing a nation's capital. Other taxes may be expected to come out of current income. Specific assets are not consumed because of death and capital gains taxes, but the assets which are sold to pay the taxes are purchased by other investors whose savings or liquid funds would otherwise have been available for new investments. Taxation which depletes a nation's capital seems extravagant.

An alternative to a presumptive realization of gain at death would be a carry-forward of the decedent's basis to his estate and heirs as is now done for gifts. Though this would appear to be more complicated than the extra tax at death, it would seem to be fairer and equally effective in unfreezing investments which show large profits. Complications would arise in dividing property in an estate among the heirs because the actual value of property to them would depend not only on its market price but also on its tax basis and the heirs' plans to sell or retain a particular piece of property and on their effective tax rates at the time of sale. Discussions with attorneys concerned with tax matters suggest that these problems may not be insuperable, however. This change would not lead to an immediate reduction in capital as would the first proposal. If the present law giving a step-up in basis at death were to be changed, the carry-forward of basis on balance would appear to be very much better than a presumptive realization of gains.

Capital Losses

The preceding sections have incidentally referred to various problems arising from the tax treatment of capital losses. In general it is reasonable that if capital gains are given a more liberal tax treatment than ordinary income, capital losses should be treated less liberally than ordinary losses. This is now accomplished by allowing losses generally to be offset against capital gains, with net losses carried over to subsequent years.

But taxpayers are at a disadvantage in balancing out capital gains and losses, because the government collects taxes on net gains while it allows no reduction in taxes for net losses which cannot be offset against current or future gains, except for the $1,000 annual deduction. It is sometimes suggested that net losses might be applied against other income but with the saving in taxes limited to the tax rate which would be applicable to a net gain, at present to a maximum of 25 per cent of the loss. This would seem to be fair and reasonable and not be particularly complicated. It would to some extent encourage risk investment. The long period for loss carry-overs seems, however, to be equally effective in most instances, and a change of this sort is not particularly important.

The limitation on the deductibility of losses was introduced in 1934 after a congressional committee determined that the partners of J. P. Morgan & Co. had not been subject to tax in 1932 because their capital losses had completely wiped out their ordinary income. In the temper of the times, any provision of a tax law which made a Morgan partner nontaxable was presumably bad, and capital loss deductions were thereafter made applicable only against capital gains. (This was the same scandalous committee hearing in which a midget was put in the lap of J. P. Morgan for publicity photographs. It is amazing that in such an atmosphere no worse tax change was conceived.)

Net capital losses up to $1,000 are currently deductible by individuals from ordinary income in computing taxable income. An increase in the $1,000 figure to $2,000 or $5,000 is frequently proposed. It would be helpful in encouraging investment and would make it unnecessary to carry forward small capital losses. A deduction of capital losses does make the tax saving from a loss greater than the tax burden on a gain, and from the standpoint of fairness this may be objectionable to some. However, the requirement that large net losses must be carried over while net gains are currently taxable and the further fact that some net losses never lead to savings in taxes suggest that the current deductibility of some losses against ordinary income gives a rough equity.

In 1958, as part of the tax-relief program for small business, the Congress adopted the recommendation of the President and the Cabinet Committee on Small Business to allow an ordinary loss deduction for losses by original investors in stock in small business. The conditions for the deduction are discussed in connection with the tax problems of small business in Chapter 9, but the principle should be noted here because it might well be applied to other sorts of investments. This is one of the very few ways in which a tax law may provide a positive stimulus to investment. For an individual in the 75 per cent tax bracket, a $10,000 investment with an equal chance of complete loss or 100 per cent gain (if any such estimate of risks were possible) is obviously not attractive. But with the gain taxed at 25 per cent and the loss deductible at 75 per cent, the net gain becomes $7,500 and the net loss $2,500, which is attractive.

The full deductibility of loss cannot be advanced on grounds of fairness, except in a very general sense that since ordinary income is taxed in full, a loss should be deductible in full. But deductibility of losses is an effective way to use government power to offset inherent barriers against particular forms of investment which it is desired to encourage on social or economic grounds. A possible additional use would be in connection with certain private investments in less developed countries.

Deductibility of capital losses as ordinary losses has two great advantages over direct government subsidy or assistance. Administratively, it does not require the creation of any new government agency or bureau or even additional government personnel. Financially, it gives relief only where losses actually occur and after the occurrence of the loss. It does not spread funds around where they may not be needed, and no one is made richer by public funds. Either one of these advantages alone should be sufficient to make this a preferable form of government assistance, if assistance is to be given in some form. Together they make the ordinary loss allowance extremely attractive.

A Proposal for a Major Reform—Tax-free Roll-over of Investments with Withdrawals of Gains Taxed as Ordinary Income

The tax law permits an owner to sell his residence at a profit without paying any tax on the gain if the proceeds are reinvested in another residence. This is widely regarded as a desirable relief provision in the law. Less well known is the fact that all taxpayers may exchange investment property and property used in a trade or business for other property of like kind without incurring a tax.

The exchange must be a direct one; a sale and purchase do not qualify. In both cases, tax is not waived; it is merely postponed by requiring the cost or tax basis of the old property to be carried over and used as the tax basis of the new property. The courts have been very liberal in interpreting "property of a like kind." Virtually all real estate, for example, is regarded as homogeneous, and a retiring farmer can exchange his farm for a city apartment house with no tax on the gain. Securities are specifically excluded from this tax-free exchange of investment property.

These precedents in the law are the basis for many suggestions to extend the tax-free exchange or roll-over to securities. This is advocated to reduce tax barriers to risky investment and more particularly to remove tax barriers to changes in investment portfolios. It would doubtless be effective in both respects. The question is whether it would be unfair to other taxpayers to permit gains to be accumulated in this way without interim taxes. Here, as is so often the case, a reform package seems possible which will tighten the law where it needs to be tightened and liberalize it where it needs to be made less onerous.

It would seem desirable to permit the tax on gains from sales of securities by individuals to be postponed if the entire proceeds are reinvested in other securities but to tax any net withdrawals of gains as ordinary income. This would improve the fairness of the law by applying full taxation to gains which are not embodied in capital. It would reduce or eliminate the adverse economic effects of taxing gains which continue to be part of one's capital. It would, however, make the law more complicated; perhaps it would not be administratively feasible. The proposal appears to have sufficient merit to justify a careful examination.

Much of the disagreement about the fairness of a lower rate of tax on capital gains comes from a difference of opinion as to what they actually are. The point of view advanced in this book is that appreciation in value is typically thought of as constituting part of capital and continues to be embodied in capital even when one investment is sold and another purchased. From this standpoint, a capital gains tax is a form of capital levy. From this point of view it also follows that a capital gain which is not continued as a part of one's capital should not receive a favorable tax treatment except in so far as it may be necessary to offset the effects of a bunching

of income. When a profit on the sale of securities is used for consumption along with ordinary income, it should in fairness be taxed
as regular income, regardless of the length of time the securities
have been held. It is only because long-term gains are ordinarily
not regarded or used as income that a lower rate of tax is theoretically justified. The lower rate may produce a rough equity by taxing
on the average the part of gains which are consumed. But if it is
possible to distinguish the uses of gains and tax them on the basis
of use, greater equity could be achieved. This is what is proposed
here.

Those who believe that even unrealized gains should ideally be
taxed on the ground that appreciation in value is as much a part of
income as salary or interest will, of course, not accept this proposal
as improving the fairness of the tax law. The reasons for rejecting
this very broad concept of income have already been given.

It is also true that if one were to permit gains to be free of tax
when they are kept in a capital fund, one should also consider
letting ordinary income be free of tax when it is put into a capital
fund. There is much to be said for such a law. The concept of a tax
on spending, on consumption rather than on income, has strong
support from distinguished economists. It is not considered in this
book because it would be such a drastic change that it is not within
the range of possible tax reform in the immediately foreseeable
future. It is enough to recognize that the more limited proposal
made here concerning capital gains would be logically consistent
with this much broader possible change. The fact that it would not
go all the way to the new concept is no reason to reject it if it is
sound within its own frame of reference.

Adoption of tax-free roll-overs for investments, though desirable
on grounds of equity and economic policy, would raise two difficult
administrative problems which require further examination. The
first problem is one of identification. When a person sells one residence and buys another, there is no problem of identification, since
one can bring only one residence at a time under the provision of
the law. Likewise the direct exchange of investment properties involves no problem. But the sale and purchase of securities would
involve a problem because an investor usually has many securities.
Should there be an attempt to trace the proceeds from a particular
sale into a particular new investment, or should there be a lumping

together of all investments with a presumption that any withdrawal would be regarded as a withdrawal of a gain to the extent of any existing realized gain?

The second problem involves indirect withdrawals of gain. If gains are to be taxed as ordinary income unless they are reinvested, it is important to prevent avoidance of the tax by indirect withdrawals. One might, for example, develop a large fortune from a single investment, sell it and buy a diversified portfolio, and then borrow indefinitely against securities for living expenses. Deductible interest would be less burdensome than the income tax on a withdrawal of gain. The problem of indirect realization exists under the present law in that one may borrow against appreciated property and, in effect, consume the appreciation without even being subject to a capital gains tax. The elimination of the deduction for interest on personal loans, previously proposed, would discourage loans of long duration.

An indirect withdrawal also might be made by selling property which has not appreciated, perhaps bonds, and using that sum for consumption while some appreciated stock is sold and the proceeds used to purchase bonds and restore a balanced portfolio. To a lesser extent this problem also exists now in that an investor may sell and live on the proceeds of sale of nonappreciated property while continuously building up his net worth in other property. In an extreme case, one might be able to combine a high standard of living financed by the sale of nonappreciated assets with a large increase in net worth through appreciation on other assets and pay neither an income nor a capital gains tax. Such a possibility suggests, in passing, one advantage of a tax based on consumption.

If a tax-free roll-over were to be adopted, it would probably be desirable to give wide latitude to the forms of reinvestment. It has sometimes been proposed that fairly strict limits be established with funds from common stock having to be reinvested in common stock. This would be undesirable because, while removing one tax force which accentuates market fluctuations, it would substitute another artificial tax influence. Though one would be more willing to sell stock which he thought was overvalued, he would be forced to buy another stock which he considered less vulnerable, thus accentuating the price movements in the "defensive" stocks. It has also been proposed that a roll-over might be permitted only if the funds received were reinvested in government bonds. No such artificial support for government securities should be needed or accepted.

A change in the law to permit tax-free roll-overs of investments, with full taxation at regular rates of any withdrawals of gains, would make the tax law fairer and reduce its adverse economic effects. Its adoption would be a major reform. The administrative problems should not be insuperable; it is to be hoped that others may join in seeking a solution to them.

Chapter 6 DEPRECIATION

The depreciation allowances on machinery and equipment authorized for tax deductions in this country by law and by publications of the Internal Revenue Service are probably the most limited in the world. The industrial countries of western Europe and Canada are much more liberal, as are the countries seeking to start industrial development. In the United States excessive reliance has been placed on historical service lives, with much controversy in the past between taxpayers and tax officials. Other countries, in order to minimize tax barriers to economic growth, have established depreciation rates for machinery and equipment which are based on life estimates probably appreciably shorter than the average lives in actual use, though they are not unrealistic at a time of great technological change. In addition to shorter life estimates, many countries also allow one or more of the following: revaluations and special allowances to offset higher replacement costs, total depreciation in excess of 100 per cent of cost regardless of price changes, initial allowances in the year of acquisition which make possible a very rapid recovery of an investment in machinery though they do not give total allowances in excess of cost, and special additional allowances above cost.

More liberal depreciation for machinery and equipment is the most urgently needed tax reform in this country, other than a revision of individual income tax rates with a tightening of the definition of taxable income. The reform in depreciation will be simpler to develop and should be less controversial. It should be undertaken immediately to help in providing the industrial base for defense requirements, increased labor productivity, a larger national income, and a better opportunity to meet the rapidly expanding foreign industrial competition in both domestic and foreign markets.

Tax reform on depreciation allowances should combine more liberal deductions and a removal of the present loophole which gives capital gains treatment to profits which may offset and arise from previous depreciation deductions. The need to treat as ordinary income any recovery of prior depreciation was discussed in the previous chapter. In the following discussion, a tightening of the law on such profits is assumed to be part of any major reform concerning depreciation.

More liberal depreciation is desirable for machinery and equipment. It is not needed for real estate, depreciation allowances on which are probably too liberal. These allowances might even be reduced, though the repeal of the capital gains provision may take care of the worst of the present unfair tax advantages achieved through real estate transactions. Principal attention in this chapter is devoted to depreciation on machinery and equipment. This is the most important form of depreciable property from the standpoint of industrial productivity.

Present United States Depreciation Allowances

Under our present law, depreciation rates on all items of depreciable property must be based on all relevant facts and circumstances for each taxpayer. The rates actually claimed and allowed are not known on any statistical basis. Though the amounts of depreciation are regularly tabulated from tax returns, information on rates has not been reported with sufficient accuracy to make tabulation possible. A survey of rates claimed and allowed, along with comments on possible changes in the law, was undertaken by the Treasury in the summer of 1960. It will provide a necessary base for appraising proposed changes in authorized rates, in terms of both their economic impact and their effect on revenues. The details of specific proposals made here might well be modified on the basis of conclusions from this investigation, which may be released before the publication date of this book.

Suggested depreciation rates are contained in *Bulletin F* of the

Internal Revenue Service, last revised in 1942. This contains several hundred suggested rates for different sorts of depreciable property in different industries. Actual rates used may be either higher or lower than those listed. Taxpayers may claim higher rates; they are virtually invited to do so when the claim can be justified by the facts. Many companies are allowed substantially higher rates than those given in *Bulletin F*. But it is also clear that taxpayers are not assured of being allowed even as much as is suggested there. Revenue agents, as well as taxpayers, may assert that facts in a particular case require different rates.

The Treasury is apparently aware of the obsolete character of many of the rates given in *Bulletin F*. It has reprinted it only with reluctance and at the insistence of taxpayer groups who request some sort of a guide, however inadequate. The reprints have continued the 1942 date of the last revision lest a current date give the bulletin more authority than it is intended to have. Material from the questionnaire described above will help in providing a basis for legislative or administrative changes in rates.

In the meantime, the depreciation rates suggested in *Bulletin F* are apparently used by many companies which are not in a position to make their own engineering studies to support higher rates. Revenue agents also at times use *Bulletin F* figures as authority to disallow claims for larger deductions, in spite of a policy that they are not to be used for that purpose. The impact of *Bulletin F* is probably heaviest on small companies, since they are usually least able to take the time and expense necessary to establish their own rates.

In spite of the fact that its rates are not binding on either taxpayers or revenue agents, the *Bulletin F* rates are significant. A few of them may be mentioned here for comparison with those in other countries to be given in the next section. Machinery and equipment in metal products and processes are typically given composite lives ranging from 15 to 25 years, with the minimum in only one industry as short as 10 and the maximum in another as long as 30. The 15- to 25-year lives are equivalent to 6⅔ to 4 per cent depreciation on a straight-line basis and 13⅓ to 8 per cent rates on the declining-balance method. The iron and steel industry is given a 25-year life including buildings, with mill machinery ranging from 20 to 30 years. Factory buildings are given lives of 33 to 44 years. A composite life of 28 years is given for all equipment of railroads, with electric locomotives having 35 years, boxcars 28 years, and passenger cars 35 years.

The straight-line method of depreciation, in which equal amounts of depreciation are taken annually for any depreciable item, was commonly used up to 1954. In that year, taxpayers were authorized to use the declining-balance method of depreciation on new property with useful lives of three years or more at depreciation rates double those applicable under straight-line depreciation. Thus, a $10,000 machine with a ten-year life would be depreciated at 10 per cent, or $1,000, a year under the straight-line method. This charges off the cost in equal amounts. Under the declining-balance method the rate would be 20 per cent applied to the remaining balance of cost, with a deduction of $2,000 in the first year, $1,600 in the second (calculated by applying the 20 per cent rate to $8,000, the original cost of $10,000 less the $2,000 depreciation in the first year), $1,280 in the third year (20 per cent of the remaining cost of $6,400 after deducting previous depreciation), with continuously decreasing amounts in successive years. Taxpayers may also use a somewhat more complicated method known as the sum-of-the-years digits which also gives higher deductions in earlier years of use.

Depreciation may not be used to write down the cost of an asset below its probable salvage value at the time is is likely to be sold by the taxpayer, which means the probable resale price and not simply scrap value. For self-drive automobile rental companies which change their fleets of cars annually, the salvage value is the sale price of a used car one year old. Salvage value is an important limitation to protect the revenue and prevent gross abuse of the tax laws by a few taxpayers. The Hertz Corporation claimed, for example, that its depreciation and salvage value should be based on an ordinary physical life of automobiles, which is three years or more. If a four-year life were used, the company would be able to get a deduction of 50 per cent in the first year under the declining-balance method. Since the market price does not decrease by that amount, an excessive depreciation deduction would have had to be allowed, offset only partially by the capital gains tax on the profit on sale. In June, 1960, the Supreme Court, in three decisions that were a notable victory for both common sense and the general taxpaying public, disallowed the Hertz contention and held that the probable selling price of the individual taxpayer, based on his own practices concerning replacement, should fix salvage value. These decisions curbed some of the worst abuses through excessive depreciation followed by capital gains. But the cases did not affect real estate transactions where a company does not have a regular practice of selling investment properties which might serve to set the probable sale price as a limit to depreciation. Though salvage value, when significant, is important to prevent abuses similar to those attempted by Hertz, it should not be applied by revenue agents when the amounts are trivial; the possible scrap-steel value of a filing cabinet which will be sold only as scrap is not important enough to justify an adjustment in the interim depreciation deductions.

In 1958, an approach used in many countries abroad was adopted here in a very limited way. All taxpayers were permitted to take a deduction of 20 per cent of their annual investment in depreciable tangible personal property up to $10,000. The cost of the asset is reduced by this amount, and the regular depreciation rate then applied to the balance for all years including the first. This is an additional allowance in the first year but does not increase total depreciation over the entire life of the property. It was proposed and adopted in the House Ways and Means Committee, with the hearty approval of the Treasury, as part of the small-business tax relief in 1958.

Foreign Allowances for Tax Depreciation

Other countries typically give shorter life estimates for depreciation than those contained in *Bulletin F* or generally known to be available here. Many of them also give additional allowances in the year of acquisition or permit revaluations to adjust for higher replacement costs. The competitive disadvantage of United States manufacturers is evident from a brief review of the depreciation allowances in other countries as they stood in June, 1960.

United Kingdom. England, often referred to on the Continent of Europe as having the least liberal allowances of the European countries, has in practice settled on basic depreciation rates of 7½, 10, 12½, and 20 per cent for various categories of industrial machinery and equipment. These basic rates are increased by 5/4 before they are applied on a declining balance basis, thus making the effective rates 9.375, 12.5, 15.625, and 25 per cent. Industrial buildings are depreciable at 2 per cent on a straight-line basis.

The 7½ to 20 per cent rates have been developed in consultation with various trade associations. Individual companies are not bound by these and may justify higher rates if their individual circumstances justify them. There is no requirement that tax depreciation has to be taken for book purposes, though in the aggregate they seem to be roughly similar.

Both business and government officials note that there is little controversy over depreciation or, as they are referred to, capital allowances. The fact that a balancing charge is imposed or allowed, as required, in the year of disposition of an asset is regarded as of basic importance. This brings back into income any profit on sale, up to original purchase price, or gives an additional deduction for previously undepreciated cost. Thus depreciation becomes purely a matter of timing, and it is frequently noted by all concerned that "it all comes out to the same thing in the long run." The fact that tax inspectors work with returns prepared by a company's independent accountants and make their inquiries to and through the accountants, having access to a company's books only in cases of suspected fraud, probably also tends to reduce controversy to a minimum, especially as to the classification of property in the 7½, 10, and 12½ per cent basic rate categories. The 20 per cent rate is usually reserved for motor vehicles.

Over and above the regular depreciation, English tax law allows initial and investment allowances on certain classes of new investment. An investment allowance is given over and above the original cost which can be recovered in full irrespective of the investment allowance. An initial allowance, by contrast, is applied against the original cost, with the regular allowances subsequently applied to the cost thus reduced. In the years since the war there have been numerous changes in these two allowances, intended to achieve both desired countercyclical stabilization and long-run increases in investment. In April, 1959, the law was liberalized by reinstating investment allowances for a part of the initial allowances previously granted.

Among the combined allowances effective in 1960 was an investment allowance of 20 per cent plus an initial allowance of 10 per cent on new machinery and plant. For machinery receiving the basic 12½ per cent rate, this gives a total allowance in the year of acquisition of slightly over 44 per cent, made up as follows: 20 per cent investment allowance, 10 per cent initial allowance, and 14+ per cent regular depreciation based on 5/4 times 12½ per cent applied to the 90 per cent of cost remaining after the initial allowance of 10 per cent. If the basic depreciation rate were 10 per cent, the first-year allowance would still be 41.25 per cent. Industrial buildings receive a 10 per cent investment allowance plus a 5 per cent initial allowance, new ships receive a 40 per cent investment allowance, and expenditures on scientific research and field equipment each receive 20 per cent.

The notable things about English depreciation are the very large allowances in the year of acquisition and the use of broad categories of depreciable property. The allowance in 1958 in the United States of 20 per cent of the first $10,000 of investment in depreciable personal property, as part of the small-business tax relief in that year, was a very small step in the direction of substantial first-year deductions; it is no more than a gesture compared with the British allowances where there are, of course, no ceilings imposed.

France. France is notable for the very short useful lives implicit in its allowed depreciation rates. Though allowable rates of depreciation for individual companies are subject to determination on the basis of the facts pertaining to its operations, discussions with trade associations have led to agreements on rates, appropriate for various industries, which are published by tax officials and which can be counted on as being acceptable. Ordinary machinery is given a 15 per cent rate, on a straight-line basis, consistent with a life of less than seven years. This rate may be increased to 20 or 30 per cent for multiple-shift operations. Furthermore, in the first year a double allowance is granted, giving 30 per cent for ordinary machinery with the remaining 70 per cent of cost depreciable at 15 per cent of original cost in less than five more years. Heavy machinery, covering such things as the equipment in a steel plant, is given 10 per cent, also with a double allowance in the first year. Factory buildings are given a 5 per cent rate and offices 2 to 4 per cent.

France also gives an initial allowance of 10 per cent on various classes of machinery. As in Great Britain, this further increases the first-year allowance. Though it does not typically equal the British figure of 40 per cent or more, it can approach that amount, and the much more rapid write-off of the remaining cost in France makes its total depreciation treatment more liberal.

In December, 1959, France authorized declining-balance depreciation, with the factor to be applied to the straight-line rates to be established later. These were announced in May, 1960. They permit straight-line rates to be increased by 1.5 for property with a life of three or four years, by 2.0 for property with a life of five or six years, and by 2.5 for property with a life of more than six years. These higher rates, if used, supplant the initial allowance and double allowance in the first year. This gives a slightly lower deduction in the first year but much higher allowances in the second and third years. Thus, property with a 10 per cent rate would get 28 per cent of cost in the first year under the straight-line system (10 per cent of initial allowance plus double the 9 per cent allowed on the balance of cost) and 9 per cent of original cost in the second, third, and all following years. By contrast, under the new method, the allowances in the first three years would be 25, 18.8, and 14 per cent, or a total of 57.8 per cent in the first three years, compared with 46 per cent under the previous method.

The most significant limitation of tax depreciation in France is said to occur because a company may not be able to afford to take on its books as much depreciation as it would be allowed for tax purposes. France, as do many other Continental countries, restricts tax depreciation to what is taken on the books. The fact that tax allowances are limited by what a company can afford to take on its books emphasizes the liberality of the tax allowances, especially in view of the use of hidden reserves and the acceptance of fluctuating depreciation charges on a company's books and in its published statements.

In addition to rapid recovery of original costs, France permits revaluation of assets by applying factors ranging from 243 for 1914 and previous years to 1.05 for 1958 to both historic cost and annual depreciation allowances since the date of acquisition. Thus even property which has been completely written off can have a restored value because the index factors applied to the depreciation will typically be less than that applied to the historic cost. Adjusted written-down value, provided it does not exceed real value at the date of computation, may be written off over its probable remaining useful life from the year of revision. Revision is allowed not only for the major inflation of the two world wars but also for intervening inflations, with a factor of 1.25 for 1951 and 1.9 for 1949.

Germany. Germany made very liberal use of special allowances for particular forms of investment including housing in the reconstruction years after World War II. They are still allowed for investment close to the Iron Curtain and for other restricted uses. Of major significance, however, is the treatment of regular depreciation, which again is very liberal by United States standards.

Though specific rates are to be determined on the basis of facts for each taxpayer, in 1958 a set of allowable rates was published to reduce controversy. Taxpayers may count on these rates and use higher rates if they can be justified, as they often are. A 10 per cent basic rate for machinery is common for straight-line calculations. The basic rates may be increased by a factor of 2.5 under declining-balance depreciation, giving a 25 per cent deduction for a machine in the first year, or about 58 per cent of cost in the first three years. (The factor of 2.5 was reduced to 2.0 in October, 1960.) The first-year allowance under the declining-balance method is limited to 25 per cent of cost (reduced to 20 per cent in 1960.) This is a significant restriction when the basic rate is more than 10 per cent, that is, when the life estimate is less than ten years. It is regarded as important by tax officials to prevent virtually complete recovery of capital outlays in the first year or two of use of an asset with a four- or five-year life.

One additional liberal aspect of German tax depreciation is the permission to take as current expenses all purchases of individual items of property with a cost of less than 600 D.M. This right is used freely by both large and small business concerns and is recognized as a generous but simplifying provision by tax officials. Its use is demonstrated by the widespread advertisement of items of office equipment and the like at 599.50 D.M. toward the end of each year. The interpretation of individual items is fairly liberal. Individual components of a set of office furniture are separable, though a typewriter frame and its carriage are not.

Tax depreciation may not exceed the depreciation taken on a company's books, with the two frequently corresponding to each other. The traditional hidden reserves are created through special reserves for bad debts or general contingencies which may be lumped together indistinguishably to show the desired current net income and net worth on the balance sheet.

Sweden. Sweden in the years immediately after World War II was the best known of all countries for its generous depreciation allowances. Any amount up to the full cost of plant, machinery, and equipment was allowed at the taxpayers' discretion provided only that this amount be taken on the books. This "method," referred to as "free" depreciation, was the ultimate in liberality. It was drastically curtailed, in comparison with previous allowances, effective in 1956, but even the present reduced allowance still leaves it the most liberal as regards the timing of deductions. Two alternatives are now available—depreciation according to plan and depreciation on a bookkeeping basis. Without describing the details of the two, the essential point is that a 20 per cent rate (consistent with a five-year life) can be applied to the historic cost of plant and equipment. The allowance may be more; the standard rule on the bookkeeping basis is 30 per cent of book value at the beginning of the year plus the cost of acquisition less realizations during the year, with the 20 per cent of historic cost as a saving alternative in case the 30 per cent rate does not permit historic cost to be reduced at 20 per cent on a straight-line basis. The principal requirement for use of the bookkeeping basis with the 20 per cent minimum rate is a method of record keeping which will permit gains arising on sales of depreciated assets to be brought into account.

Over and above this liberal depreciation of actual cost, Swedish law permits deductions of up to 40 per cent of business profits for reserves to stabilize business. Forty per cent of the 40 per cent, or 16 per cent of profits, must be invested with the Riksbank, with the company free to use the remaining balance as it pleases, including the purchase of depreciable property. The conditions vary for utilization of that part of the reserve required to be placed with the Riksbank. Thirty per cent of the total reserve, that is, three-quarters of the amount so placed, may be withdrawn after five years without question; prior authorization and authorization to use the balance may be given by the Royal Labour Market Board, depending on the levels of economic activity and employment, for a variety of investments, including not only new capital equipment but repairs of existing buildings, employees' housing, and accumulation of raw material or finished inventories. When a reserve is utilized with

permission of the Labour Market Board, an additional deduction is
allowed of 10 per cent of the amount withdrawn from the tax-free
reserve. Assets financed from the investment reserve are naturally
presumed to be fully written off, however, and are thus not subject
to double depreciation.

Perhaps the most notable feature of the Swedish treatment is that
this most liberal of all programs has been developed under Social
Democratic-Labor-Agrarian governments. The extreme liberality
was adopted to foster investment and increase the productivity of
labor. By no stretch of the imagination could it be said to represent
favored treatment of a politically powerful group.

Switzerland. Actual tax depreciation in Switzerland is difficult to
ascertain because of the control exercised by the twenty-two cantons in the administration of the income tax. The Federal tax is
typically much less than the combined cantonal and communal
income taxes, and the communal authorities collect the entire tax.
The Federal authorities have a right of review for the Federal component, but this is seldom exercised in fact.

For purposes of the Federal tax, depreciation rates have been
established which will be accepted without question. These are
fixed on a declining balance basis and include figures of 5 per cent
for industrial buildings, 20 per cent on plant and machinery, 25 per
cent on patents and good will. The usual form of balancing changes
on disposition is required, though a profit on sale may be immediately applied against the cost of similar property acquired, thereby
avoiding an immediate tax at the expense of future depreciation
deductions.

The foregoing rates apparently are merely a point of departure
for negotiation with cantonal officials. First, these rates, which according to the Federal policy should be reduced by half when
applied on a straight-line basis, may in fact be allowed on a straight-
line basis, an obvious major concession. Substantially faster rates
may also be allowed when an investment is deemed important to
the canton where it is proposed to be made.

Many of the cantons have also granted concessions involving
outright tax exemption for various companies and on the income
from new investment. In the late 1950s a concordat was developed
among most of the cantons to prohibit such concessions, but restrictions on negotiations on depreciation are not included in the con-

cordat. Thus, agreements for very rapid depreciation, limited only by what a company can take on its own books, remain common and once established are usually accepted for Federal as well as cantonal taxes. The requirement that tax depreciation must be taken on the books is of little practical significance because of the full discretion of management in setting depreciation and the multitude of hidden reserves deemed appropriate. The plant and machinery account is often ostentatiously shown without any monetary value simply by the letters p.m. (pro memoria), in a manner reminiscent of the New England textile mills' use of a figure of $1 in the days before systematic depreciation in this country.

Concepts of Depreciation

Depreciation spreads the cost of a long-lived asset, such as a machine or a building, over its useful life. It is necessary to recognize depreciation to get a fair measure of net income. Though there is no controversy on the need to recognize depreciation, there are several ways of spreading the total amount over the service life.

If a machine costing $10,000 is used for ten years in manufacturing and then disposed of as valueless junk, the original outlay of $10,000 must be taken into account as part of the cost of production for the entire period. Failure to do so would overstate profits by $10,000; the outlay for the machine is as true a part of cost as the outlay for immediately consumed raw material or the labor embodied in the product. But should the $10,000 be regarded as a cost of the year when the machine is purchased or the year when it is sold, or should it be spread over the ten-year period, and if it is to be spread, should it be done in equal annual amounts or according to some other systematic plan? There are good reasons for all approaches, but some are better than others.

It was long the practice in some industries to regard the entire price of a depreciable asset as an expense of the year of acquisition. This was the conservative thing to do because of uncertainty as to its useful life. Until the capital outlay was recovered, there was no assurance of a net income and, in a sense, no true net income. One still finds people in New England companies who tell of remembering when the policy was to show the plant at not more than $1 or to see to it that the book figure of plant account never increased in spite of large new capital investments.

Immediate expensing of the costs of capital equipment gave a conservative balance sheet and net worth for creditors. But since the machine probably would be useful for several years, it understated the income of the years when depreciable assets were acquired and overstated the income of other years. This was misleading to investors and gave insiders an unfair advantage. Income could be wiped out and deficits created by large purchases of equipment which would be the source of large incomes in future years; ordinary stockholders would be discouraged and sell their stock; insiders could buy it up at bargain prices.

The other extreme in allocating the cost of depreciable property was to ignore it until the property was actually retired from use. As long as the property was in use, it was a source of income and it could not be known in advance just when it would no longer be useful. This method, known as retirement accounting, was especially attractive to the railroads, which built their lines ahead of existing traffic and counted on future population and economic growth to make the venture profitable. If the entire cost of the depreciable asset had been charged as an expense in the first year, or even if it had been spread over the life of the asset, the operation would have shown continuous deficits and financing would not have been possible. By waiting until assets were retired from use, traffic would have grown to a point where the original costs of assets retired could be absorbed and a net income still shown. After a company became sufficiently mature to begin to retire assets, the retirements could be spread over the years to give a fairly smooth retirement expense roughly comparable to annual depreciation charges. As long as the company continued to retire and replace assets, its income, after the initial period of growth when income ignored the cost of capital equipment, would be reasonable; in its final years, a company would have large retirement expenses and losses, but final years were not expected to occur. The retirement method was used by railroads for their roadbeds until World War II, and the method of transition to ordinary depreciation accounting was not finally settled until 1958, when an amendment to the tax law was finally adopted by the Congress which resolved in a reasonable manner a technical point under litigation involving many hundreds of millions of dollars in income taxes for the railroads.

With increasing emphasis on income reports for investors and on consistency over the years to show changes in profitability, both of the methods involving a charge to expense in a single year became unacceptable. The first method understated income in years of growth and overstated subsequent income; the retirement method did just the reverse. Both are misleading. It is now generally recognized that the cost of depreciable property used to produce income should be spread over its useful life. But there are at least three methods to spread the total, and each of the three has some logical support.

The straight-line method spreads the total equally over the life of property. It is simple and sensible and appealing for both of those attributes. It was the conventional method adopted in this country when accountants and businessmen became concerned about more scientific depreciation analysis. It will probably always be considered a proper method.

In other countries, the declining-balance method previously discussed was the conventional method adopted. This is also a simple method. It may have one incidental advantage in reducing the stated value of assets more rapidly in early years when they are, in fact, declining more rapidly in market value. This tends to keep the balance sheet figure in line with the market value of depreciable assets, whereas under the straight-line method they may be overstated. The declining-balance method also tends to give an even cost for the combined figures for depreciation and maintenance which together may be regarded as total cost of using depreciable assets. Maintenance expense usually increases in later years. If depreciation expense is declining at the same time, the sum of the two will be more even over the years and give a fairer measure of net income. Other methods are used to give larger deductions in early years of use, such as the sum-of-the-year digits plan mentioned before or systems which allocate half the cost to the first third of the probable life and half the remainder to the next third. These methods are reasonable and acceptable for business purposes and should continue to be acceptable for tax purposes.

A third method of spreading the cost of a depreciable asset over its useful life assumes that funds arising through depreciation will be used profitably in a business and that these profits should be added to the depreciation itself to recoup the original cost of the asset. Thus depreciation in the early years is relatively small, increasing each year by the interest imputed to a theoretical depreciation fund consisting of previous depreciation deductions and interest accruals. This is referred to as the sinking fund method of depreciation accounting. It is interesting as a theoretical concept but has little practical application, though it does call attention to the fact that in any business which earns its depreciation, funds do arise prior to the actual retirement of an asset. It is not known to be used for tax purposes. This method has the disadvantage of stating the net value of depreciable assets on the balance sheet at amounts well above their actual secondhand value.

The foregoing description of alternative methods of allocating the cost of depreciable assets over time has been given to show that there is no one "correct" method, with all others being distortions of the truth. Different methods are appropriate under different circumstances to meet different purposes.

An entirely different approach to depreciation is sometimes proposed. Depreciation is thought of as providing a source of funds to replace capital equipment. This is the concept which supports the idea of calculating depreciation on replacement cost. Under inflation, new capital equipment costs more than that which is being retired and an increasing total dollar investment is necessary to maintain the existing productive capacity of a plant. If one conceives of an investment as representing a given capacity, with depreciation intended to record the exhaustion of the capacity over time and to replace it when necessary, then it follows that depreciation should be related to the cost of replacement. A departure from monetary measurements of investments and incomes, with an attempt to convert them into real investments and real incomes, opens an endless field for adjustments and differences of opinion as to what adjustments should be made. It is a concept and approach which seems justified only in extreme situations.

But whatever the method of depreciation used and whatever concept underlies it, one fact is significant. Depreciation is a noncash expense, which means that funds arising from a business operation are greater than they appear to be at first sight by the amount of the depreciation. To simplify the analysis, one may assume that inventories, receivables, and outstanding debts are the same at the end of the year as they were at the beginning and that a company has earned $5,000 during the year. One would first expect that available cash had also increased by $5,000. If the company had taken $1,000 depreciation in the year, however, profits were less by this amount but the depreciation did not involve any outflow of funds. Thus, funds "became available through depreciation" to the extent of an additional $1,000. In financial analysis, depreciation is always added to net income as a source of funds.

In another sense, one can make the same point by considering the sequence of events if one starts with $10,000 in cash, then buys a machine for that price and depreciates it at $1,000 a year over ten years. If one were just to break even in the operation, there would be $1,000 of funds arising each year which, if they were kept segregated, would mount up to the $10,000 original cash by the time the machine was scrapped at the end of ten years. It is in this way that the inclusion of depreciation among the expenses of operations "provides" funds to replace an original investment. The operations themselves, of course, provide the funds; since the depreciation does not represent a current cash expense, the funds actually provided by operations are understated by the amount of the depreciation. The addition of depreciation to net income gives a corrected figure for total funds provided by operations.

Funds arising from depreciation are not ordinarily segregated and kept separate for the replacement of a specific asset. They never really are distinct from any other flows of funds. Current funds, regardless of source, in excess of the needs of the business are ordinarily used for expansion. Security analysts are giving increasing attention to the cash flow per share of stock as an important item of information along with the traditional earnings per share. Depreciation is usually the principal reason for difference between the two. In some companies, typically those with large fixed assets subject to depreciation, the cash flow per share may be two or three times the earnings per share. The cash flow is an indication of funds available for distribution to stockholders (if surplus is adequate to cover dividends) or to reinvest in new assets in the business. A hotel company, for example, with a cash flow several times its annual income, based to a considerable extent on depreciation of existing hotels, is in a position to buy additional hotels or otherwise expand its business to a much greater extent than would be expected if one looked only at the figures for net income and dividends.

In a mature company with fairly steady annual retirements of old machines and purchases of new ones, the current depreciation may just about cover the cost of the new machines if there has been no increase in the cost of replacement from inflation. For a company with much new equipment and few retirements, however, the funds arising through depreciation are available for expansion which may continue until retirements and necessary replacements during a year catch up to the year's depreciation charge. If a company has only a single asset which will last for fifty to seventy-five years, as a large office building, the funds arising through interim depreciation charges will finance other investments over many years. If, in fact, there is no real plan ever to tear down the building, and if, in fact, its value is maintained in spite of greater age because inflation increases construction costs for new buildings, then the depreciation may be and is thought of as "tax-free income" in many investors' calculations.

This analysis explains much of the tax advantage in real estate investments. Available cash from operations is distributed instead of being used for expansion. To the extent that it exceeds net income, that is, to the extent that it arises through depreciation, it is not taxable income to the stockholder of a corporation or the owner of a syndicate interest. The "tax-free income" attitude of the investor is valid as long as the day of reckoning, the ultimate replacement of the building, is postponed. When this time finally comes, the source of all income, both taxable and tax-free, will cease to exist, and unless the tax-free part has been set aside for new investment, it will turn out that one has squandered one's capital.

But for periods such as those of the past fifteen years, depreciation on real estate has been a source of tax abuse. Inflation, far from justifying higher depreciation to cover higher replacement costs, has really been nonexistent in fact, and even normal depreciation has been excessive. Certainly the declining-balance method for buildings has turned out to be unduly generous. For companies with one or a few very long-lived assets, the sinking fund concept of depreciation might be appropriate. The denial of any depreciation deductions in Great Britain on buildings other than factories becomes comprehensible under the combined circumstances of real estate costs, incomes, and market prices during the postwar period.

Economic Significance of Depreciation Allowances

The principal economic significance of depreciation is that it "provides" funds to replace capital equipment in the manner just described. In spite of the peculiar and distinctive characteristics of real estate, most depreciable assets have a definite and fairly short useful life. Rapid obsolescence means that they should be replaced frequently. New machinery, ranging from railroad locomotives through ordinary machine tools to textile machinery, is offered with improvements such that the new items can pay for themselves in relatively short periods. The lower costs with new machines permit price reductions or justify wage increases without price increases. The rebuilding of war-destroyed factories in western Europe and Japan, not to mention Russia, has given our competitors in many respects newer, more modern equipment to work with than we have in this country, where it was reported that 60 per cent of our machine tools were over 10 years old in 1958, up from 38 per cent in 1945.

The increase in replacement cost of capital equipment has meant that depreciation is inadequate to maintain capacity in a mature company. The fact that depreciation makes funds available prior to the time that specific assets have to be replaced can help, in a very rough way, to offset the inadequacy in its aggregate amount. Though one may not accept the theory that depreciation should be based on replacement cost, one may be very glad of any practical method by which business concerns can maintain their productive capacity without having to raise new funds or use retained earnings. These latter sources of funds should be available for expansion; it would be a sorry state of affairs indeed if they had to be absorbed just to keep even. The faster the depreciation deductions, the greater the flow of internal funds from business operations and the greater the prospects of securing modern efficient plants.

It is also true that in many instances a decision to retire an old piece of equipment depends on whether it has been fully depreciated. In a dispassionate scientific calculation, it is irrelevant whether the old item has been depreciated because the investment in it is properly regarded as a "sunk cost." Whenever the costs of using new equipment, including depreciation on it, are less than the current cash costs of using the old equipment, a replacement should be made. In a more precise and elaborate way one may say that whenever the present value of the net cash flows from new equipment exceed the present value of the net cash flows from the old equipment, the replacement should be made, recognizing that for the new equipment there is an immediate cash outlay to be made to get it while the outlay for the old equipment was made in the past and does not enter the current present-value calculations. But concepts of this sort are as abstruse to many businessmen as they must be to many readers of this book.

The idea that a machine which has not been fully depreciated has not "paid its way" or "returned its cost" is an appealing one. In many companies, it is still true that a piece of property which is not fully depreciated is not yet ready for replacement. Thus, in a practical sense, faster depreciation is likely to set the stage for faster replacement. And since many companies use the same depreciation rates on their own books as they use for taxes, though they are not required to do so, the shorter the estimated lives used for tax purposes, the greater the willingness to replace obsolescent machinery.

Depreciation also has economic significance because of uncertainty about the future. Risks and prospects for income can be seen more clearly in the near future than for remote periods. If a machine can be depreciated over ten years and has a good prospect of earning enough to pay its capital cost and give a reasonable profit, a businessman is more likely to risk the investment than if the depreciation is spread over fifteen years. This is a reasonable decision if one regards the fact of full depreciation before retirement as significant. If one makes his decisions on the period over which an investment is recovered, assuming that all available funds are applied against the investment until it is covered, or if one makes decisions on the basis of the present value of future cash flows, the difference between a fifteen- and ten-year estimate of useful life for depreciation would not be significant. But it has already been indicated why many businessmen do not and for a long time to come probably will not think in these theoretical terms. The fact that full depreciation can be covered and the investment recovered over a shorter period of time is an understandable inducement to commit funds to the investment. The shorter the term, the greater one's confidence in his own estimates of the prospects.

Faster depreciation also facilitates financing of new capital outlays. Funds arising through depreciation may be used to repay debt incurred to purchase a capital asset. The greater the depreciation, the faster the debt can be repaid or the greater the amount of debt that can be repaid in a given period of time. Banks ordinarily make loans for five years at most. If property is depreciated evenly over twenty years, the depreciation would "provide" funds to repay a five-year term loan for only one-quarter of the cost; if depreciation was speeded up and extended over only ten years, a five-year term loan would cover half the cost. Increased use of declining-balance depreciation after it was authorized in the tax law in 1954 apparently permitted the financing of more capital equipment by term bank loans. This was especially important for small businesses which could not sell long-term bonds.

It should be apparent that at any given selling price, larger depreciation charges mean smaller profits; more funds provided through depreciation mean less funds provided by net income. The net cash flow is not changed by a shift between the components. But the composition of the cash flow is significant. Net income is presumptively available for dividends; funds from depreciation are not, except in very special cases like the single-building real estate companies mentioned previously. Funds from depreciation are presumptively available for and even destined for the purchase of new fixed assets or for the retirement of debt on existing assets. And the retirement of debt on some assets restores borrowing capacity to borrow again to purchase new assets. Depreciation is a source of funds especially likely to be used for replacement and expansion of capital equipment.

Faster depreciation also increases the opportunity for capital investment by shifting taxes to later years. In the previous paragraph, it was stated that more depreciation meant less net income with the implication that the two were interchangeable. But if the faster depreciation is allowed as a tax deduction, it makes current taxes less and, if the rate of investment is not maintained, future taxes greater. In the meantime, more funds are available for business use, and they are available in the form which is most likely to be used to purchase new capital equipment. Faster depreciation and lower corporate income tax rates as alternative tax changes to increase capital investment are compared in Chapter 7 dealing with corporate taxation. Further consideration is left to that point.

The analysis in this section has given some of the reasons why other countries have used liberal depreciation allowances to encourage new investment and thereby increase productivity and economic growth. The final section of this chapter will cover the possible changes in our own tax law to improve our economic growth. In comparison with what other countries have done, the changes proposed in this analysis are modest indeed. They might be considered to give no more than realistic depreciation.

Proposed Changes in United States Tax Allowances for Depreciation

The following discussion covers the proposals commonly advanced in this country for more liberal depreciation. The two most generous ones, adjustments for higher replacement costs and depreciation in excess of 100 per cent of actual costs, are rejected as unnecessary and inappropriate under existing circumstances. What is proposed here is simply a general authorization for faster depreciation than is now taken by many companies and the use of a relatively small number of categories of depreciable property to make the calculations simpler. As a safeguard to prevent abuses and protect the *bona fides* of tax deductions, depreciation should not be allowed for tax purposes in excess of what is taken on a company's books for its own business purposes. This change in the law, as stated previously, should be adopted only as part of a general reform which would also tax as ordinary income, instead of capital gain, any profits on the sale of depreciated property up to the original purchase price.

Depreciation Limited to Historical Cost. The problems involved in converting an income measured in monetary terms into real income are formidable. In the calculation of depreciation on capital equipment, the selection of the appropriate price index and adjustments to reflect increased efficiency of new machines would both open up new areas of controversy. Identical machinery is frequently not available, and if it were, it would not be purchased, because new models are more efficient. But how much of the higher price of the new model reflects a truly higher cost and how much reflects higher speed, smaller wastage, less frequent repairs, and greater automation?

When a country has had a drastic inflation, some adjustment in the basis of capital assets and depreciation is necessary, as was the case in France. Rough adjustments give rough justice, and rough justice is better than gross inequity. It does not appear, however, that the inflation in this country, inexcusable though much of it has been and deplorable though all of it has been, has gone far enough to justify embarking on price-level adjustments for depreciation now. The fact that faster depreciation on actual cost can meet some of the problems of higher replacement cost reinforces this conclusion. Since there is so much discussion of replacement-cost depreciation, however, it deserves more specific comment.

Adjustments for higher replacement cost might be made in many ways. If it were to be done, the method by which an additional allowance for the difference between original cost and replacement cost (however that is measured) is given when a retirement is made and a replacement occurs seems the most acceptable. This gives the allowance only when there actually is a replacement, which is both fair and sound economic policy. There is certainly no reason to give more depreciation to a company owning a single office building when the company distributes all its available funds and apparently proposes to go out of existence when the building is finally torn down.

The alternative method of adjusting annual allowances on an interim basis may not even serve its intended purpose if the rise in replacement cost occurs toward the end of the life of an asset. Consider a machine costing $10,000 with a ten-year life which has been depreciated on a straight-line basis for eight years. In the ninth year assume a 50 per cent increase in prices, to give simple illustrative figures. The ordinary depreciation in that year, as in all other years, would be $1,000. Adjusted for higher replacement cost, it would be $1,500. If prices stay steady in the tenth year, there would again be depreciation of $1,500, or a total for the ten years of $11,000. The extra $500 in each of the last two years would fall far short of covering the extra $5,000 needed for the higher replacement cost if that is the intent. Alternatively one might say that in the ninth and tenth years the annual depreciation should be $3,500, which is the amount necessary to bring total depreciation, which was $8,000 at the beginning of the ninth year, up to the full replacement cost of $15,000 at the end of the tenth year. Interim adjustments of this sort unnecessarily complicate the calculations; a single final one, if there is to be any adjustment at all, is simpler and confines the benefit to cases of actual replacement.

A larger deduction at the time of replacement would discriminate in favor of established companies in comparison with new or rapidly expanding companies. The latter must get their funds for new assets from new sources, new security issues, or retained earnings. Their depreciation in the first years of use of new property is only the normal depreciation, and their taxable income and taxes are also what might be called normal. The established company replacing old equipment would get an extra deduction for the excess of replacement cost over original cost, its taxes would be commensurately less, and it would have to rely less heavily on new funds than the expanding company. It is, of course, the purpose of the extra deduction to permit replacement without recourse to new funds, but the differential tax burden on the two companies in the year of acquisitions of machinery is nonetheless discriminatory.

The use of debt to finance a good deal of the capital equipment in some industries would also raise problems of fairness if replacement-cost depreciation were adopted. Debt gives leverage to the common stock equity. The leverage would give a windfall gain to the holders of common stock if depreciation is based on replacement cost. An example of a company with 1 million dollars of fixed assets and $500,000 each of debt and common stock equity will give a simplified example. If the replacement cost doubles and an extra deduction is allowed for it, there would be funds to provide 2 million dollars of fixed assets; with $500,000 of debt the money value represented by each share of stock would have trebled. If the company had been financed entirely by stock with no debt, the money value represented by each share of stock would only have doubled. Adjustment for differing debt ratios would seem to be required for fairness but would be unduly complicated.

Another interesting aspect of debt in a financial structure would arise if the replacement cost fell. In the foregoing example, if the replacement cost fell by 50 per cent, allowable depreciation would presumably be adjusted downward and only $500,000 of assets would be required on replacement. This amount would be necessary to cover the debt, however, and the common stock interest would have been completely wiped out. Proponents of replacement-cost depreciation usually ignore the possibility of decreases in replacement costs, and they are perhaps justified in doing so in view of the many inflationary pressures existing in the world. But a little reflection on the implication of replacement-cost depreciation if it were to be applied consistently sometimes discourages them from further support of the proposal, especially if their company has a high debt ratio.[1]

Depreciation Limited to 100 per cent of Cost. In spite of the good precedents abroad for giving investment allowances in excess of the cost of depreciable assets, they do not seem to be necessary here under present circumstances. At least, we should first see what the results are of faster depreciation of cost.

The use of extra allowances can be directed to particular categories of investment which it is desired to encourage. By that very fact, these allowances become an instrument of economic planning and are not consistent with a relatively neutral tax system. But if subsidies are to be given, extra investment allowances have the advantage of giving them without creating any new government organization which will have a vested interest in its own continued existence and expansion. They also are available equally to old and new companies, avoiding the sort of discrimination noted above under replacement-cost depreciation.

[1] The authorization in the tax law to use last-in first-out (lifo) inventory accounting is sometimes cited as a precedent for replacement-cost depreciation. It is true that nominal inventory profits arising from inflation are kept from entering taxable income by lifo accounting, but this was not the purpose of the provision when it was first adopted in the tax law in 1937. The purpose was to prevent undue fluctuations in reported income from cyclical price changes. It was fortuitously available to insulate business from the inflationary profits in inventory which started to build up with World War II. One should also note that more dollars are required even in the cash account, as well as in receivables and fixed assets, to carry on a given volume of business after inflation. If an increase in the monetary investment in fixed assets is to be permitted tax-free to maintain their real value, what should be done to permit tax-free earnings to cover the increased amount of cash needed to handle the weekly payroll and the increased receivables necessary to finance the same volume of sales at a higher price level?

Faster Depreciation of Actual Costs. From all standpoints, faster depreciation should, generally speaking, be allowed on industrial plant and equipment. In the absence of adequate information of the rates now being used by all companies, the new authorized rates may be no higher than those actually used in some instances now. But they should be substantially higher than those contained in *Bulletin F,* which set an effective limit on depreciation allowances in many companies. Estimated lives should not be set at such an extreme figure as five years, as was done for wartime emergency amortization. Rates should be related to actual service lives but kept on the short side of both historical experience and prospective lives. Rates allowed in other countries should not be ignored in view of international competition. an eight- to ten-year life presumption for machinery might be reasonable, with fifteen or at most twenty years for the heaviest equipment. A twenty-year life for railroad locomotives and ten or fifteen years for other rolling stock might also be desirable.

It should not be regarded as improper or scandalous if a good deal of depreciable property is used beyond the time it is fully depreciated. An acceptance of this proposition is basic for effective depreciation reform. Actual life beyond full depreciation must not be taken as evidence that depreciation has been excessive. For reasons already given, it is likely that faster depreciation will in time lead to faster replacement and thus tend to bring the actual life down to the assumed life. This is the intended result. It is vastly better than the present situation, where slow depreciation delays replacements and tends to bring the actual life up to the assumed lives. Assumed lives shorter than actual lives are reasonable and proper.

The authorized rates of depreciation should not be the maximum rates allowable. Taxpayers should be able to use higher rates if their particular circumstances justify them. But the authorized rates should be sufficiently high to cover the most ambitious plans and prospects for rapid replacement and improvement of capital equipment by most companies.

The authorized depreciation rates should be available to all taxpayers, and their use should not be subject to challenge by revenue agents. If the rates were fixed in the Internal Revenue Code, they would be removed from administrative control but the Congress would be subject to continual pressure by lobby groups for special treatment. They might be established by administrative action. The Congress should be assured, however, that they will be established on a reasonable basis, and the Administration should be assured that rates of the sort described here would not be subject to congressional criticism.

If rates could be worked out jointly by the Treasury and the Congress and specifically referred to with approval in the committee reports on legislation concerning depreciation, they could be made effective as a Treasury regulation on the date new legislation was effective. This would relieve Congress of pressure to change detailed rates, while giving a congressional directive to establish rates consistent with the intended objective. Subsequent changes could then be made as they seemed necessary by administrative action consistent with the congressional policy. The choice between statutory and administrative establishment of rates should be made in the light of the legislative development at the time this aspect of the tax reform is made. However it is done, specific rates must be authorized. It is not enough to direct revenue agents to give more consideration to taxpayers' estimates. All taxpayers should be put in the same position to get the same allowances.

Broad Categories of Property. In the interests of simplicity, and to reduce controversy, relatively few categories of property should be established for depreciation. Fifteen or twenty categories should be sufficient, and most companies would use only a few of these.[2] The refinements from more detailed classifications do not justify the extra work required. Many companies now use fairly broad categories, and amazingly enough, a good many use a single composite rate for all depreciable property from the shortest lived automobile to the longest lived right of way or transmission line. A single composite rate is too broad and too hard to adjust to reflect changes in the mix between short-lived and long-lived assets. Records should be kept by the year of acquisition to assure identification and proper treatment of gains and losses on disposition.[3]

If a general revision of rates were considered too formidable to

[2] Broad categories of depreciable property have been used in Canada, apparently with complete success.

[3] In many European countries, where such records are regularly required, the year of acquisition is delightfully called the "vintage year."

undertake at one time, the new system might be applied first to a few types of property only. If new rates were established for machinery and equipment and perhaps railroad rolling stock, they would be available for the sorts of depreciable assets most important in increasing productivity. Rates for other types of depreciable property could be developed in later years.

Tax Depreciation Limited to Book Depreciation. The depreciation taken for tax purposes should not exceed what has been taken on a company's own books and used in its published reports. A good deal of thought was given to making this a requirement in 1954 for the use of declining-balance depreciation, but it was not done because of some of the complications and extreme restrictions imposed previously on the use of lifo inventory accounting. In retrospect, it seems that it was a mistake not to have made tax depreciation conditional upon book depreciation of an equal or greater amount in 1954. It should be done now as part of the reform in tax depreciation.

Some people argue that a requirement that tax depreciation must not exceed book depreciation should be the only limitation on the depreciation deduction. In large companies with many stockholders this might well be an adequate limitation. Excessive deductions would be prevented by the impact of the large depreciation on reported earnings. But in the vastly more numerous closely controlled companies and partnerships, reported earnings are not important or at least not important enough to outweigh the advantages of tax savings through too rapid depreciation deductions. To protect the revenue and to maintain substantial equality among companies, established rates of the sort described above would be necessary.

Though there is great difference of opinion within the accounting profession, the prevailing policy at present requires companies which take more depreciation for tax purposes than they do on their books to set up a "reserve for future taxes." Though the larger present tax deductions will be followed by smaller future deductions on specific items of property, and hence higher taxes, the reserve item on the balance sheet is confusing to many. If a company merely maintains its total dollar investment in depreciable assets by systematic replacements, it will have successive new assets with new depreciation deductions to balance the declining deductions on old assets. Thus, there will be a fairly steady rolling-over of the components of the "reserve," with no net reduction in it except in the most improbable circumstances. Some accounting firms urge their clients not to take tax depreciation in excess of book depreciation, and some firms also oppose the use of the "reserve for future taxes." Many difficulties and much confusion would be eliminated by the requirement that tax depreciation could not exceed depreciation taken on the books.

Security analysts have been slow in recognizing the importance of differences in depreciation accounting in comparing companies within an industry. The use of cash-flow projections is a step toward recognition of some of its implications; it would be significant even if all companies used the same depreciation rates. If standard rates were established for tax purposes and widely used for both tax and book purposes, financial statements would be more comparable than they are now. It might then be decided that any substantial divergences from the allowable tax rates should be noted in a footnote to financial statements, giving a much better basis for analysis than is now generally available. If a requirement to indicate substantial divergences from allowable tax rates ever did develop, it would come through the evolution of accounting practice, not as a part of tax legislation.

Larger depreciation charges on a company's own books, arising from more liberal tax depreciation, might have significant economic implications in two areas not usually considered in connection with this reform in the tax law. It could affect a company's prospects for external financing through new stock issues and the pricing of its products. In the absence of extensive research and analysis, the exact results in both of these respects are uncertain; the relationships are noted here to show the far-reaching ramifications of a change in depreciation allowances.

A reduction in reported earnings per share would tend to lower the market price of stock and thereby discourage financing by new stock issues. But with reduced taxes, there would be larger cash flows per share, as described above, and this would tend to increase the price of the stock. The net result of these two opposing influences would depend on the extent to which investors shift their attention from the traditional earnings per share to cash flows.

Higher depreciation charges would tend to increase the prices charged for products to the extent that book depreciation is incorporated into cost figures and costs are a basis for pricing. But better capital equipment, fostered by the more liberal tax depreciation, would tend to reduce costs through greater efficiency, again with an uncertain net result.

The only substantial objection to a requirement that tax depreciation cannot exceed book depreciation would come from some of the public utility companies which have tried to play both ends against the middle in their depreciation accounting. They desire to take the highest possible depreciation for tax purposes in order to save current taxes, a perfectly proper desire. They would also be glad to take high depreciation on their books and thereby reduce their incomes and show the need for higher rates if they could do so without having to reduce the stated value of their assets and their invested capital, which in turn constitutes the base on which their allowable income is fixed. Different utility commissions have different policies with respect to tax depreciation, book depreciation, reported allowable net income, and the rate base. The subject is too specialized to develop here. A requirement that tax depreciation be limited to book depreciation would under present rules preclude some utilities from taking faster depreciation. But they should not be permitted to do so anyway if they do not take it consistently and carry it through to all its implications, including its rate base.

A good precedent for the regulatory bodies seems to have been set by the Illinois Supreme Court in a 1960 decision which permitted Illinois utilities to take declining-balance depreciation provided it is deducted from the rate base. In the words of the Commonwealth Edison Company, "This decision, in effect, approves the practice we have followed from the beginning." The policy and attitude of Commonwealth Edison set a good precedent for utility companies.

The limitation of tax depreciation to book depreciation for utility companies would also help to close a present loophole by which a large part of some dividends are tax exempt to stockholders.[4] This comes about because the tax status of dividends depends upon the earnings and profits of a company, which in turn is influenced by the deduction for depreciation. If tax deductions for depreciation

[4] Thirty-six per cent of the Detroit Edison Company dividend was tax exempt in 1959.

are larger than the book deductions permitted or required by a state utility commission, then the sum of earnings and profits will be less than the surplus shown on the books. The surplus on the public books makes a dividend distribution legal; the smaller sum of earnings and profits on the tax books makes part of it qualify as a return of capital to the stockholders. It is altogether unfair to the general public that some taxpayers should get partially tax-free dividends when the distributions are covered by current earnings as reported to the public, the stockholders, and the regulatory authorities. This situation needs correction; a limitation of tax depreciation to book depreciation would help but not be adequate to close the loophole.

These rather technical points concerning some of the public utility companies cannot be fully examined here. They are raised and described in as simple a manner as possible to suggest that the protests which some representatives of utility companies will make when they are required to limit their tax depreciation to the depreciation taken on their books should be appraised against these other more subtle aspects of their tax depreciation.

Ignore Salvage Value. With the profit from any excessive depreciation taxed as ordinary income, it should be possible to ignore salvage value in calculating depreciation, except perhaps in extreme cases involving the regular sale of little-used property. This would be a major simplification.

Special First-year Depreciation Deductions. The faster depreciation proposed above need not, under present circumstances, be supplemented by special first-year deductions similar to those widely used in Great Britain and western Europe. The allowance of a deduction of 20 per cent of the first $10,000 invested in depreciable personal property by the tax legislation in 1958 was a desirable relief to small business. It was approved by the Treasury Department as a sound general concept in the law, the application of which might be extended in the future. If it were not possible to make the general reform in depreciation rates proposed here, an immediate extension of this treatment would be desirable as the next best alternative. With adequate reform in the rates, the extension is perhaps not necessary. But the present provision should be continued in the law in its present limited form, available for broader application. This provision, which is not available for real estate, introduces a useful precedent for distinguishing between real estate and other forms of property.

Use of Variable Deductions for Contercyclical Purposes. It is often proposed that the tax depreciation to be allowed on new depreciable assets should be varied from time to time to slow down a boom and foster expansion in a recession. This idea has a certain appeal as an element of fiscal policy. If one had sufficient confidence in the ability to predict the dominant forces influencing the business situation and action could be taken immediately, the policy might have merit. The lag in giving allowances and the additional lag in making new commitments of capital make it possible, however, that the final result might accentuate rather than smooth fluctuations in capital investments. It is, furthermore, doubtful how effective a temporary change in depreciation allowances would be in modifying the timing of capital investment. Certainty and stability of rates are important for long-range planning; the unsettling influence of short-term variations might nullify the intended benefits.

The proposal made in this book is for a long-run reform through faster depreciation for tax purposes on machinery and equipment at all times. This is a major item in tax reform, with certain value in facilitating long-term growth. Proposals to make another major change of uncertain value in the interests of greater stability should be postponed for further examination.

If variations in depreciation deductions for countercyclical purposes were to be made, they could be done most effectively by a variable first-year allowance. A 15 or 20 per cent first-year allowance, of the sort described in the preceding section, might be established as a normal provision of the law. This normal first-year allowance could be increased or decreased as the circumstances seemed to require. A variation in the first-year allowance would have a more immediate impact on business decisions and available funds than would an adjustment in the regular rates of depreciation for new depreciable property. If the regular rates were changed, the effects on deductions would be spread fairly evenly over the entire life of the property; if the first-year allowance were changed, the effect would be concentrated in the year of acquisition, where the impact is desired.

Variations in first-year depreciation allowances for countercyclical purposes would be incompatible with a requirement that tax depreciation could not exceed the depreciation taken on a company's own books. Consistency in book depreciation is necessary to avoid distortions in income reported to stockholders and the public. Accordingly, if special allowances were to be given either for countercyclical purposes or on a continuing basis as a subsidy for investment, it might be preferable to allow them as an additional deduction over and above total cost. Any such allowances would not and in fact could not be recorded on a company's own books. In this respect investment allowances would avoid the complications caused by variable or unusual first-year allowances which are treated as part of the total recovery of original cost. As already indicated, it is questionable whether so fundamental a departure from tax neutrality is needed. Certainly the basic reform in regular depreciation rates and simplification in categories should be adopted before any experiments are made with new tax gadgets.

One final point should be made on the countercyclical aspects of depreciation. If we ever again need to give emergency amortization to encourage private investment in depreciable assets in a defense emergency, we should consider, as an alternative or a supplement, the policy of denying depreciation deductions to nonapproved investments during the emergency period. This was done by Canada during the war in Korea. Since such a period is one when resources are strained in any case, action to slow down less important capital investments is desirable. A postponement of depreciation on nonapproved projects would be useful for this purpose and would tend to have investments concentrated in approved areas.

Chapter 7 CORPORATE INCOME TAXATION

Its Economic Effects—Double Taxation of Dividend Income

It is uncertain whether the ultimate burden of the corporation income tax rests on stockholders or consumers or is in some way diffused generally throughout the population. It is as surprising as it is disturbing that there should be such uncertainty about our second most important revenue source. The corporation income tax provides over a quarter of the total Federal revenue, with a yield of 20 billion to 21 billion dollars in seven of the nine years 1952 to 1960, and 17 billion dollars in the other two years. It should cause more concern than it apparently does to rely so heavily on a tax whose incidence and consequences are so uncertain. The explanation for the lack of concern lies in the political implications and, one may perhaps say, even the political advantages of the uncertainty.

If it were certain that the tax did rest on the corporation, relief from the double tax on the dividends of shareholders could be advanced more firmly, though perhaps no more effectively than it has been. If it were certain that the tax was shifted to consumers, it could be attacked more firmly as a 20-billion-dollar excise which simultaneously (1) supports inefficient companies by taxing their more effective competitors in proportion to their greater efficiency, (2) discourages economic expansion by increasing the rate of return necessary from new plant and equipment to justify a capital outlay, and (3) burdens consumers capriciously and in ways which, if known, might be regarded as thoroughly inequitable.

This formidable list of adverse consequences of corporation income taxation requires explanation. In some respects the statements even appear to be self-contradictory. This analysis is contained in the first part of this chapter. It is more theoretical than any other section of the book; readers who find theoretical analysis distasteful may prefer to skip this part. The discussion will not, however, attempt to resolve the uncertainty as to whether the corporation income tax is borne by stockholders or consumers. The arguments on both sides are presented, but a conclusion is one of the major unsolved problems in economics and promises to remain unsolved for the foreseeable future.

Economic Effects of Corporation Income Taxation

Though the corporation income tax seems to have bad effects, whatever its incidence, it is a major source of revenue and our economic system has in one way or another somehow adjusted to its existence. Some proposals for reform themselves contain undesirable implications. But though one may expect continuation of the tax, it should not be regarded complacently. Its consequences should be understood, especially its probable adverse effects on economic expansion.

The traditional belief in economic theory and popular opinion is that the corporation income tax cannot be shifted forward to consumers. Prices under competition are theoretically in equilibrium when they just cover the cost of the last increment of production—at the point where marginal cost and marginal revenue are equal, in the economist's language. At that point there is no net income from the final increment of production, hence no income tax, and hence it is thought there is no chance for the tax to be reflected in price. In a monopoly situation, the seller is presumed to set prices to maximize his profits, and any tax fixed as a percentage of the profits, either proportionately or progressively, will not change the price at which the net profits will be at a maximum. A maximum income before tax will yield the maximum net income after tax, and the same price and volume of sales are still preferable however the income is reduced by income tax. Thus, under both competition and monopoly, the tax theoretically rests on the corporation.

Statistical analysis and common observation confirm the existence at almost all times of some companies which just break even with no net profits. Many profitable companies also have some no-profit production in some lines of activity. If one accepts the idea that price is determined by high-cost production, the proposition that corporate income taxes rest on the corporation and the stockholders is confirmed.

In spite of the statistics and the logic, the real issue is whether the high costs of no-profit production determine prices, at any given level of demand, or the lower costs of profitable firms plus the income taxes on their profits are more significant. In the latter case, income taxes may be considered an element of cost by profitable firms, and the prices established by profitable firms which reflect costs plus taxes give inefficient firms an opportunity to exist which they would not otherwise have. The income tax may, it is contended, support a "price umbrella" over the marginal producers. With lower taxes, the efficient producers would sell at lower prices and the producer who just breaks even at the higher price would be forced out of business.

Discussions among economists concerning the incidence of the corporation income tax are almost as extensive as the discussion of price theory itself. The income tax may be regarded as simply reducing profits which are determined by forces quite unrelated to the tax. Costs, demand, volume, and prices are all uninfluenced by the rate of tax or even by its existence; profits are determined by these factors and are then reduced to the extent of any income tax. This has been the classical view in economic analysis. Alternatively, the corporation income tax may be regarded as an element of cost, with business decisions on prices and on investment of capital in plant and equipment based on planned rates of return after taxes. To the extent that dominant profitable firms in an industry make the decisions in this way and set prices which marginal firms merely follow, the tax may be shifted forward.

It appears that there is some truth in each of these opposing positions. The proverbial phrase "It all depends" is especially appropriate. At the one extreme, it is hard to see how the corporation income tax can be reflected in the price of wheat or other farm products, in spite of the fact that a good deal of the nation's farm activity is now incorporated. Competition from nonincorporated farmers and, more importantly, the fact that, once a farm is developed, direct costs of production are usually sufficiently low to encourage production of something rather than nothing make it unlikely that there would be any restraint in production and hence any chance to raise prices because of a corporation income tax. At the other extreme, an industry dominated by a few companies may be operated to secure a "going," normal, or "fair" rate of return on its investment; a lower rate is not acceptable and a higher rate not sought because of public relations, employee relations, or a fear that it would encourage other companies to enter the field. Under these circumstances, a corporation income tax is likely to be reflected in prices. It is uncertain how American business is distributed between these two extremes. Unsatisfactory though it is, the only practical generalization is that the burden of the corporation income tax falls to some extent on consumers and to some extent on corporate stockholders. The competitive position of a company within an industry, price policies, and the business situation all influence the distribution of the burden between consumers and stockholders, and short-run burdens may be different from long-run burdens. No more extended analysis on the subject will be given here, since it would only elaborate on the relevant factors without making the conclusion more precise.

Regardless of its incidence, the results of the corporation income tax are undesirable. If one could, with present knowledge, start fresh to build a tax system, it is unlikely that the corporation income tax would be given the importance it has. But there is enough truth in the saying that "Any old tax is a good tax and any new tax is a bad tax" to make it doubtful whether even the most ambitious program for tax reform should propose that any other source of revenue be substituted for it; an alternative to provide 20 billion dollars of revenue a year is not readily available. The bad consequences of the tax should nonetheless be recognized, even if one has decided that it will be necessary to live with them for some time.

If the traditional belief that the burden of the corporation income tax falls on the corporation and its stockholders were wholly correct, the tax would appear to be especially repressive. All other forms of income arising from a corporation are subject to tax at only one level. Wages, salaries, rent, interest, and royalties are all deductible in computing a corporation's taxable income. They are all taxable to their respective recipients, but taxable only once. The net income of the corporation, by contrast, is taxable to the corporation, most of it at the high rate of 52 per cent, and then to the extent that it is distributed as dividends, it is taxed again to stockholders.

An unshifted corporation income tax, by definition, reduces net corporate income by the amount of the tax. Lower income means lower retained earnings or dividends or both. It is improbable that dividends alone would be curtailed because of the tax; retained earnings are also less than they otherwise would be. In the long run, there is no reason to suppose that dividends and retained earnings would not be affected proportionately by lower earnings. A curtailment of retained earnings is as important as it is obvious in limiting economic growth.

It seems peculiarly unfortunate to single out the return on equity capital for the only instance of double taxation in a tax system, since equity capital provides the base on which capital investment and increased productivity depend. It is typically the scarcest form of capital. Equity capital alone can finance corporate growth, regardless of the availability of debt capital, but debt capital alone cannot be used and will not, in fact, continue to be made available in the absence of equity capital. Retained earnings are by far the most important source of equity capital; after the recovery from the Depression, when new common stock issues were negligible and retained earnings were negligible if not negative, retained earnings have been several times as large as new common stock issues. One can only repeat that to the extent the corporation income tax is not shifted to consumers, it reduces retained earnings in proportion to the tax rate unless it reduces dividends more than proportionately, which seems unlikely. With retained earnings ranging from 6.7 billion to 11.8 billion dollars in the years 1955 to 1959, out of total personal and corporate savings of 29.3 billion to 34.3 billion dollars during the same years, anything which reduces retained earnings significantly is important to the whole country, not simply to the stockholders and managements of the companies involved.

The individual income tax tends to encourage the retention rather than the distribution of corporate earnings. Stockholders who have to give up most of their dividends in individual income taxes logically prefer to have a corporation retain its income even if it cannot be used very profitably. If a stockholder pays 80 per cent of a dividend in tax, a 2 per cent return on a corporation use of retained income gives the same return in dollars that would be earned by a 10 per cent return on the net investment which could be made by an individual after paying his 80 per cent tax on a dividend.[1] To be sure, the income is still in the corporation and not in the hands of the stockholder and a tax may have to be paid when it is realized by the individual, but this tax may be at a capital gains rate, and it may be obviated by a step-up in the basis of stock at death. In the meantime, a stockholder's equitable interest in corporate assets increases much more rapidly than his directly owned assets could increase if the corporate earnings had been paid out as dividends. This tax advantage of corporate retention of earnings in closely controlled corporations made it necessary to adopt the penalty tax on undistributed income or personal holding companies and the more general penalty tax on unreasonable accumulation of surplus.

A reduction in retainable earnings by the corporation income tax thus may be partially offset by the effect of the individual income tax in discouraging distribution of corporate income. This is significant only when a corporation is closely controlled and owned by high-bracket stockholders; it is not important for the great bulk of corporate income which is earned by widely owned companies whose stockholders range from tax-exempt organizations to the wealthier individuals and where the tax status of stockholders does not appear to be a major influence on dividend policies.

An interesting but infrequent result of the tax penalty on distributed corporate earnings appears when wealthy investors prefer to hold a special class of stock which pays no dividends rather than the regular stock in the same company which pays dividends.

[1] Invested at 2 per cent, $100,000 of corporate funds gives $2,000 income before tax; if the $100,000 is paid in a dividend, only $20,000 is left for investment after the 80 per cent individual tax, and at 10 per cent this also gives $2,000 income before tax. The advantage of the corporate investment is immediately compounded by the tax on the income from the new investment; the $2,000 is reduced to $960 by the 52 per cent corporate tax (but only to $1,844 if the income is a dividend from another corporation and subject to the 7.8 per cent effective rate on intercorporate dividends), while the $2,000 income to the individual is reduced to $400 by the individual income tax.

Two classes of common stock are sometimes created when a closely controlled corporation first sells stock to the public. The shares are identical in all respects except that one class does not pay dividends, though it is convertible into the class which does. The high-bracket investors prefer to forego dividends because a partial interest in the earnings which are thereby retained is considered more valuable than the net dividends which would be left after the individual tax.[2]

An unshifted corporation income tax not only directly restricts the accumulation of equity capital through retention of earnings but also indirectly discourages increases in equity capital through new issues of common stock. The analysis here is somewhat involved. The fact that corporation income is less than it would have been to the extent of the tax means that retained corporate earnings or dividends or both are less than they otherwise would have been. Lower earnings and dividends also mean that the price of corporate stock is less than it otherwise would have been. This is so because common stock is only one of many alternative investments for most investors. Lower earnings and dividends per share as a result of an unshifted corporate tax make stock less attractive than it otherwise would be in comparison with other investments, and its price will be less than it would have been. If there were perfect fluidity of investment funds, the price would be expected to be less by whatever amount is necessary to maintain the going yields and price-earnings ratios of stocks. The substance and complexity of this statement can be explained by an illustration.

If bonds of a given quality yielded 4 per cent and stock of a given quality yielded 5 per cent and sold at ten times earnings with no tax on the corporation income, what theoretically might be the effect of a new 20 per cent corporate income tax? With the available alternative of bonds and other investments, it would be expected that the price would drop 20 per cent if the tax fell equally on dividends and retained earnings. At a 20 per cent lower price, the yield on the stock would be 5 per cent and the price-earnings ratio 10, and

---

[2] If the owner of 75 per cent of the stock of a company is subject to an 80 per cent tax on his dividends, he would have only $20,000 left from a dividend of $100,000. If the $100,000 were retained, the equity interest of the minority stockholders would be increased by $25,000 but the interest of the majority stockholder would increase by $75,000. It is reasonable to prefer to have other stockholders get $25,000 than to let taxes get $80,000, even if the $75,000 left is still in corporate solution.

the relative attraction of the bond investment and the stock investment would be as it was before the tax. Such a fall in price would reduce the capital value of the investment of the owner of the stock when the tax was imposed or when it was proposed and the expectation of it made the price less than it otherwise would have been. A subsequent purchaser would bear no burden of the tax because the rate of return on his investment would be as high as it would have been otherwise. The process by which the full burden of a recurring tax is imposed on those who own property when the tax is first levied through a reduction in value is known as the capitalization of a tax.

The foregoing simplified analysis of the impact of a corporation income tax is subject to many reservations and variations. A listing of the principal ones will indicate why there is uncertainty about the exact consequences of the tax even if it is assumed that it is not shifted to consumers. The reservations can be put in the form of questions. Does a tax reduce retained earnings and dividends proportionately or does it fall primarily on one or the other? The answer doubtless varies from company to company and over time. Are earnings or dividends of greater importance in determining the price of stock? This is a subject of major inquiries by others; the results of which will give a better basis for appraising the effect of reduced earnings on the price of stock. To what extent is there really fluidity in investment funds? If investors are committed to stocks and will not consider alternatives, the effect of the tax on corporate earnings will not be reflected in the price of stock. Is a tax considered permanent or temporary? To the extent that it is regarded as temporary, the prospect of higher net earnings in the future will help to maintain the price of stock; this is significant under a wartime excess profits tax.

In the preceding analysis, reference has been made to corporate income and stock price lower "than they otherwise would have been." This awkward phrase has been used because major increases in the corporate income tax rate in this country have usually come at times when incomes before taxes were rising rapidly. This was notably the case at the start of World War II when war activity finally produced a business recovery that had been impeded by mistaken government policies in the preceding years and at the time of the Korean War when inflationary pressures were strong. Because of these coincidences in timing, there has not been an occasion when one can with assurance say that corporate net income has been actually reduced in absolute terms by a corporate tax increase. At other times, changes in the tax rate have been so small as to be obscured by ordinary fluctuations in corporate income before tax. One might argue that the absence of large reductions in net income even when taxes were increased substantially proves that the taxes were shifted to consumers, but this is not necessarily so because of the existence of other strong forces to account for the maintenance of the income after tax. It is thus more accurate historically to speak of earnings and stock prices less "than they otherwise would have been."

The conclusion to this point is that an unshifted corporate income tax makes stock prices somewhat less than they would be otherwise. Theoretically under previously stated assumptions they might be expected to be less in proportion to the tax; actually the reduction would be likely to be somewhat less than this. What, in turn, is the effect of lower prices of stock? It will not discourage investors from buying stock. In fact, the lower price is presumed to neutralize the effect of the tax to prospective purchasers. There is thus no shift by investors from stock, with its doubly taxed income, to bonds or other investments the income of which is taxed only once. But the lower the price of corporate stock, the less disposed corporate management is to finance by new stock issues—at least managements should be reluctant to issue stock at prices which dilute the interests of existing stockholders. Again a complete tax analysis impinges on another area in which concepts and theory are still in the process of development; the subject here is the cost of equity capital and its significance in corporate financing.

Though some aspects of the analysis of the cost of equity capital are involved, one basic proposition is sufficient for the discussion here. It is simply that the greater the number of shares which have to be issued to secure any given amount of capital, the more likely it is that the interest of existing stockholders will be adversely affected. Unless the earnings per share of stock would be at least as large as they would have been without the new issue of stock, it is better to refrain from expansion regardless of the increase in total dollar earnings. An increase of 50 per cent in total income is undesirable if it is achieved by new financing which doubles the amount of stock outstanding, since earnings per share are reduced by one-quarter. Sometimes professional managements may be so impressed with mere size or with total net income that they give insufficient attention to the interests of individual stockholders, but this seldom occurs, and constant emphasis on earnings per share of stock among investment analysts discourages any tendency to increase total income at the expense of earnings per share.

The significance of an unshifted corporation income tax on corporate expansion should now be clear. To the extent that the price of stock is lower than it would be, it is more difficult to expand through new common stock issues without decreasing earnings per share. The effect of the tax thus is not to discourage investors from buying stock; lower prices will restore a competitive equilibrium with alternative investments. But lower prices discourage new financing by stock issues because it takes more shares to secure any specific amount of new capital funds. The opportunity to increase earnings per share through expansion financed by new stock issues is reduced. This is a major result of an unshifted corporation income tax. Its practical significance depends on the level of stock prices.

When earnings are fairly good and price-earnings ratios are very high, as they were late in 1959 and early in 1960, the chances of an adverse effect on earnings per share from a new stock issue are not great. Any reasonably profitable use of new funds would produce sufficient earnings to maintain earnings per share. For the glamour companies with stocks selling at fifty to one hundred or more times earnings, mergers with companies as yet untouched by glamour provided the increased earnings per share on which the glamour was founded. If a company whose stock is selling at one hundred times earnings can acquire a company with earnings as large as its own but whose stock is selling at ten times earnings through an exchange of stock, it need increase its own stock outstanding by only 10 per cent to double its total earnings and earnings per share rise by over 81 per cent. This is an extreme but not fantastic example of the possibilities open to imaginative managements of companies with stocks selling at abnormally high price-earnings ratios. Under such market situations, the fact of an unshifted corporation income tax which kept earnings and the prices of stock lower than they otherwise would have been is obviously not much of an impediment to any sort of action.

In other circumstances, lower stock prices may be a major barrier to financing. When stocks are selling at five to ten times earnings, as was common from 1946 to 1952, a new issue of stock will typically not produce a proportionate increase in earnings. The price-earnings ratio indicates the rate of return which must be earned after taxes on new capital to maintain earnings per share. At a 5 to 1 ratio, new funds must produce new earnings at 20 per cent after taxes, or at over 40 per cent before a 52 per cent corporate tax, if earnings per share are not to fall as a result of the new issue; at a 10 to 1 price-earnings ratio, the new funds must produce new earnings at 10 per cent after taxes, or more than 20 per cent before the 52 per cent corporate tax, to avoid dilution.[3]

In brief, an unshifted corporation income tax reduces corporate net income and earnings per share. This, in turn, means that stock prices are somewhat less than they would be otherwise. Lower prices discourage expansion through new stock issues, but other factors affecting the market may either offset or accentuate the effects of the tax. In a buoyant market, expansion through stock financing can still be very attractive to some companies; in a depressed market, it would be unattractive even if there were no reduction in earnings through taxes. The unfavorable influence of an unshifted tax always exists; it may or may not be a significant barrier to financing. And it must always be remembered that limited expansion through new stock issues is not evidence that stock prices are so low that they make financing unattractive. A predisposition to limit expansion to what can be supported by retained earnings regardless of stock prices and inherent management difficulties in too rapid expansion always limit the speed of growth.

[3] The prospects of avoiding dilution from a new stock issue can also be appraised roughly by comparing the price of stock with the value of the net assets represented by it. During most of the 1930s and 1940s and well into the 1950s, in many industries common stock typically sold for less than its book value, which in the postwar period at least was typically much less than the current value of the net corporate assets which stockholders equitably own. Such a situation means that an increase in stock will not provide a proportionate increase in earning assets, and this presumptively means that earnings per share will be reduced by new financing. Conversely, when stock can be sold at a price well above the value of the assets which it represents, new capital funds can be expected to yield enough income to increase earnings per share.

In summary, to the extent that the corporation income tax is not shifted to consumers, it directly reduces corporate savings in the form of retained earnings and indirectly discourages new issues of common stock. Since retained earnings and common stock issues are the only sources of corporate equity capital, an unshifted tax restricts the base for capital investment. It is especially hard to see why newly developing countries which are desperately short of capital impose corporation income taxes, at least on retained earnings. A tax on distributed earnings at either the corporate or the individual level is understandable, but retained earnings are the most obvious source of savings for economic expansion and the source most likely to be used immediately in actual productive investment. In any country concerned with its economic growth, an unshifted corporate income tax, especially because of its effect on retained earnings, is inconsistent with other policies designed to encourage economic expansion, though allowances for rapid depreciation may be a partial offset to the repressive effects of the tax itself.

Though the economic effects of the corporation income tax are bad, if the tax is not shifted to consumers, a failure to tax corporate earnings would make the tax system unfair. There is a clear conflict between the objectives of fairness and economic growth. Most other forms of income are taxed. The only notable exceptions are interest from municipal bonds, the great bulk of the investment income of life insurance companies which, even after the important reform in 1959, are still never taxed either to the companies or to policyholders, and employers' contributions to and income of pension funds, which constitute savings on which the tax is postponed until pensions are received. If there were no corporation income tax, savings in the form of retained corporate earnings would be untaxed. Important though savings are, it may be questioned whether saved income should be made entirely tax exempt. At least, if a tax incentive is to be given to savings, from the standpoint of fairness it is doubtful that it should be given to corporate savings alone.

In the less developed countries, savings are so critically important that general inducements should be given for them, but this can best be done by reliance on consumption taxation rather than income taxation. Under such a plan, exemption of corporate retained earnings and even of all corporate income would be fair. In other countries, where savings are also needed but less urgently so, the objectives of fairness and economic growth must be balanced against each other. There is a conspicuous conflict here between the tax policies required to meet these two objectives. The subject will be discussed further in the analysis of alternative methods of giving relief for double taxation of dividend income. First, however, the general appraisal of the economic effects of the corporation income tax must be concluded.

To the extent that the corporation income tax is shifted forward to consumers through higher prices, the nature of its effects can be described quite simply, though precise measurements of them are not possible. Since the tax applies only where there is net income, its effect is to raise the prices of the products of the more profitable, presumably the more efficient, concerns. In a sense, this has an equalizing effect by raising the prices of the more efficient producers and thereby permitting less efficient producers to receive enough to meet their higher costs. From another standpoint, the shifted tax tends to prevent consumers from receiving the benefits from the lower costs of efficient producers which they would ordinarily secure in even a moderately competitive economy.

A shifted corporation income tax is thus a capricious excise tax, the burden of which falls in uncertain and indeterminate ways on consumers and which shelters inefficient producers. This is hardly a tax which, under any such description, would be politically attractive. Its political appeal lies in the very uncertainty as to its incidence. There is first uncertainty as to whether it is shifted. To the extent that it is thought not to be shifted to consumers, it is acceptable because of a too frequent though mistaken attitude that corporations, like governments, are sources of unlimited wealth and that stockholders are proper subjects for discriminatory tax burdens anyway. These beliefs may even make an unshifted corporation income tax positively attractive to some people. To the extent that the tax is shifted, its uncertainty obscures its burden. It is the supreme example of a hidden excise tax. A general sales tax at rates between 10 and 15 per cent, depending on the coverage, would be necessary to produce an equal amount of revenue. The corporation income tax is not only a hidden excise; it is popularly presumed not to be an excise tax at all. Whatever the incidence, it is hard to imagine a more attractive set of specifications for political acceptability of a tax.[4]

After these somewhat cryptic comments, made in a terse form for the sake of emphasis, on the economic disadvantages and political advantages of both unshifted and shifted corporation income taxes, one more economic consequence must be described. It is an important one, and somewhat surprisingly, it exists whether the tax is shifted or not.

A corporation income tax raises the cutoff point which must be in prospect to justify new capital outlays by a corporation. This discourages the use of funds in making investments. From an economic standpoint, the corporation income tax may be doubly bad. To the extent that it is not shifted, it decreases the availability of funds for corporate investment, and whether shifted or not it discourages the investment of the funds that are available.

Corporate managements decide on investments of available funds by comparing the prospective returns from alternative uses in several different ways. The comparison may be in terms of expected rates of return or the present value of future cash flows or the duration of the pay-back period necessary to recover the original outlay. The return may be compared with the cost of capital, also calculated according to any of several formulas, to determine the desirable scale of new financing and expansion. But whatever the concept of the return on investment, the corporation income tax reduces the net return; more significantly, one may say that the tax increases the gross return which must be earned to yield any given or desired net return. At a 50 per cent corporate tax, it takes a 40 per cent return to give a 20 per cent net return; it takes a two-year

---

[4] It is interesting and somewhat amusing to note that in Russia there is reported to be extensive theoretical discussion about the incidence of the "turn-over tax," a payment required to be made on the turnover of products in each stage of production and distribution. It is apparently part of the communist dogma to believe that these payments which are the principal source of funds to finance general government activities are not a burden on consumers because they are imposed on the "business" entities which carry on production and distribution. It is hard to imagine that the practice of deceit against a country's own citizens could be extended to a more esoteric subject than tax incidence. Our honest confusion and uncertainty on the incidence of the corporation income tax is a pleasant and healthy contrast to a pretense that a general hidden sales tax imposes no burden on the general population.

pay back of an investment before tax to give a four-year pay back after taxes. Under the economist's frequent assumption that all other things are equal, these higher rates of return raise the level at which projects are acceptable; the tax means that otherwise acceptable projects are rejected.

The influence on the cutoff point for new projects does not depend on the incidence of the tax. Even if it is shifted, the effect is not the same as for an ordinary excise tax. An excise tax is a specific identifiable cost which, like material or direct labor costs, enters into total costs which are compared with total receipts or into unit costs compared with unit prices to determine profit margins. Rates of return, pay-back periods, and cutoff points for investments are all determined in the first instance on an after-tax basis. The income tax comes out of pretax returns and profit margins. To be sure, if shifted, the tax will make prices higher than they otherwise would be, but it does not do so by increasing identifiable costs. Before-tax and after-tax rates of return and profit margins exist only under an income tax. Their full significance requires much more thorough analysis than it has received thus far or than would be feasible in this book. The effects of before-tax and after-tax rates of returns and cutoff points must be examined under various sets of assumptions. If one assumes a given amount of available funds from internal sources, for example, and further assumes that they will all be used for corporate investments of one sort or another, the existence of the tax may not change either the priorities or the aggregate amount of investment. Such a conclusion would contradict the previous statements about the repressive effect of a new scale of before-tax rates of return, but the assumptions are by no means generally valid and merely indicate the range of possible results of the tax. Though the uncertainty on this aspect of the problem is annoying, the need for further analysis to examine all the possibilities and determine which are likely to be the more significant helps keep the subject of taxation from being duller than it is.

The corporation income tax produces between 400 million and 500 million dollars of revenue for each percentage point of tax when corporate profits before tax are in the 40-billion- to 50-billion-dollar range. A reduction in the tax rate would be extremely expensive in terms of the immediate revenue loss. It is for this reason that it was stated earlier that a substantial reduction in the corporation income tax does not appear to be feasible as part of a self-financing tax reform. This conclusion should not be the basis for complacency, however. In view of its bad economic consequences and capricious and uncertain incidence, plans for long-term reform should include reduction in the corporation income tax. The average tax rate on dividends is 40 to 45 per cent. The corporate tax at 52 per cent thus not only imposes a double tax on distributed earnings but taxes retained earnings at a higher rate than that which is imposed directly on the owners of corporate stock. In spite of the fact that some of the corporate tax is probably shifted to consumers, a corporate rate applying to both retained and distributed earnings which is above the average tax rate applied to stockholders on distributed earnings seems particularly onerous. A first object might be to bring the corporate rate down to this level with the tax rate on retained earnings no higher than the second tax imposed on stockholders on distributed earnings.

A reduction in the corporate tax rate is less important than more realistic depreciation allowances. For reasons discussed previously, funds arising through depreciation are especially likely to be spent on new and more efficient capital equipment. To the extent that larger tax allowances for depreciation will lead to larger deductions on a company's own books, there is a compound impact. Not only is the cash drain for taxes less, but the internal funds arising through depreciation, and not subject to distribution to stockholders, are greater. A reduction in the corporate rate itself does not have this double effect. To the extent that the tax is shifted to consumers, a reduction in the corporate tax will lead to lower prices rather than an increase in net income and available funds of the corporation. The amount foregone by the Treasury from more realistic depreciation allowances thus seems much more likely to be spent in ways that will increase national productivity and thereby promptly increase tax revenue than would a similar amount foregone by a reduction in the corporate tax rate itself, useful though such a reduction would be.

Capital Gains and Losses of Corporations

Corporations, as well as individuals, are permitted to use a 25 per cent tax rate or net long-term capital gains. Net capital losses may be carried forward for five years. The capital gains tax on corporations produces about 500 million dollars in annual revenue. There would appear to be a good many advantages in removing the differential rate on capital gain for corporations and taxing all corporate income gains and profits at the same rate. The additional revenue from the full taxation of capital gains would permit a reduction in the general corporate tax rate from 52 to 50 or 51 per cent without loss of revenue.

Elimination of the differential tax would be a major simplification in corporate taxation and remove the existing inducements to convert ordinary income into capital gains. With all profits and gains taxed at the same rate, there would be no advantage in setting up special transactions to bring profits into a form qualifying for special treatment or in attempting to get the tax law amended to provide the special treatment on still another type of profit.

More fundamentally, the reasons which require differentiation in tax rates for individuals do not seem to apply to corporations. One of the major improvements of accounting in reporting corporate income during the past generation has been to bring almost all results into the income account and largely eliminate the practice of direct changes and credits to surplus which at one time were acceptable and even thought desirable. Profits, gains, and losses of all sorts and periods are regarded as sufficiently homogeneous to be finally brought together in the all-important measure of earnings per share. Nonrecurring gains and losses are distinguished from operating income and losses, but this is for analytical purposes, and ultimately they are combined to give a single figure for earnings. This is usually regarded as misleading if it is not all-inclusive.

A corporation, as an impersonal entity, is incapable of making the distinction between spendable income and embodied capital which individuals do, and stockholders do not make that distinction indirectly through corporations. As far as investors are concerned, the corporation is a source of income and appreciation and a distribution of a realized corporate gain may be the source of the income or a retention of operating income the source of appreciation. There seems little reason for the tax law to make a distinction which is not firmly embedded in either corporate accounting or investors' attitudes.

The corporation income tax did not give a special rate to capital gains until 1942. The adoption then of the special category may have been due to the belief that the high regular rates during World War II were temporary. The application of temporary high rates to nonrecurring gains would be inequitable and also discourage free movements of property which were desirable to encourage transfers to whoever could use it most productively in the war effort. This point was discussed in an earlier chapter in describing the origin of the special role on gains from the sale of depreciable assets. But it is now apparent that the war rates were not temporary, and this reason for a differential tax rate is no longer significant.

The proposal to remove the differential tax treatment of capital gains for corporations is made primarily in the interest of simplification and the elimination of an inducement to tax maneuvers. The special rate is not inequitable; there is enough importance to the distinction between ordinary income and nonrecurring capital gains to give some validity to tax differentiation. But the distinction between income and capital gain for corporations does not rest on the same solid ground as it does for individuals. The denial of capital gains treatment for the profit made possible by excessive depreciation should be adopted as part of the tax reform on depreciation. This is probably the source of a large part of the total capital gains for corporations, though it is minor for individuals. The idea of going all the way by removing the capital gains category from corporate income tax calculations is appealing. There seem to be stronger reasons for making the change than for leaving the law as it is.

Alternative Methods of Relief from Double Taxation of Dividend Income

It has already been stated that if the corporation income tax is not shifted forward to consumers, dividend income is uniquely subject to double taxation. All other forms of income arising from business operations are deductible to the payer and taxable only to the payee. Corporate income is taxable to the corporation, and when distributed, the dividends paid from the corporate net income are again subject to tax in the hands of individual stockholders. Such double taxation is both unfair and unsound economically for reasons described in the preceding section. Various methods of relief have been proposed and adopted in different countries; this is the subject of the present section. Let it be emphasized once and for all that to the extent the tax is shifted forward to the consumer in higher prices, relief from double taxation is not needed from the standpoint of fairness, though some mitigation of the bad economic effects of the tax may still be desirable to encourage growth even if the result were somewhat inequitable. The following discussion is based on the conclusion that to a substantial extent the corporation income tax is not shifted forward to consumers. Thus some relief is needed for both equity and economic reasons. Since it is not feasible either to determine the extent of unshifted burden in individual companies or to give selective relief to individual companies or their shareholders, only methods for general relief are presented.

Taxation of Dividends Only at Individual Surtax Rates. Double taxation of dividend income was very simply avoided in the original 1913 income tax in this country. Corporate income was taxed at 1 per cent; this was also the normal rate imposed on individual incomes, with higher surtaxes going up to 6 per cent on the largest incomes. Very sensibly, the law provided that dividends, since they were paid from corporate income already taxed at 1 per cent, would not be subject to the normal individual tax at the same rate but would be subject to surtaxes. This treatment forthrightly prevented any penalty of double taxation. All income was taxed at the normal rate in either corporate or individual hands, and distributed corporate earnings were included in an individual's total income and subject to the progressive surtax imposed on him. This treatment tacitly assumed that the corporate tax was not shifted to consumers. It is a great misfortune that this original approach was ever disrupted. It was fully effective for only a few years, though the concept underlying it lasted until 1936 and was restored, in a very limited way, in 1954.

During World War I, the corporate tax rate was raised to 12 per cent, not counting the excess profits tax, while the normal individual rate rose only to 6 per cent, with combined normal and surtax going to a maximum of 77 per cent. In the 1920s and up until 1936, the corporate rate varied between 10 and 13¾ per cent, while the individual normal rate varied from ½ of 1 to 4 per cent. Dividends continued to be exempt from the normal individual tax throughout this period, but since the corporate tax was several times the individual tax, there was a large double tax penalty on dividend income. Double taxation was avoided in theory and to some extent in practice.

In 1936, President Roosevelt recommended a complete change in the taxation of corporations and dividends; dividends were to be deductible in computing corporate taxable income and fully taxable to individuals; net corporate income after dividends was to be subject to a high penalty tax. The objective was to force distribution of corporate earnings and have stockholders decide how much, if any, of the increased dividends should be saved and where and how much, if any, of the saved dividends should be reinvested in corporate stock. This would have imposed a penalty on retained earnings and reduced still further the low level of corporate investment. The notion that corporate income should be distributed to stockholders and investment decision be made by them was consistent with the punitive attitude toward business which prevailed at the time and led to policies which helped to prolong the depression until World War II. It ignored the realities of economic life, which clearly indicated that retained earnings could not be replaced in any foreseeable period by new individual savings, first because individuals would not save from increased dividends as much as corporations lost in retained earnings and, second, because corporations would not issue and individuals would not buy as much stock as would be needed to replace retained earnings.

The Congress was wiser than the administration and refused to adopt the full program, but in the legislative confusion which developed, an unfortunate program was adopted. The corporate income tax rate was raised from 13¾ to 15 per cent on incomes above $40,000, an undistributed profits tax was adopted at rates ranging from 7 to 27 per cent, and dividends were made subject to the individual normal tax as well as the surtax. Thus double taxation of dividend income was imposed in full. The penalty tax on undistributed income was so bad, especially because it was discovered as a surprise to some that taxable income is not synonymous with disposable funds, that it was reduced in 1938 and repealed in 1939. But the full double taxation of dividend income was continued until 1954.

In the intervening years, most proposals for tax reform included relief from double taxation of dividend income as a major necessity. In the light of subsequent events, the most notable recommendation for relief of double taxation was made in the House Ways and Means Committee minority where a report in opposition to the general tax reduction was adopted in 1948; this minority favored tax reform to general tax reduction and cited relief from double taxation of dividends as a major item. Politics being what it is, it was regarded as more amusing than embarrassing that many of the same members signed another minority report in 1954 opposing relief for double taxation of dividends. Before the reasons for adopting the particular method of relief used in 1954 are described, the alternatives should be reviewed.

Presumptive Partnership Approach

Theorists sometimes propose that all corporate income should be imputed to stockholders who would include their respective shares in their taxable income. The corporation itself would pay no tax. This would be similar to the tax treatment of partnerships, the income of which is attributed to the various partners in accordance with the partnership agreement. Though the idea is appealing on theoretical grounds, it would raise such monstrous administrative problems that it does not deserve serious or lengthy attention. With hundreds of thousands of stockholders in a single corporation and many of them holding their stock for only part of a year, the first problem would be to decide how to allocate the corporate income. Would it be done at the end of the year to stockholders of record of that date? If so, there would be a great rush to sell stock and be "uninvested" on that critical date. Or if income is retroactively spread over a year by some formula, a man selling stock in January would find out a year or more later how much if any "income" he had had through his stock ownership.

Most important of all, stockholders in a corporation cannot make direct arrangements as a condition for ownership of stock to withdraw at least as much as is necessary to pay the personal tax on attributed income. In partnerships, the participants can and do agree among themselves on such withdrawals of profits as may be appropriate and necessary and different partners can be treated differently. But dividends must be declared on a uniform basis. Stockholders subject to high marginal tax rates would need to have almost all their shares of the income paid to them just to cover the individual tax on the corporate earnings imputed to them. Tax-exempt stockholders would need no funds for taxes on imputed income. The conflicting pressures on directors and the situation in the security markets would be little short of chaotic.

Presumption That the Corporate Tax Is a Withholding on Individuals. In the United Kingdom, the income tax is regarded as applicable simultaneously to individuals and corporations. The tax paid by corporations is deemed to be paid on behalf of their stockholders, who report as taxable income their proportionate share of the pretax corporate income from which the dividend was paid, compute their individual tax on that amount, and then apply the tax paid by the corporation as an offset against it. Dividends are "grossed up" by adding back to them the tax paid by the corporation on the income from which the dividend is paid. If the individual rate is the same as the rate paid by the corporation, there is no individual tax due; if the individual rate is higher, a balance is due; if the individual rate is lower, a refund is received.

An example may clarify the process just described. If the basic income tax rate is 40 per cent, a corporation pays 40 per cent on all its taxable income. A dividend represents 60 per cent of pretax corporate earnings, and a stockholder reports the full amount of pretax earnings as individual income. A stockholder receiving a £60 cash dividend would report £100 of individual taxable income. He would then compute his individual tax on his total income including the £100 and apply as a credit against it the £40 paid by the corporation which is deemed to be withheld on his behalf. If the tax attributable to the £100 is just equal to £40, no further payment is due; if the tax attributable to the £100 is greater, say £70, then an additional £30 is paid; if the tax is less than £40, say £25, then the taxpayer is entitled to a refund of £15 or may use that amount as an offset on his tax on other income.

This British concept and approach are reasonable on the assumption that the entire corporate tax is borne by the corporation and its shareholders. It treats the corporation as a joint venture by imputing to each stockholder his proportionate share of the pretax corporate income from which dividends are paid. Undistributed corporate income is taxed at the basic income tax rate; it is not imputed to stockholders and hence not subject to higher progressive rates or to a lower rate if the stockholder is not himself subject to the full normal rate. The use of a single normal rate of tax applicable to individuals and corporations is a fundamental feature of this British approach. With relatively few shareholders and with virtually all of them presumably subject to at least the normal tax on all their dividend income, the administrative problem of refunds was not great in the early years of the tax. As the number of shareholders increases, and as special rebates are given which makes even the marginal tax rate lower than the normal rate for many taxpayers, refunds become more numerous.[5]

The original British concept of a simple income tax, with the part of it imposed on corporations treated as a withholding tax on stockholders to the extent profits are distributed, has been used widely in the British Commonwealth. Some have gone even further in avoiding double taxation of dividend income. In Hong Kong, corporate income is taxed at 10 per cent, which is also the maximum rate for the individual income tax. Since dividends come from income already taxed at the maximum rate, they are exempt from the individual income tax. This is the sort of sensible and forthright approach which gives Hong Kong one of the best tax climates in the world, except for the tax-haven countries whose principal products are corporate charters and postage stamps. New Zealand also for many years completely avoided double taxation, though it did so by taxing corporations as separate entities rather than imposing a

[5] The British tax law has, in recent years, superimposed a profits tax on the regular income tax. This profits tax is regarded as a tax on the corporation as a separate entity. It is not deemed to be withheld, it is not influenced by dividends or retention of earnings, and it is not creditable by stockholders against their individual taxes. It breaks the logical and consistent pattern of refraining completely from double taxation of dividend income. Regardless of its incidence, the profits tax seems an undesirable one on which to place increasing reliance, constituting as it does to some extent a hidden excise tax and to some extent a tax on retained earnings. One may assume that to the extent that the profits tax is not shifted, it will in the first instance reduce retained earnings more than dividends, since dividends in England, as here, once established are not readily reduced. When a budget surplus is needed as a deflationary force in an economy, neither of the results of a higher profits tax seems consistent with the main objective of fiscal policy. A hidden excise is more likely to create pressure for wage increases than identifiable excises, and retained earnings are desirable to offset a deficiency in national savings.

general normal income tax rate on them. With corporate income having been taxed once, dividends paid from after-tax corporate income
were not again subject to tax in the hands of stockholders. A double
tax imposed in New Zealand during the last decade is the subject
of criticism on grounds of both equity and economic policy. A proposal to substitute taxation of dividends and a low tax on retained
earnings to help offset capital erosion and the maintenance of physical capital resources was not adopted; the present full double tax
discourages corporate savings.[6]

The British approach often has been suggested as a method of
relief from double taxation of dividend income in this country. It
has a strong theoretical appeal and has been referred to as the only
"intellectually satisfying" form of relief. In spite of the appeal of
intellectual satisfaction, it was not recommended by the Treasury
for this country in 1954 for several reasons. Corporations have been
regarded as separate taxable entities in this country; the corporation
income tax was imposed in 1909 four years before the individual
income tax was adopted. The concept of corporations as joint ventures with no separate tax capacity simply does not fit with our
attitude toward them. This point can be made more telling if one
thinks of tax-exempt stockholders. It is not likely that relief from
double taxation in this country would be thought of as going as
far as making the corporate income itself tax exempt to the extent
that it is attributable to stock owned by a university, and yet that
is what follows from British approach. Relief in this country was
intended to mitigate the double tax, not to give full tax exemption
or to make the Treasury actually pay refunds of the corporate tax
to low-bracket or tax-exempt stockholders.

Though the British approach is logical and understandable when

---

[6] An excerpt from an editorial in one of the leading papers in New Zealand,
observed during a brief visit to the country as a tourist, will give the flavor of
the world-wide concern with the problem of double taxation of dividend income. "Until Mr. Nordmeyer [Minister of Finance] came along no-one had
had the idea of taxing the same income twice. Most people would perhaps think
it dishonest. Still less would they contemplate the additional tax imposed by
Mr. Nordmeyer to stop companies from ploughing back some of their profits
to increase their turnover to earn greater future revenue for themselves—and for
the taxgatherer. Mr. Nordmeyer has not, of course, bothered to explain how this
retention tax squares with appeal for savings to counteract inflation. . . ." *The
Press*, Christchurch, New Zealand, Aug. 12, 1959.

fully applied, relief in this country in 1954 was to be limited, both because of budget limitations and because of the fact that the tax was to some extent shifted to consumers and hence full "relief" to stockholders would shift the balance of equity from its previous discrimination against them to a discrimination in favor of them. The fact that the corporate rate at 52 per cent was so much higher than the basic individual rate at 20 per cent was a further argument against the withholding presumption; most stockholders would have been entitled to refunds under full relief.

Under less than full relief, as required by both equity and revenue considerations, the partial grossing up of the dividend would be inexplicably arbitrary and hardly intelligible to taxpayers. A provision which required a taxpayer to increase his cash dividends by 10, 15, or 20 per cent and then to deduct this amount from his tax would seem to many people another device to confuse the taxpayer and obscure the logic, if any, in the tax law. A good many taxpayers would probably not even be clear as to whether the net result reduced or increased the tax or left it unchanged. The objective of simplicity would preclude the introduction of a partial application of the British method of avoiding double taxation of dividend income, acceptable though the concept may be where a tax system has included it consistently and where it was first adopted when tax rates were very low.

Relief by Deduction of Dividends in Computing Corporate Taxable Income. Instead of relief being given to stockholders in recognition of the tax paid by the corporation, the relief may be given to the corporation by allowing a deduction for dividends paid, with dividends fully taxable to stockholders. This approach is appealing in its simplicity and by the fact that it gives a superficial neutrality to debt and equity financing. Against these advantages is the overwhelming disadvantage that deductibility of dividends, though intended as a relief measure, would convert the corporate tax into one exclusively on retained earnings. Such a tax penalizes small and rapidly growing companies which must rely on retained earnings for expansion. At the corporate level, the "relief" varies with the proportion of income distributed. A mature company with no need to retain earnings could pay its entire income out in dividends and pay no corporate tax. A company needing to retain all its income because of great opportunities for growth would be taxed on all its income. Viewed in this light this would be a bad provision in the tax law of a country still concerned with its economic development.

It is interesting to consider how the attitude toward a provision of the tax law can be influenced by the name applied to it and the point of view from which it is regarded. The 1936 penalty tax on undistributed income gave a deduction for dividends paid, but the combined effect was a penalty, not relief. A new deduction, proposed as such, would be regarded as relief in the first instance, and since it would not involve an increase in tax rates, it would give relief in the form of a tax reduction to companies in proportion to their distribution of income. But for the companies which could not or should not distribute much of their annual income, there would be little or no relief and the net effect would come to be regarded as a tax barrier to growth.

In spite of the fact that the net result is a tax penalty on retained earnings, the first effect of a new deduction for dividends paid, with the rate on retained corporate income staying the same, is likely to be an increase in retained earnings, since it is unlikely that the entire savings in taxes would immediately be paid out in additional dividends. But as noted, the companies paying no dividends, presumably the ones with the greatest need for retained earnings, would have no reduction in taxes to use for any purposes. The immediate result of a deduction for dividends paid would depend on whether the first impact was to increase or decrease the total tax paid by corporations through a combination of change in the corporate tax rate and the proportion of income distributed. An increase in taxes would decrease both dividends and retained earnings, and a decrease in taxes would increase both. In this country the policy of maintaining fairly steady dividends in many companies would probably throw most of the immediate impact on retained earnings in both cases.

Germany gave a substantial deduction for dividends paid in the late 1950s, making the corporation income tax rate 51 per cent on retained earnings and 15 per cent on distributed earnings. The purpose there was an ulterior one to encourage the development of the security markets. A tax inducement to distribute corporate income would, it was felt, put stockholders in a position to save more from increased dividends and then invest the savings in new securities while at the same time putting corporations in a position where they would need to issue additional shares to offset the ultimate reduction in retained earnings. The differential tax in favor of distributed earnings in Germany is a controversial subject there, and its adoption did not appear to create any enthusiasm in other countries to follow the German example.

Deferral of Corporate Tax until Dividends Are Paid. The reverse of the German approach was adopted in this country in the new tax treatment of life insurance companies in 1959; it sets a precedent which might properly be considered for general application. One segment of the corporate tax is imposed only when earnings are distributed. The only justification for deferral of the tax was that the companies needed the funds for expansion. There is no theoretical or equitable reason for this special provision in the law, but if this pragmatic one is acceptable for life insurance companies, it should be adopted generally.

As a matter of economic policy, a lower tax or imposition of part of a total tax on corporate income as it is earned, with an additional tax or the balance of the tax imposed when earnings are distributed, makes a great deal of sense when economic expansion is desired. If it is deemed fair to postpone part of the tax on life insurance companies, as it apparently is, the same treatment should be acceptable for other industries where additional capital funds may be expected to increase the national income in ways that they do not do in the life insurance industry.

If the favorable tax treatment given to life insurance companies were to be extended, the additional tax at the time dividends were paid might be treated as a withholding tax on behalf of stockholders. Since it would be a tax payable by a corporation with reference to dividend distributions, rather than on current earnings, the concept of a withholding approach is appropriate. Under such a combination of taxes, the tax on all earnings might be set at 25 per cent, with another 20 per cent on dividends, or a total of 45 per cent on distributed earnings. Again under the assumption that one could start to build a tax system afresh, this would appear to be preferable to the existing system, but it would involve too much loss of revenue to be appropriately considered as part of the sort of self-financing reform proposed in the rest of this book. Essentially it would simply amount to a reduction in the corporate rate of tax with a withholding tax on dividends. In spite of the undesirable features of corporation income taxation, reduction on this scale in this area should not have priority over other forms. But the completely new concept adopted in 1959 for life insurance companies should be kept in mind for general application. In other industries its economic benefits would be greater and its discrimination in favor of savers and investors no more inequitable.

Present Partial Relief for Double Taxation of Dividend Income. In 1954, the present $50 exemption and 4 per cent credit for dividend income was adopted as part of a general tax reform. The exemption was designed to give full relief for very small stockholders. Consistent with the policy of treating corporations as taxable entities, no rebate or allowance was made for the corporate tax; the exemption simply recognizes that since dividends are paid from income already taxed to the corporation at rates much higher than applicable to individuals with small incomes, the dividend should not be taxed again to them. The 4 per cent credit is a shortcut method on the tax form to give exemption from four percentage points of the individual tax. This is modest relief, indeed, in view of the 52 per cent tax already paid by the corporation. This method is substantially similar to that used prior to 1936 when dividends were exempt from the individual normal tax. The distinction between normal and surtax was dropped in 1954 as a matter of simplification. If one regards the bottom rate of 20 per cent as the equivalent of the normal tax, the 4 per cent credit is the same thing as waiving the individual tax to the extent of one-fifth of the normal tax while maintaining the other four-fifths of the normal tax and all the surtax.

Descriptions of the partial relief from the double taxation of dividends are subject to the same numbers game previously noted in connection with changes in individual tax rates themselves. The relief can be described in terms of changes in tax rates, absolute or proportionate, and changes in net income, absolute and proportionate. A comparison of the credit against tax adopted in 1954 with a credit (deduction) against taxable dividend income will show the different ways the relief can be regarded. The following

Comparison of Effects of 10 Per Cent Credit against Tax with 20 Per Cent Credit against $1,000 of Dividend at Varying Tax Rates *

Tax and net dividend with no credit			10% credit against tax ($100 reduction in tax)				20% credit against income ($200 reduction in taxable dividend)			
Marginal tax rate	Tax	Net dividend	Net tax	% reduction in tax	Net dividend	% increase in net dividend	Net tax	% reduction in tax	Net dividend	% increase in net dividend
20%	$200	$800	$100	50	$900	12.5	$160	20	$840	5
50	500	500	400	20	600	20	400	20	600	20
90	900	100	800	11	200	100	720	20	280	180

* The revenue loss from a 20 per cent credit against income is roughly comparable to that from a 10 per cent credit against tax.

table compares a 10 per cent credit against tax with a 20 per cent credit against income, which would involve roughly comparable revenue losses.[7]

The credit against the tax gives an equal dollar amount of reduction in tax for a given amount of dividend income, regardless of the marginal tax rate. The percentage reduction in tax is larger for small taxpayers than for large taxpayers; the percentage of increase in income is larger for large taxpayers than for small ones. By contrast, the credit against income gives a larger dollar reduction in tax and larger increase in income to larger taxpayers. The percentage reduction in tax is the same at all levels, and the proportionate increase in income is very much larger for large taxpayers. The equal rather than larger dollar increase at all income levels and the smaller percentage reduction in tax at large income levels made the credit against the tax seem more equitable than the credit against income, and it was accordingly recommended by the Treasury and adopted by the Congress. It is obviously difficult to explain all the alternative ways of viewing tax relief in a political debate. Each protagonist is likely to seize upon whatever measure—absolute increase in income or decrease in tax or proportionate increase in income or decrease in tax—best supports the position he wants to take. Sometimes there seems to be confusion on the results of the method proposed or criticized, even on the elementary fact that a deduction from income gives more relief to high-bracket taxpayers than a deduction from tax.[8]

[7] In planning tax relief, about double the number of percentage points credit could be given if the credit were allowed against income as if it were allowed against the tax for any available amount of relief allowable in the budget.

[8] Two remarks by Senator Paul Douglas during the Senate debate on the tax reform bill are interesting. On Mar. 30, 1954, he stated: "If dividends are to be deducted from anything, it might be argued that they should be deducted from taxable income. But this bill introduces a monstrosity into the theory of taxation, in that it permits 10 per cent of the dividends received to be deducted from taxes, not from taxable income." (*Congressional Record*, 83d Cong., 2d Sess., p. 3850.) Almost three months later, on June 29, 1954, in the final debate on the bill, he returned to the same aspect of the bill with the remark that: "When I began my normal study of the proposals and discovered that . . . the percentage was to be deducted, not from taxable income, but from the tax itself, I rubbed my eyes in disbelief. My friends said it was impossible. Yes, it would seem impossible but, unfortunately, it was true." (*Ibid.*, p. 8783.)

Unless Senator Douglas was, in fact, arguing for a higher degree of relief for

The present dividend credit has been attacked as a loophole, and its repeal was voted in the Senate in both 1959 and 1960. Fortunately, the repeal was not accepted by the House conferees. The very limited 4 per cent credit here is extremely modest relief compared with the 20 per cent credit against tax given in Canada. Though there is doubt as to the exact distribution of the burden of the corporation income tax, a 4 per cent credit after a 52 per cent corporation tax gives relief only to the extent of one-thirteenth of the corporate tax; this is far below the minimum fraction of the aggregate corporate tax which is likely to rest on the corporation and its stockholders.

The complete imposition of double taxation on dividend income in 1936 was regarded as a punitive act against stockholders and characteristic of its period. The limited relief in 1954 had a symbolic importance greater than its monetary significance in reversing this punitive approach. The repeal of the relief would also have a disproportionate importance. To deny any relief for the only form of double taxation in the country is conspicuously unfair. When this income is from a source that is vital for economic growth, unrelieved double taxation is conspicuously unwise. The denial of relief in 1936 came from confusion in a complicated piece of legislation. The denial proposed in 1959 and 1960 was much worse because it was designed for that specific purpose. If political opportunism triumphs over equity and economic policy on this matter, it would be understandable if it destroyed the tax morale of those dividend recipients who comprehended the nature of the double tax imposed on them. Nor would repeal of the relief help the tax morale of those concerned with genuine tax reform, since this calls for more equity, not increased inequities, in the law.

---

higher bracket taxpayers, which seems unlikely, it appears that the actual implications of the difference between a deduction from tax and a deduction from income are less obvious than was supposed by most of those concerned with the tax legislation.

Chapter 8 TAXATION OF CORPORATE MERGERS
AND DISTRIBUTIONS

This chapter and the next deal with several unrelated problems in the taxation of business, especially corporations. The subjects are more specialized than those in preceding chapters. The aspects of the tax law discussed here are of great importance to those immediately affected by them, but many of them are not important to most taxpayers. They do, however, have significant implications for public policy. Though these topics would require lengthy analysis in a book for businessmen concerned with the tax factors bearing on their management decisions, the fundamental issues in public policy can be presented briefly. The purpose here, as in the rest of this book, is simply to review in broad terms our tax law from the standpoint of tax reform. In some of the following areas reform is urgently needed; in others, though the situation under the present law is by no means ideal, it is not clear that possible changes would give a net improvement.

Mergers

The present tax law gives a distinct advantage to a merger over the outright sale of a closely controlled business. This preferential treatment of mergers may not be entirely in the public interest. This opinion is not based on any bias against mergers as such. They are often the only way to secure continuity when a company has "run out" of management and cannot secure new management. Mergers may increase competition by permitting small and medium-sized companies to become effective competitors. Mergers may be the cheapest and most efficient way to secure diversification, and diversification may reduce costs and help to stabilize the economy as well as a company's activities. But in spite of these and other favorable results, mergers have their undesirable consequences as well. They may restrict competition. By eliminating independently owned and managed companies, they substitute salaried managers, who may be transients, for settled owner-managers who are more likely to participate sincerely in a community's activities and add stability to a social structure.

But it would be presumptuous here to try to pass judgment on mergers, and it is not necessary to do so. Unless there were strong social or economic reasons to encourage mergers, which is not the case, the tax law concerning them should be neutral. It is not neutral, and this is what makes the law questionable as a matter of public policy. Neutrality could be achieved by removing the present favorable treatment of mergers or by giving a comparable tax treatment to the proceeds of sales of business. Each of the alternatives should be considered, but first the present law must be described briefly for those not familiar with it.

The tax law properly makes provision for nontaxable exchanges of stock and securities in corporate reorganizations. When a company in reorganization exchanges new stock for old stock, or when a corporation chartered in one state changes to operate under a new charter in another state and stockholders turn in their old shares for new ones, there has been no real change in an investment, no new funds are available with which to pay a tax, and the imposition of a tax would stand in the way of desirable and even necessary changes in the form and capital structures of existing business concerns. The law conforms to a common-sense view by permitting the exchanges of stock and securities to be made without an immediate tax burden. But the law postpones the tax; it does not give tax exemption. This is achieved by making the security holder carry forward the cost of his original stock and use it in computing the ultimate gain or loss on sale of the new stock. If stock is originally purchased for $1,000 and later exchanged in a reorganization for new stock worth $2,000, there is no immediate tax, but when the new stock is sold, the gain or loss is calculated against the original cost of $1,000. If it is sold for $4,000, the taxable gain would be $3,000.

As described thus far, the law seems fair and consistent with sound economic policy. The problem arises from the definition of a reorganization, which is not limited to distress situations, to mere changes of identity, or even to recapitalizations of a single corporation. The definition of reorganization for tax purposes includes mergers and consolidations of virtually all sorts. This means that if the owner of stock in one company exchanges it for stock in another company as a result of a merger or in a new successor company, the exchange will be tax-free. This is in contrast to a sale of the stock to new owners, where the profit is immediately taxable at capital gains rates. For the owners of a very successful closely controlled corporation, whose original investment was small, an offer of stock in a merger is worth almost one-third more than a cash offer of equal value as long as they are willing to continue to hold the new stock as an investment. If the new stock is held until death, the heirs get a stepped-up basis and the capital gains tax is never due.

This tax advantage of disposing of a company by a merger rather than a sale is stressed in proposals for mergers. It is doubtful if the tax advantages of mergers induce many controlling groups of stockholders to dispose of companies that they would not dispose of anyway, but once the decision is made to dispose of a company, the advantage of a merger may control the method of disposition. When the stock offered is in a company with a good enough record and prospects to be held indefinitely, those who might want to buy the company for cash and incidentally keep it as an independent business entity will have to bid up to one-third more to offset the tax advantage given to mergers. The inducement to mergers seems unfortunate.

The law could be changed in either of two ways. Most obviously, the definition of tax-free reorganizations could be tightened to limit it to exchanges involving recapitalizations of a single company or a single predecessor and a single successor corporation. This would be regarded as a drastic change by those who have grown up under the present broad definition, but it would not seem unduly restrictive to those who are not tax specialists. The present broad definition is a surprise to nonexperts when they first learn of it as well as to tax specialists in other countries. The alternative change in the law would be to permit a tax-free sale of stock when the entire company is sold, provided that the proceeds are reinvested and the basis of the old stock is carried forward to the new investment. This would eliminate the present tax advantage of mergers and in fact give an advantage to cash sales because it would permit a diversified portfolio of securities to be acquired instead of a single stock, which, no matter how diversified the company may be, is less attractive for most investors.

The only strong argument against the tighter definition is that it would discourage original investment in new ventures which are now made in anticipation of ultimate disposition through merger. With a reasonable treatment of capital gains, this inducement to mergers should not be necessary. The tax-free sale and carry-over of basis would be logical if the roll-over proposed in Chapter 5 were adopted; in fact it would be provided automatically and subject to the desirable limitation that net withdrawals of gain would be taxed as ordinary income. The tax inducement to mergers described here does not require attention immediately. If and when the mergers need to be restrained, the removal of the tax advantage which they now have would be desirable.

Loss Carry-overs in Mergers

The present loss carry-forward of five years and carry-back of three years is needed to prevent tax discrimination against companies with fluctuating incomes. The denial of loss carry-backs and carry-forwards in the 1930s was unfair and bad economic policy. Even at tax rates of slightly more than 10 per cent, losses were so large in some years that the modest tax on modest incomes in good years exceeded the total net income of a five-year period for many companies.

The loss carry-back is useful for established companies; it entitles them to refunds of prior years' taxes for current losses. An income of a million dollars followed by a loss of $250,000 gives a net income of only $750,000; a refund is due to bring the tax for the two years down to what it would have been if the $750,000 had been earned over the two years with no losses. The refund gives a company cash when it may most need it, though cash is not necessarily short in a recession; many companies become quite liquid through liquidation of inventory and receivables and postponement of capital expenditures. But a loss carry-back is of no use to a newly established company, since there are no profitable years to which it may be carried back. The loss carry-forward can be important to them to permit them to recoup their initial losses and pay taxes only when they have earned an aggregate net income. A long loss carry-forward is necessary to allow for the lengthy periods which it takes some companies to become profitable. Loss carry-backs and carry-forwards are somewhat complicated, but the sacrifice of simplicity is much more than offset by increased fairness and reduced tax barriers to investment and economic growth. Fortunately, the complications affect only those who secure the benefits, and for them it is a small price to pay.

Though loss carry-backs and carry-forwards are desirable, they may be abused. When a corporate shell with no assets and a long record of losses is purchased for a nominal price or acquired through merger, there is a proper resentment against having the new owners get the tax benefit of the old losses to apply against the profits of a completely unrelated business, with no relief or payment to the old owners who incurred the losses. The phrase "trafficking in losses" describes the substance and gives the flavor of the sort of manipulations which are offered in advertisements in the financial press. The problem is where should the line be drawn between the bona fide use of a loss carry-over and a tax shenanigan. A review of the possible degrees of change in ownership and activity will indicate the difficulty of fixing a really good cutoff point.

If a company changes its product line, from wagons to automobiles or from automobiles to missiles, no one would be likely to object to its rights to apply the losses from the declining phase against the profits from the new activity. Nor would anyone be likely to object to the use of a loss carry-over if a company fired an old management and brought in a new management. The fact that some stock changed hands would also not seem to justify a denial of loss carry-over to a company; with any appreciable number of stockholders some stock will inevitably change hands over any appreciable period of time. If one accepts the three foregoing propositions, then it also seems to follow that the combination of the three changes should not automatically disqualify a company from a loss carry-over. A concern which brings in a new management and shifts its product line while some stock is changing hands would seem entitled to its loss carry-forward; changes such as these are a normal part of business development. And yet if a new group buys up a defunct interurban railway company and under its charter manufactures bowling alleys or Fiberglas boats, the loss carry-over seems objectionable, even though it is just a change of product, management, and stock ownership. The problem is one of degree, and where there are no clear qualitative distinctions, no line can be thoroughly satisfactory.

In 1954 the law was tightened to deny a carry-over of loss when 50 per cent of a company's stock is purchased within a year by ten or fewer stockholders, with a family group counting as a single stockholder, and the corporation has not continued to carry on substantially the same trade or business. This restriction is intended to prevent the use of loss carry-overs where new owners purchased a corporation for its losses rather than as a going concern. A different limitation occurs if a corporation with a loss carry-over is acquired by another corporation through a merger. In these cases, unless the stockholders of the loss company have a 20 per cent equity interest in the continuing corporation, the loss carry-over is reduced by 5 per cent for each one percentage point by which the stock interest falls below 20 per cent. If the stockholders of the loss corporation have only 10 per cent of the stock of the surviving corporation, the loss carry-over is cut in half; if they have only 1 per cent, the carry-over is reduced by 95 per cent. The purpose of this limitation is to restrict the benefits of the loss carry-over in a situation where the owners of the corporation which incurred losses are in a position to secure only a negligible part of the tax benefits from them.

The percentage figures for change and continuity of ownership adopted in 1954 were arbitrary ones; other figures might have been selected with equal justification. The intent in each case was to prevent the more flagrant abuse of sales of loss carry-overs by denying or restricting them when the old owners of a corporation were no longer in a position to get the principal tax benefit from them. It is by no means clear that the line drawn in the present law is the best one that could be drawn, but unfortunately a better one has not been described.

Under one proposed change, loss carry-overs would be available to successor owners or corporations with no restrictions whatsoever. It is reasonably argued in support of this proposal that full availability would assure market prices for corporate shells substantially equal to the tax benefits from their losses. A corporation with no assets except a loss carry-over of 1 million dollars would give a tax saving of $520,000 to any other company acquiring it. It would be respectable to acquire it entirely for its tax benefit, and competition among potential users of this "tax rebate" would assure former owners of a price approaching $520,000. Unrestricted uses of acquired loss carry-over would thus assure owners of the corporation which suffered a loss a recovery of the tax benefits from it whether they continued in business or sold out, and those using an acquired loss carry-over would not get any appreciable windfall from it because they would have had to pay approximately the full value. If the proposed change in the law had this result, the government would, in effect, have underwritten and refunded approximately 52 per cent of the net losses, as measured by negative taxable income, of corporate ventures. This is hardly a policy to be adopted through a technical amendment to the tax law without extensive discussion.

Reactions to the proposal for unrestricted use of acquired loss carry-over are not based on logic alone. Some of us are so offended by maneuver and manipulation that the idea of transferable tax deduction, even if it is transferred for value, is repugnant. It seems one thing to have an investor or a business get generous allowances for its own losses, as in the regular loss carry-back and carry-over or the proposed liberalization of deductions for capital losses on an individual's own investment, and quite another thing to have transferable rights for tax reductions. One might comment on an analogous situation with the statement that, "The fact that the dependency deduction for my child would be worth more to you with your high tax bracket than it is to me doesn't mean that you should be able to claim him as your dependent even if I sell you the right to do so for full value." This is perhaps too subtle a point, and the analogy will be denied by many. But loss carry-overs seem to be attributes of particular businesses or corporations, and more extensive "trafficking" in them, even if the balance or advantage is shifted from the buyers to the sellers, seems objectionable. It is because of this quite subjective feeling that liberalization in the law on the use of acquired loss carry-overs is opposed here.

If any change is to be made in the law, it should be tightened. Unfortunately, the greater the restrictions on the use of loss carry-overs, the lower the price that will be paid, the greater the windfall to the buyer, and the less the benefit to those who owned the company when the losses were sustained. This is, indeed, a troublesome subject. It and some of the problems in the taxation of income from foreign sources are the only ones in the whole area of taxation on which it is regretfully admitted here that, though the present law seems unsatisfactory, no better alternative is suggested. Continued discussion of the issues may produce new approaches to the problem.

Divisive Reorganizations

A divisive reorganization is the reverse of a merger. One corporate entity is broken up into two or more separate businesses. This may be done by continuing the old corporation unchanged and giving its stockholders the stock in a newly created corporation to carry on some aspects of the business or by setting up two or more new corporations and liquidating the old one. Spin-offs, split-ups, and split-offs are the legal terms which describe the various forms of divisive reorganizations; the precise characteristics of each need not be reviewed here, since they are treated similarly under the law and the public policy issues are equally applicable to all of them.

Some restrictions on divisive reorganizations are necessary to prevent flagrant tax abuses. Though the name and general descriptions suggest an infrequent and improbable sort of transaction, in the absence of a preventive provision in the tax law, divisive reorganizations would become a method of distributing earnings in most closely controlled corporations and perhaps some widely owned ones as well. It would be done in the following manner: Instead of paying out cash dividends, the funds would be invested in securities of other corporations which the stockholders might like to own individually or perhaps in real estate of some other form of property related to the business. The investments would then be transferred to a subsidiary corporation; in due course the stock of the subsidiary would be spun off, split off, or distributed in a stock split to the stockholders of the original corporation; and the new corporation would then be liquidated. The net result would be that the stockholders would still own the original business as a going concern and would have received, subject only to capital gains tax, the securities or other property which they wanted to own individually. If the corporate earnings had been distributed to them originally in cash, they would have been taxed as a dividend. By a roundabout process, the stockholders would be given direct personal ownership of just what they would like to have. With the difference between ordinary income and capital gains tax rates, a high-bracket stockholder might receive over five times as much.

This situation is one of the many examples where the use of a series of steps, each one reasonably taxed when viewed by itself, adds up to an unreasonable total result. The transfer of assets to a subsidiary corporation is not taxable. This is reasonable, and a contrary rule would impede normal business transactions which are not thought of as creating income in a business sense and which produce no new assets with which to pay taxes. Somewhat more debatable is the proposition that a splitting of an investment into two pieces should not be regarded as a taxable event. There is no increase in the value of underlying assets. A composite of assets has been rearranged, and two pieces of paper, that is, stock in two corporations, represent the same equitable interest which one piece of paper represented previously. The imposition of a tax at the time of such a division would seem harsh. From the standpoint of social policy, there is nothing about the splitting of an investment which should be discouraged. This is the reverse of a merger, and if a merger is not regarded as constituting a realization of income or capital gain by comparing the value of the new stock with that of the old stock surrendered, the splitting up of a company would seem to be even less appropriate for treatment as a taxable event from the standpoint of social policy. And finally, the liquidation of a company is reasonably regarded as involving only capital gains and losses. An enterprise and investment are completely terminated. In the absence of misuse of a corporate form of business to accumulate earnings at the corporate tax rate with the expectation of dissolving the corporation, an abuse which has made necessary the complicated provision of the law dealing with collapsible corporations, the ultimate winding up of a business seems to justify a capital gain treatment. It is the combined effect of the successive steps which is objectionable.

The law was tightened substantially in 1954 and may need further restriction. The limitation is imposed at the stage of the divisive organization by providing that it is to be nontaxable only when the corporation whose stock is distributed conducts an active trade or business which has been in existence for at least five years and when the distributing corporation also continues to conduct an active trade or business. It is further provided that a company owning or trading in securities is not conducting an active trade or business nor is a company which owns real estate used by the principal company. By these limitations, corporate earnings can no longer be used to buy investments and turn them over to an investment subsidiary whose stock is distributed to the original stockholders. The limitations also preclude the separate incorporation of factory buildings, with its stock distributed to the shareholders of the parent company, the building then sold under a lease-back arrangement, and the proceeds of the sale of the building finally distributed as a capital gain. But it is still possible under the law for a company to be split into its two or more separate operating components, with stockholders receiving separate stock in each and dividing the cost of their respective original investments among the separate parts in proportion to the market value at the time the distribution of stock in the subordinate corporations is made.

Many legitimate business reasons exist for corporate divisions, quite unrelated to taxation. Separate managements may be desirable, separate incorporation may make it possible to secure new management for one which would not be available in a single company, or a division may make outside financing available or acceptable in a single company. When divisive reorganizations are desirable for such reasons as these, tax barriers should not be placed in their way. But the temptation to abuse is great, and if it is found that separate businesses are frequently developed or acquired with the expectation that they will qualify for later nontaxable divisions, the law should be further tightened by treating the value of whatever is received in the way of stock or property as an ordinary dividend.

Special Problems in Corporate Distributions to Stockholders

The law contains several complicated provisions concerning the tax treatment of corporate distributions to stockholders. Most of them are necessary to prevent abuse which would otherwise exist, but sometimes the results are unduly harsh and the preventive measure needs to be amended to give relief. Some of the problems will seem surprising to those familiar only with straightforward business practices.

The tax law provides that any distribution by a corporation to its stockholders is presumed to be a distribution of its earnings and profits, and hence a taxable dividend, to the extent that there are current earnings and profits or earnings and profits accumulated since 1913, when the income tax became constitutional. The purpose of this provision is to prevent a company from distributing its earnings under the guise of a return of capital. Without it, companies might never pay a dividend but each year retire some fraction of their stock; each stockholder would have fewer shares, but his proportionate ownership would be the same. Every few years the stock could be split 10 or 100 for 1 (a nontaxable transaction, since it merely subdivides an existing investment into more units) to put stockholders in a position where they would continue to have whole shares for continued retirement.

The law further provides that in addition to ordinary cash dividends other things of value distributed to stockholders are to be taxed as dividends to the extent of their fair market value. This is necessary to prevent a corporation from buying various items, be they groceries or marketable securities, and distributing them in kind to stockholders.

The problem under either or both of the foregoing general rules is to distinguish between transactions which are subterfuges for a cash distribution and those where a distribution occurs because of a genuine business situation or is even compelled by a court action. Suppose, for example, that one of two properties owned and operated by a company for many years is destroyed by fire and it is decided that it should not be replaced with the proceeds of the fire insurance; the company will continue with only one property and distribute the insurance proceeds to its stockholders. In ordinary investment terms this would be thought of as a partial liquidation, as would a decision to dispose of one of the divisions of a diversified enterprise. When, for example, the Pullman Company was required under an antitrust action to discontinue either the manufacture or operation of sleeping cars, it chose to sell its cars to the railroad companies. If it had distributed the proceeds of this sale to its stockholders, this action would certainly have been thought of in a business and financial sense as a partial liquidation. Should the distribution have been treated as a payment of a dividend for tax purposes to the extent of earnings and profits accumulated since 1913? This would seem to be unduly harsh.

Another type of situation occurs when a corporation redeems all the stock of one or more stockholders. This may be necessary when different owners or the heirs of the founders of a business come to a parting of the ways on basic policies. It may be necessary to buy out one group to assure continuation of the business enterprise. Should the group whose stock is retired be deemed to have received a dividend to the extent of the earnings and profits of the corporation since 1913? This again seems unduly harsh.

The concept of a partial liquidation has been recognized in the tax law for many years, but the definition had been developed by court decisions and was somewhat uncertain prior to 1954 when objective tests were provided in the law. Since a partial liquidation may produce the same results as a divisive reorganization, provisions respecting the two procedures were made to conform to each other. If they were not equally strict, the more liberal route would be taken to secure a desired result. The same requirement for the discontinuance of a separate active trade or business conducted for at least five years is the standard for both divisive reorganizations and partial liquidations. It was felt that abuse, through the purchase of assets for the purpose of later distribution under the pretence of liquidation, would not be significant if the only assets which could qualify for a partial liquidation consisted of an active trade or business. The risks of operating losses over a five-year period and the interim management problems would discourage shenanigans as long as the purchase and sale of securities was excluded from the definition of an active trade or business.

The second genuine situation which seemed to justify relief was the complete retirement of the stock of one group of stockholders. This also is treated as a partial liquidation, with the stockholders taxable only on a capital gain to the extent that the amount received on retirement of the stock exceeds the cost or other tax basis of the stock. But the framers of the law had to make it complicated in order to prevent anticipated abuses of a sort which would never occur to ordinary managements and ordinary stockholders but which would be very attractive in some closely controlled companies. For example, if there were no limitations on the rule that a complete retirement of a stockholder's stock qualified as a partial liquidation, one might expect that in a family business a father's stock would be retired, on a capital gains basis, while his children continued to own their stock, which would then constitute the entire equity. Once a generation, the older generation could receive whatever distribution was desired from the earnings of the business while the company continued to be owned by the prospective heirs, with no dividend ever paid. By arranging the retirement price of the stock to be less than the amount represented by its proportionate share of the assets, there could also be a concealed gift; a low price for the retired stock would minimize the advantage of the dividend taxed as a capital gain but increase the value of the children's stock with no actual transfer to them. If a father and his children each own half the stock in a business worth 1 million dollars, and the father's stock is retired for $250,000, the value of the children's stock is increased from $500,000 to $750,000 with no apparent transfer from the father. The concealed gift is a separate tax problem. The partial liquidation is limited by making a complete retirement of stock qualify only if a whole family has its stock retired. Retirement of the stock of one spouse, a parent, or a child alone does not qualify.

With a little more ingenuity, successive retirements might be arranged when there are several families owning a closely controlled corporation. Ordinary dividends would never be paid, but every few years all the stock of one family could be retired at an agreed price, and the family then by prearrangement be permitted later to buy a little new stock at an agreed price. In successive years, the stock of other families would be retired, and they in turn again could buy into the corporation. At the end of each cycle, each family would have had its stock retired once, at prices which covered all the accumulated earnings which would have been paid in ordinary dividends, and by later repurchases of stock each family would end up with the same proportionate ownership of the company that they had at the beginning. The framers of the law anticipated this maneuver with a requirement that to qualify for a partial liquidation, a stock retirement could not be followed by a repurchase of stock in the corporation. The law in effect says, "You can get capital gains treatment if you get out of a company but it has to be a complete withdrawal of an investment; you and your family have to get out together and stay out." Thus must the law be made complicated to forestall abuse.

Some argue that no partial liquidations should be entitled to capital gains; the general rule that as long as a corporation has any earnings and profits, all distributions to stockholders should be deemed to be dividends should be applied with no exceptions. This is certainly an understandable point of view, and its adoption would simplify the law. Opinions differ as to its equity. Some believe that as long as a corporation has accumulated earnings, any distribution to any stockholders should be deemed to be a distribution of those earnings and taxed as a dividend. This seems to others to be unduly legalistic. Situations arise where a genuine curtailment of a business is practically regarded as a partial realization of an investment by all stockholders or where some stockholders withdraw their investment; in these situations it is felt that it is equitable for the tax law to conform to ordinary financial attitudes even at the expense of complications. The latter view is the one adopted here. Complexity should not be criticized, because it is a necessary price to pay to prevent abuse and it affects only those who seek to come under the relief provisions. Because of the real possibility of abuse, the requirements for qualification should be strict; if there are to be any changes in the present law, they should tighten and not loosen the definition of partial liquidations and divisive reorganizations. The experience under the 1954 standards has not yet demonstrated the need for major changes in this area.

In the meantime, the general rule that all distributions to stockholders must be treated as dividends to the extent that a corporation has accumulated earnings and profits may be harsh and inequitable when distributions are forced. The decision by the Supreme Court that the ownership of General Motors stock by the Du Pont Company is contrary to the antitrust laws gives a good example of the problem. When the stock was purchased in 1917 to 1922, there was apparently no thought by anyone that it was illegal; the antitrust action was not filed until 1949. Taxation of the value of the General Motors shares as ordinary dividends, if they were distributed to Du Pont shareholders, would doubtless force the sale of large amounts of the stock to secure cash to pay the tax. This would decrease the value of General Motors stock, to the disadvantage not only of the Du Pont stockholders receiving it but also to the other General Motors stockholders who are bystanders in the entire proceedings. Because of these harsh results, the District Court wisely declined to follow the recommendations of the Justice Department to require distribution of the stock and accepted a proposal to transfer voting rights instead, a decision which was appealed by the Justice Department.

Whatever one may think of the merits of the antitrust decision itself and of the insistence for distribution of the stock in this particular case, the problem is one which justifies relief if it can be given without creating an opportunity for abuse. General permission to make tax-free distributions under antitrust or other similar decrees would not be acceptable, because some companies wanting to distribute excess cash would first buy stock the holding of which was expected to be successfully challenged by the Justice Department. The companies would then happily distribute the stock to their shareholders, who could sell it and pay only a capital gains tax on part of the proceeds. Some way must be found to forestall intentional violation of the antitrust laws to secure a tax advantage.

The most sensible proposal made thus far is to tax stock distributed under an antitrust decree as a dividend only to the extent of its cost to the distributing corporation. This appears to have a useful self-policing effect. If stock were purchased with the expectation that distribution would be required, the interval between purchase and distribution would not be long and the cost would probably be about the same as the value on distribution. There would thus be no tax advantage over a distribution of cash. When there is a long interval between purchase and distribution, it is reasonable to presume that the distribution is made necessary by a new interpretation of our ever-changing concepts of the meaning of antitrust laws and that no tax abuse was intended. A further provision that the tax relief would be available only if recommended by the Justice Department and approved by the Court on the ground that no tax avoidance was intended would seem to preclude abuse while granting needed relief. Under this proposal, for example, the Du Pont stockholders would be deemed to have a taxable dividend to the extent of the cost to the Du Pont Company of the General

Motors stock which they receive; they would then apportion the cost of their Du Pont stock between the Du Pont stock which they keep and the General Motors stock they receive in proportion to their respective market values of the date of distribution and add to the tax basis of the General Motors stock the amount currently taxable as a dividend. The distribution would thus be treated as a partial liquidation, which it is, but with a full immediate tax on that part of the value which represented the actual outlay of corporate funds on the property distributed.

Stock Dividends

New practices in the use of annual stock dividends may, at some future time, require a change in the provisions of the tax law concerning them. The area is one of outstanding current interest in both corporate finance and investment analysis. The full potentialities of annual stock dividends, with provision made for stockholders to sell some or all of their dividend stock on a regular basis and receive cash taxable only as a capital gain, have been seen by some corporate managements, but the ultimate logical plan has not yet been presented to stockholders by any corporation, and the market has not yet been reasonably responsive to the limited plans which have been adopted. Before the present possibilities are analyzed from the standpoint of corporations and investors, the development of the tax law concerning stock dividends will be described. In no other field has there been greater change. The changing concepts in the law and the evolving business practices under the law really make a fascinating tale.

A stock dividend is a distribution of new stock in a company to its own stockholders; usually but not necessarily it is paid in additional shares of common on existing common stock. It differs from a stock split only in the bookkeeping and certain technicalities. In a stock split, the aggregate amount in the existing capital stock account is not changed; it is simply represented by more shares, with the stated value of each share reduced in proportion to the increase in the number of total shares. With a stock dividend, the stated capital per share is maintained by a transfer to capital from a surplus account and an increase in the aggregate stated capital. This difference is of no practical significance whatsoever to investors, except in the rare case where future dividends, cash or stock, would be limited because of the previous capitalization of surplus. Since it is available free funds, and not legal surplus, which usually determines cash dividends, the shift from surplus to capital in the books, which, of course, does not affect available cash or any other asset, really has little bearing on subsequent dividends.

Under the original income tax, stock dividends were taxed as ordinary dividends to the extent of their fair market value. They were treated as any other dividends in kind, including dividends paid in the stock of other companies. In 1920, the Supreme Court in one of the most celebrated tax cases, *Eisner v. Macomber,* held that a stock dividend did not constitute income under the Sixteenth Amendment, which authorized income taxation. The Court ruled that the stock dividend merely divided an existing equity interest into more shares with no fundamental change in it or realization of it. The decision conformed to financial opinion and was regarded as bringing good sense into the tax law.

The Congress amended the law in accordance with the decision to exclude stock dividends from taxable income. With this exclusion the cost or other tax basis of an original investment in stock was allocated between the old and new stock in proportion to the fair market value when the new stock was received, and gain or loss on subsequent sale of part of the stock was calculated against this allocated basis. In a stock dividend paid in common stock on common stock, it was not even necessary to ascertain the fair market value. After the stock dividend was paid, the original cost was simply divided by the larger number of shares to determine the future basis per share. After a 50 per cent stock dividend, an original cost of say $7,500 for 100 shares, or $75 per share, would be spread over 150 shares, or at $50 per share. If the stock dividend was paid in preferred on common stock or in common on preferred, the allocation of cost over the aggregate market value at the time of issuance of the stock dividend was required.

The law was seemingly settled for seventeen years until the Supreme Court in 1937 in another much quoted case, *Koshland v. Helvering,* ruled in a case of a dividend in preferred stock on common stock that the preferred stock was taxable as income under the Constitution. The Court supported the taxpayer's claim to use the fair market value of a dividend in preferred stock when it was received as its basis in computing subsequent gain or loss rather than using an allocated fraction of the cost of the common stock on which the preferred stock dividend was paid. The Court distinguished the *Koshland* case from *Eisner* on the ground that the preferred stock dividend gave new rights to the common stockholders by permitting them to share in the priorities of preferred stockholders, whose rights were thereby diluted.

Congress, not wanting to be trapped again by a Supreme Court opinion the full implications of which it might not appreciate, simply amended the law to make stock dividends taxable to the extent that they could be taxed under the Constitution and left it up to the taxpayers and the courts to work out the line of demarcation between taxable and nontaxable stock dividends. It was an interesting episode in the division of powers under the Constitution. The court ruling on one set of facts in *Eisner* was taken as a generalization by the legislature; seventeen years later the Court gave a contrary ruling on another set of facts, which really were quite distinguishable. A casual observer of the process would say that the Court stood ready to give opinions as asked but was unconcerned about misinterpretations until it was asked another question and that the legislature acted as though it was tired of piecemeal enlightenment and abrogated its usual desire to make a law specific; the result must seem somewhat amusing to one unfamiliar with our constitutional structure.

The *Koshland* decision was very timely because in 1937 it became suddenly important to be able to pay taxable stock dividends under the undistributed profits tax then briefly in effect. For companies with current earnings but without equivalent free cash, a not uncommon situation in the brief business revival of 1936 and early 1937, a taxable stock dividend relieved the companies of responsibility for the penalty tax though it forced stockholders to provide cash from other sources to pay the tax on a noncash form of income. There was, however, uncertainty as to just what preferred stock dividends on common stock were taxable. The *Koshland* case dealt with a situation where preferred stock was already outstanding. If none were outstanding, a new issue distributed as a dividend would not appear to give common stockholders any new rights. Though the preferred stock would come ahead of the common, each common stockholder would have his pro rata share of these new rights, which would still be subordinate to the rights of all others. But how much preferred stock had to be previously outstanding to give common stockholders receiving new shares of preferred a significant improvement in their priorities and hence make the new stock taxable? A series of cases established fairly clear lines, but taxpayers had to operate with unfortunate uncertainty in the meantime.

The law as fixed in 1937 and clarified in subsequent years continued unchanged for another seventeen years until 1954. In the latter part of this period, a new abuse known as the "preferred stock bail-out" was developed by ingenious tax experts. A company with accumulated earnings available for distribution to stockholders first issued a nontaxable preferred stock dividend in callable preferred stock, an easy enough thing to do when no preferred stock was previously outstanding or when the new preferred was subordinated to all others. The stockholders then sold their preferred stock in a block to an intermediary for slightly less than its call price, realizing a capital gain in the process. The corporation then called the stock and paid the intermediary the call price. The intermediary was perhaps a life insurance company or a friendly foundation or university anxious to pick up a small gain on a brief investment. All this could be done at no risk between Christmas and New Year's, and the courts sanctioned it, since each step was separate.

The net result was that the company had distributed cash, the common stockholders had cash, and both the capital structure and each stockholder's share of the stock were unchanged. The composite result was a triumph of form over substance. The final adverse court rulings against the claim of the Treasury that form should not be permitted thus to triumph were made while the Internal Revenue Code of 1954 was under consideration in the Congress and quick action was necessary to prevent preferred stock bail-outs from being widely used to supplant cash dividends.

The change finally made in the law in accordance with the recommendation of the Treasury was twofold. All stock dividends were first made nontaxable, whether they gave new rights or not, thus wiping out the distinction among different sorts of preferred stock dividends developed under the Court decisions following the *Koshland* case. But the axe fell on the shenanigans with a provision that the proceeds of the sale of a preferred stock received as a dividend were to be taxed as ordinary income. Before recommending this drastic rule, the Treasury at first proposed a high penalty tax on the redemption within ten years of preferred stock issued as a dividend, but this period was recognized as a short one in the financial planning in closely controlled corporations, and it would have given statutory sanction to a once-a-decade preferred stock bail-out, and the more drastic rule was later recommended and adopted in the Senate.

Because, however, preferred stock dividends are often useful in rearranging the interests in capital structures of closely controlled corporations and are used with no plan or actuality of tax avoidance, various escape clauses were put into the final rule. The owners of a corporation may want to leave preferred stock to their wives or daughters and common stock to their sons. Or they may want to use a preferred stock dividend to secure a prior claim for most of the present value of a company and thereby give the common stock a sufficiently low value to permit a new management group to secure a substantial fraction of it with the limited funds it may have to invest. In this last situation a preferred stock dividend may be necessary to get a new management group to come into a company and prevent a merger when the old group retires. In a company with a 1-million-dollar equity, a new group with $50,000 to invest could secure only a 5 per cent interest. If a $900,000 preferred stock dividend is paid, the common stock equity is reduced to $100,000, and with their $50,000 the new group can buy a half interest in the future growth for which they will be responsible.

These special situations do not lead to tax abuses, and a tax penalty on the action described may force mergers of independent companies. Therefore relief provisions waive the ordinary income rule if a stockholder sells all his stock, both common and preferred, or if the preferred stock is sold by an heir, or if it can be established that the issuance and sale of preferred stock was not part of a plan to avoid taxes. This aspect of the law seems reasonably satisfactory. The complications were made necessary by manipulations, and the innocent unfortunately must be careful to come within the precise qualifications for relief.

We come at last to the new, interesting use of stock dividends. A generation or two ago, common stock dividends were paid infrequently and were usually large in relation to outstanding stock. Dividends of 50 or even of 100 per cent or multiples thereof were used as alternatives to stock splits in order to reduce the price per share to a level more attractive in the market. A 400 per cent stock dividend on a stock selling at $250 would theoretically reduce the price to $50 and in practice probably to a somewhat higher figure, since many investors shun very high-priced stocks which they can buy only in odd lots. It was under circumstances such as these that the Supreme Court gave its opinion in the *Eisner* case that dividends in common stock on common stock do not constitute income. But in the intervening years, business uses of stock dividends have changed.

Many companies now issue stock dividends in lieu of or in addition to cash dividends. Companies regularly make provision for stockholders to sell their fractional shares or buy enough to round them up to full shares. One major utility company announced in the fall of 1958 a new policy by which it would continue but not increase its 50-cent quarterly cash dividend but would in the future pay an annual stock dividend sufficient to absorb substantially all annual income above $2. This company also gave stockholders an opportunity to specify in advance whether they wanted to have sold on their behalf some or all of their full shares and receive a check for the proceeds. The cash thus received would be taxable as a capital gain, to the extent that the total amount exceeded the allocated basis of the original stock purchase.

With a little imagination one may anticipate the next steps to be taken. Why should a company not drop all cash dividends and adopt a policy of paying stock dividends equivalent, say, to half the annual earnings, rounded to some even percentage, an amount about equivalent to what it would have paid in cash? Why should it not further permit stockholders to provide standing orders, subject to change, to have dividend stock sold on their behalf with the cash proceeds remitted to them? This would seem to be the best of all worlds from all standpoints except the national revenue, and it might even be beneficial there by permitting faster economic growth through greater retention of earnings. The corporations would not need to pay out any cash dividends. Stockholders could regularly receive cash each year, only part of which would be taxable and that only as a capital gain and could do so without disturbing their total existing investments by selling off part of their original stock each year. To the extent that stockholders sell their dividend stock and get money for consumption by absorbing funds from the equity capital market, the entire set of transactions in aggregate national terms would be somewhat similar to the results of cash dividends and new security issues.

To be sure, a stockholder may secure substantially the same result now by buying stock in a corporation which does not pay cash dividends and then selling each year a small fraction of his stock which he may even select on the basis of annual corporate earnings to enable him to "withdraw" indirectly whatever he desires. This analogy is made again and again by those who see no reason to consider a change in the long-established rule that a dividend in common stock on common stock is not income, regardless of how it is handled by stockholders. And those who hold this view may be right. But custom and tradition are strong in investment management, and the fact that two procedures are logical alternatives to each other may not make them practical alternatives. An overt action to sell even a small part of one's existing stock and spend the proceeds is generally regarded as an encroachment on capital, even though the book value and market value of the remaining shares are increased by retained earnings. Furthermore, and less importantly, an investor holding round lots in hundred-share units finds it annoying to sell off a few shares a year, and the reduction in the number of shares, to restate the first point, emphasizes the idea of living on capital. By contrast, a standing order to sell all or some part of a regular stock dividend requires no overt action by the stockholder. His round-lot holding is undisturbed and may even be increased if he sells only part of his dividend stock. The order to sell, once given, puts him in a position to receive a cash flow with virtually all the outward attributes of a cash dividend except that it is vastly more attractive from the tax standpoint. It seems probable that attitudes could change and systematic sale of part or all of dividend stock could come to be regarded as prudent and not involving an invasion of capital. The combined advantages to corporations and stockholders are so great that systematic attempts to educate investors to the advantages would seem to be probable.

For tax-exempt investors, the universities, foundations, pension trusts, and charities, stock dividends are no more attractive than cash dividends, since there is no tax to pay in either case. On balance the cash dividend is probably preferable to them, since it makes it unnecessary to decide how much dividend stock to sell. For trustees, stock dividends in lieu of cash dividends may be quite unattractive because of conflicts of interest between life beneficiaries and remaindermen. If the stock dividend is regarded as part of the body of the trust, it gives no income for those with a life interest. If it is regarded as current income, stock dividends in excess of current earnings will deplete the capital. The very existence of stock dividends complicates the investment decisions of trustees. For companies particularly concerned with having their stock attractive to trustees and tax-exempt investors, the stock dividend procedure will not be attractive. But fortunately individual investors are still generally more important than institutional ones, and for all individual investors the use of readily salable stock dividends offers tremendous tax advantages.

The use of stock dividends makes it necessary for investment analysts to adjust reported income figures. With the great and proper interest by investors in growth in earnings per share, an inadequate analysis of the implications of stock dividends will actually detract from the attractiveness of stock as the statistics are usually presented. With a larger number of shares outstanding each year as a result of annual stock dividends, the reported earnings per share are less than they otherwise would be. To give real comparability to companies not paying stock dividends, an adjustment must be made to show the combined earnings on an investment, including those on the dividend shares. Alternatively, past earnings per share must be revised downward to reflect the greater number of shares outstanding after the stock dividends. If earnings increase by 10 per cent annually, a company with no stock dividend will have its earnings per share increase by 10 per cent annually; it would be an attractive growth stock. If the same company were to issue a 10 per cent annual stock dividend, its earnings per share would remain constant; it would give no evidence of growth in a statistical analysis where stock dividends are recorded in a footnote with only the more sophisticated investors making the necessary adjustments in earnings per share to determine the real growth.

The most intriguing aspect of a policy of issuing only stock dividends is to attempt to anticipate the market appraisal of stock which has no expectation of cash dividends. As long as companies are growing, the absence of current cash dividends does not appear to detract from common stocks now. Investors are content and even eager to buy stock which represents a share in an ever-increasing equity and ever-increasing earnings per share, regardless of the prospect for cash distributions. But though remote, cash dividends are ultimately expected when growth tapers off. Stock which represents only a share of ever-increasing equity under a policy of no cash dividends has not been submitted to a test in the market. Logically it might seem unattractive, since there is no feasible way to realize on the underlying value except by sale to other stockholders who would be in the same position. But logic might not prevail. As long as there is no absolute bar to ultimate cash distribution with a chance that the company will change its policy and pay out cash, the salable stock dividends provide a more attractive substitute for stockholders wanting cash and the stock would be more attractive to those who want maximum growth. A whole new set of investor attitudes may be expected to develop.[1]

It is because of the excessive reliance by investors on unadjusted earnings per share that the suggestion was made above for a company to issue a stock dividend related to the cash dividends that would have been paid. When a stock dividend equal to all the earnings of a year is issued or a combined cash and stock dividend equal to them, the growth in earnings per share will be reduced because there will be no increase in capital per share. Earnings per

[1] An ingenious combination of advantages was provided by a utility company which created two classes of stock in a recapitalization. One paid cash dividends and the other equivalent stock dividends, with the latter stock convertible into the former. Any stockholder could thus get cash dividends if he converted his stock and renounced his right to future stock dividends. The availability of cash dividends might be regarded as holding up the price of the stock which paid stock dividends. The dual stock arrangement permitted both cash dividends and retained earnings to be increased, since the cash is paid only on part of the stock. The higher cash dividends might lift the price of the stock paying them and with it the other convertible stock. The higher retained earnings would also tend to increase the price of stocks by providing a base for larger earnings per share. Though one company received a favorable Treasury ruling on a recapitalization to secure this result, a more thorough consideration led to a position in the Treasury regulations that a stock dividend on a stock convertible into a stock paying cash dividends is taxable as a dividend. Under the statute stock dividends in lieu of cash dividends are taxable as dividends, and the arrangement described here is held to come under this provision of the law.

share would then be limited to that arising from higher profitability or higher leverage, but not by a greater capital investment per share. If the stock dividend were confined to what would have been paid in cash, then the dilution of equity per share would be no greater than the direct reduction in equity per share from a cash payment. Book value and earnings per share would continue to grow as they would with a cash dividend, and the company's total earnings and adjusted earnings per share would increase faster because of larger total funds to use in the business.[2]

No change in the tax law is called for at present. A change would require a review of the constitutional issue established in *Eisner v. Macomber* in 1920, and the Court might hold to the position it took then. But the small, frequent stock dividends discussed here are quite different from the large, infrequent ones of forty years ago. Perhaps their present use would make them so like income that a tax on them would be constitutional. If so, and if a policy to tax them were deemed desirable, the most appropriate change would probably be to tax as income the fair market value of stock received as a stock dividend if it amounts to less than some specified modest percentage or occurs more frequently than once a decade. Such a provision would leave untouched the traditional treatment of large and infrequent stock dividends, while making them taxable when they are used in a way that makes them substitutes for taxable cash dividends.

But even if they do become a substitute for taxable cash dividends, the tax law should perhaps be left unchanged. Retained earnings are important for economic growth. Reasonable relief

[2] Commonwealth Edison, by paying a combined cash and stock dividend equal to its annual income per share, might appear to have cut itself off from increased invested capital per share and reduced its future growth in unadjusted earnings per share. It does, however, properly show both historical and adjusted earnings per share in many of its financial reports. More significantly in its case, a stock dividend was probably an alternative to an increased cash dividend because of customary pay-out ratios of dividends to earnings. The stock dividend, by permitting a greater retention of earnings, thus reduces and perhaps eliminates the need to sell new common stock to finance expansion and thereby avoids the dilution in earnings which occurs when new stock is sold, as it must be, below the current market price. A stock dividend capitalized at the current market price requires a smaller number of shares for a given amount of capital than would be necessary with stock sold at a lower price; earnings per share are thus kept higher than they otherwise would be.

from some double taxation of dividend income seems unlikely, and the very modest relief now given is in recurring jeopardy. Conceptually a stock dividend is merely a redivision of an investment and the sale of a dividend is a disinvestment. It would be ironic indeed if stock dividends and the proceeds from their sale continued to be nontaxable even if they were extensively used as substitutes for cash dividends while cash dividends continued to be subject to a discriminatory double tax burden. Perhaps a rough justice to investors in common stock might be achieved in this way. In the meantime the whole area deserves attention in articles in the special journals; as was stated before, it is in many respects the most intriguing subject for theoretical analysis and practical developments in corporate finance and investment analysis now confronting us. Increased use of frequent small stock dividends, if it occurs, will be largely based on their tax advantages; their use would require a review of tax policy though not necessarily any change in it.[3]

[3] The tax treatment of stock dividends is also a matter of current controversy abroad. In Switzerland, stock dividends and new shares issued in a stock split are taxed as current income. Stock dividends and stock splits are therefore seldom made. The result is that stock of successful companies reaches prices in the thousands of francs a share, making them prohibitively expensive for small investors. Financial intermediaries buy whole shares and sell certificates of beneficial interest for fractional shares, collecting the dividends on whole shares and paying out pro rata distributions on fractional shares. In 1959, Germany changed its law, which had been similar to that of Switzerland, to make stock dividends, *gratis aktien*, nontaxable. This was done to encourage stock splits and bring share prices down to a level where they could be bought by small investors. The change in Germany is cited in Switzerland and elsewhere as a precedent for similar changes, which would appear to be eminently desirable. It would be most unfortunate if the law in the United States ever went to the extreme position of making all stock dividends taxable.

Chapter 9 SPECIAL PROBLEMS IN TAXATION OF BUSINESS INCOME

*Cooperatives—Savings and Loan Associations
and Mutual Savings Banks—Depletion in Oil and
Mining—Small Business—Investment Companies*

This chapter deals with special tax rules given to particular forms of business or industries. The topics are more specialized than those in the preceding chapter, since their application is, in most instances, quite limited. They all present significant issues in public policy which are presented here briefly.

Cooperatives

Under the present tax law, cooperatives are given deductions in computing their taxable incomes for cash distributions to their patrons and also for the face value of certificates of beneficial interest in retained earnings given to their members. Since the certificates of beneficial interest do not need to draw interest or ever be redeemed in cash, cooperatives can operate in a manner which, in effect, makes them completely tax exempt. They can retain any and all of their earnings for expansion tax free by giving members certificates of beneficial interest in the retained earnings. This gives them a tremendous tax advantage over competitive taxpaying business, which can retain only net earnings after payment of income taxes. This discrimination against ordinary taxpaying business is unfair. It also destroys the revenue base over the years, as taxable businesses are forced to convert themselves into or sell out to cooperatives. Taxation of net increases in retained earnings of cooperatives is necessary from the standpoint of both equity and economic policy.

Cooperatives may be regarded as falling under various legal concepts. Originally they were joint ventures by a few people. Funds were advanced by the members or built up by retaining some of the proceeds of the sales of the products grown by members and marketed through the cooperatives. Retained earnings were thought of as being advances from the members, even though under the by-laws of the cooperative the members had no individual right to withdraw them. But cooperatives are no longer simply small associations of neighbors to do jointly what they cannot do alone. Many of them are large, even dominant corporate enterprises with professional management who may be as interested in the aggrandizement of their businesses as the private entrepreneur. These comments are not intended to reflect on the usefulness of cooperatives in many times and places. They can have great value in breaking the monopoly of a village money lender or in providing seed or orderly marketing for crops. But when cooperatives outgrow the stage of self-help neighborhood associations, as so many of them have done in this country, they should no longer be permitted to hide behind a name with sentimental overtones and unfair tax advantages.

The present laxity in taxing cooperatives is not authorized by statute and is contrary to congressional intent. When the law was last revised on the taxation of cooperatives in 1950, it was intended that all net income, after deductions for patronage refunds, would be currently taxable either to the cooperatives or to their members. The legislation took account of the position of the Treasury at that time that certificates of beneficial interest were taxable to members at their face value when received. Retained earnings were thus taxable at the corporate rate if members were not given any certificates of beneficial interest in them; if certificates were issued, the members would be taxed. One way or another all retained earnings were supposedly taxable.

Some individual members of cooperatives objected to being taxed on the face value of certificates which in some instances were non-interest-bearing, nonnegotiable, and nonredeemable except at the discretion of the managements of cooperatives. A series of court cases resulted which held that where certificates had no determinable market value, members could not be currently taxed on receipt of them. This opened the way to avoid current taxation of retained earnings. Under the Court decisions which had overturned the Treasury position, by issuing the certificates so restricted that there was no market value, the cooperative would still get a deduction under the statute but the members were not taxable.

Some cooperatives acted fully in accord with the intent of the 1950 law by making sure that their certificates were not unduly restricted, by calling to the attention of their members the fact that they were individually taxable, and by providing members with cash distribution sufficient to cover the tax payable on the face value of certificates at the bottom tax brackets. Other cooperatives were more than pleased at the new situation of no tax on anybody and made full use of its advantages by imposing restrictions on certificates to make them nontaxable to members.[1]

The present situation is intolerable. It exists only because of the sensitive character of any legislation relating to agriculture. Large substantial cooperatives which make large capital investments and go into processing and manufacturing do not need and should not have tax preference. The desirable solution would be to tax cooperatives as the corporations which they are on their net retained earnings.

Some business groups advocate that even current cash patronage refunds should not be allowed as deductions to cooperatives. It can be argued that cash rebates at the end of a year are really a distribution of profits and should not be allowed as deductions any more than dividends to stockholders are deductible. But this goes as far in attempting to impose a penalty tax against cooperatives as the present law goes in imposing a penalty tax on ordinary business. Other companies can give cash rebates to customers without having

---

[1] A temptation already existed for the unscrupulous managers who are fortunately rare. The owner of a dairy company in the Middle West offered to provide affidavits that he was solicited by a cooperative group to convert his company into a cooperative with the inducement that he could then issue non-interest-bearing, callable but nonredeemable transferable certificates of beneficial interest which would sell for 30 or 40 cents on the dollar and which he could then buy up privately and call for payment every few years on an irregular schedule.

them treated as distributions of profits, and the fact that customers are members and hence something like stockholders should not put the patronage refunds of cooperatives into any special category.

Taxation of cooperatives on their retained earnings, as is here proposed, would appear to be a good middle ground. It would restore tax neutrality to competing businesses with respect to their ability to expand from retained earnings. This is the feature of the present differential tax treatment which most effectively undermines taxpaying businesses and destroys the tax base in those industries where cooperatives have expanded rapidly. The representatives of cooperatives argue for tax-free retention of earnings for a twelve- or fourteen-year cycle, which is the period used by some of them before redemption of certificates of beneficial interest in the ordinary course of business. A period of tax-free retention of earnings seems no more justified for cooperatives than for other businesses. It would be equally welcome to all sorts of organizations but no more justified for one than for another. The one exception which might be considered would be some special allowance for very small cooperatives which may be presumed still to be meeting the original self-help objectives of cooperatives.

Savings and Loan Associations and Mutual Savings Banks

Savings and loan associations and mutual savings banks are also given an unreasonable tax advantage over competitive taxpaying banks. The tax preference here takes the form of an allowance for a "bad-debt reserve" of 12 per cent of deposits. This compares with the reserves allowed to ordinary banks which are based on the experience of individual banks and average less than 2½ per cent of loans. These "reserves" allowed to mutual organizations in effect permit them to build up their capital funds free of tax. While total allowable reserves substantially exceed the actual reserves for the mutuals, in many instances individual organizations are at or approaching the ceiling and pay some income tax.

Commercial banks have traditionally been supposed to have total capital resources—capital, surplus, and undivided profits—equal to 10 per cent of deposits, a level few of them have maintained during the past generation. If they were given the same arbitrarily generous tax treatment that their competitors receive, they would be able to secure all needed capital resources from tax-exempt earnings. As it is, they must build up capital funds from after-tax earnings or the sales of stock to be purchased from someone's after-tax income. The differential treatment is neither fair nor conducive to reasonable competition.

The reserves of savings and loan associations and mutual savings banks, hereafter referred to together as mutual banks, are not allocated to individual depositors. Thus their reserves are associated even more with the business entity than are the retained earnings of cooperatives, which are often rolled over and paid out to members in redemption of certificates of beneficial interest after lengthy use by the cooperative. The mutual banks neither allocate nor eventually pay out their reserves; the reserves become the permanent capital reserve of the organization.

Mutuality is sometimes cited as a reason for not taxing the mutual banks. Since there are no stockholders to profit ultimately and since reserves are not allocated to depositors, one might argue that there is no one to tax. The simple solution is to tax the business entities, which is done under the present law in the infrequent instances where they show taxable income.

The mutual banks have also gone far beyond their original purpose of a neighborly pooling of cash and making loans to members to meet special needs. The savings and loan associations are especially active in soliciting corporations and pension funds in one part of the country for deposits to be made 3,000 miles away. In some states they have attempted to secure legal authorization to extend their functions to provide additional services in order to make themselves even more competitive with ordinary banks.

The usual proposed change in the law is a reduction in the allowable tax-free reserve, perhaps to 5 per cent. Since reserves required by statute or prudence exceed this figure, most mutual banks would become taxable, at least after further growth of deposits brought the present reserves to a minimum acceptable percentage. Many of the mutual banks in the meantime might be even more effective competitors of the savings departments of the commercial banks. A mutual bank with a 12 per cent reserve might be content to operate with a 10 per cent reserve and for a while would be in a position to spend or distribute all earnings and show no taxable income. As some of their officers have recognized, when they first became conscious of 48-cent dollars (the net after-tax cost of a dollar spent on a deductible item), they might become even more active in advertising or increase distributions of interest. The possibility of more active short-run competition from mutual banks as a result of new taxability is recognized by representatives of commercial banks.

Fundamental differences in the nature and distribution of the assets held give the mutual banks a competitive advantage over commercial banks apart from the difference in tax treatment. This is especially true of the savings and loan associations, and their advantage is accentuated by their virtually exclusive investment in mortgages with very small secondary reserves of government securities. A reduction in tax-free reserves of the savings and loan associations might be accompanied by legislation to strengthen them by requiring liquidity in assets or larger reserve funds on an after-tax basis. But legislation on these points should be considered on its own merits. It is mentioned here merely to indicate that there are other ways than tax favoritism to foster financial soundness in the savings and loan associations.

Some representatives of commercial banks have argued that all ordinary banks should be permitted to build up liberal bad-debt reserves set at an arbitrary level; the figure of 5 per cent of eligible loans has been proposed. This would be modest compared with the 12 per cent of deposits allowed the mutual banks and would still require the commercial banks to provide some new capital funds to protect expanding deposits from after-tax sources. But the revenue cost is prohibitive. An increase in the bad-debt reserves of all banks from the present average figure of under 2½ per cent of loans to 5 per cent would involve a revenue loss of over 1 billion dollars. Even if the build-up were spread over several years, the loss of revenue from a benefit to a single industry would be excessive. This example indicates how costly and really impossible it is to try to extend tax favoritism, originally given to a small group, to all those who can make an equally good case for comparable treatment.

The commercial banks do have a special problem in their own bad-debt reserves which justifies a change in the law. For many years, they were permitted to calculate their bad-debt reserve on the basis of a moving average of their experience for the preceding twenty years and to deduct amounts sufficient to maintain such reserves. In the early 1950s, as the losses of the early 1930s began to drop out of the period covered by the averages, many banks found a ceiling closing in on them and were suddenly no longer able to take any bad-debt-reserve deductions. To relieve this situation temporarily, permission was granted in 1954 to freeze the twenty-year period to include the years of large losses. It was recognized at the time that this would give an unreasonable result ultimately because it put a premium on a high-loss experience incurred under different conditions and different management.

The time has now come to resolve this problem and remove the incongruous tax advantage which some banks now have because their prior earlier managements made bad loans thirty years ago. This advantage should be wiped out. It would seem reasonable to extend to each bank the right to develop a bad-debt reserve up to the national average. This would be a distinctive provision for a single industry, justified by the unique importance of banking and the fact that even the most ambitious plans to curtail the tax advantages of the mutual banks do not contemplate really equal treatment. Banks would no longer be permitted higher reserves on the basis of larger losses in the distant past. Those with higher than average reserves could maintain them in dollar terms, with the expectation that expanding deposits over the years would bring the reserve in percentage terms down to the level allowable under the general rule, at which point they would again take deductions for allowable additions to reserves as deposits continued to grow. The apparent average reserve is between 2 and 2½ per cent of loans. The standard might be set at 2½ per cent, or to use a round figure, it might be set at 3 per cent, with the build-up spread over several years for banks which now do not use bad-debt reserves or have very small ones.

Depletion

The country is entitled to a good dispassionate study of the proper tax allowances for depletion in the mining and oil and gas industries. The reasons usually advanced in support of percentage depletion seem to be largely specious and misleading. Much of the objection to percentage depletion may be based on resentment against the arguments which have been used to support it. It may be that there is some justification for special tax allowances for extractive industries because of the existence of highly competitive world markets for homogeneous products and for defense requirements. But the problem has never been well analyzed from this point of view.

The tax law permits depletion to be calculated on either of two methods. The cost of a property may be spread over the estimated number of units to be mined or pumped from it, with a deduction allowed in computing taxable income to recover the capital cost. This is referred to as cost depletion. It is closely analogous to depreciation based on units of production. A recovery of cost is proper and necessary to show a true net income. No one objects to depletion which allocates the cost of property in any reasonable method over the products extracted from it.

The law also allows percentage depletion which is set at 27½ per cent of gross income and 50 per cent of net income from an oil or gas property, whichever is smaller. Other extractive industries are allowed smaller percentages of gross income but the same 50 per cent of net income. Under percentage depletion, the total depletion allowance is in no way related to the capital cost of a property. Total depletion may, and frequently does, amount to many times the total capital cost of a property.

The rationale for percentage depletion is apparently based on the proposition that natural resources are distinctive in being physically exhaustible. Depletion based on cost is not enough. Because of this absolute physical consumption of the products, it is argued, owners should be entitled to depletion allowances which in some way reflect the exhaustion of the substance and value of an irreplaceable resource.

In the development of the tax law, percentage depletion was introduced in 1926 as a simplification for depletion based on discovery value which had been introduced in the Revenue Act of 1918 to encourage discovery and production of natural resources during World War I.[2] Under the discovery-value concept, the value of a property within thirty days after its discovery could be taken as the depletion base and allocated over the probable number

[2] The Revenue Act of 1918 was not actually passed until 1919, some months after the end of the war, but the momentum for the special allowance carried over.

of units of product. This provision led to extensive controversy and litigation. Opinions as to value within thirty days of discovery differed greatly, especially with the inevitable benefit of hindsight, which was always available by the time a case got into the courts. There were also conflicts of opinions as to what constituted a discovery. Was a new well beside an old one in a proven field a new discovery, and if not, how far away from a producing well did it have to be drilled to create a discovery? Was it a discovery if a vein in a mine was broken by a vertical displacement and one "found" a vein, which happened to be the same one, 10 feet higher up the fault line? The new provision of the law was a boon to expert witnesses as well to the extractive industries.

Percentage depletion was adopted to give about the same amount of depletion as was available to successful discoveries but to do so in a simple way which would avoid administrative complications. The 27½ per cent figure on gross income of oil and gas does not represent any precise scientific accuracy in selecting an allowable figure. It was merely a compromise between 25 per cent and 30 per cent, the two figures used in the bills in the two branches of the Congress and resolved in a conference committee.

Percentage depletion has the advantage of simplicity. But its logical justification is elusive to those not initiated into the mystical aspects of the oil and mining industries. When an ordinary tax expert confesses his inability really to comprehend why miners and producers of oil and gas should have a tax rate which is only half of the general rate, regardless of either the cost or value of the property being used, those fully indoctrinated with percentage depletion seem to take it as evidence of the intellectual inadequacy of the outsiders and patiently explain that only full and lengthy participation in the affairs of the industry can produce enlightenment.

Exact analogies are difficult because of the physical exhaustion of a natural resource in the oil and mining industries. But the concept of recovery of cost rather than value is basic in both accounting and income taxation. There are other activities where value may exceed cost. A hit song, a best-seller book, and a successful model of an automobile are all exhaustible. Their value in terms of future income is above the costs attributable to them, but their owners have not yet suggested that they be allowed percentage depletion or discovery-value depletion to reflect the exhaustion of a unique and physically irreplaceable property. An argument for percentage depletion would seem to be no less valid in these cases. One might also argue that the professional income of a talented person comes from an exhaustible and irreplaceable resource and should be subject to a depletion deduction in computing taxable income. Proposals have in fact been made to allow individuals to take depreciation on themselves, but even here the base is often thought of in terms of the cost of developing a talent, including education expense and income foregone during years of education and training.

The limit of 50 per cent of net income was adopted to prevent percentage depletion from making the income from oil and mining completely tax exempt in some instances. The net income limitation is effective on the less profitable properties. In oil and gas production, whenever costs rise about 45 per cent of gross income, the 27½ per cent allowance of gross income will exceed 50 per cent of net income and the latter limitation is operative. If costs are 80 per cent of gross before depletion, a depletion of 50 per cent of net would be only 10 per cent of gross income. Depletion allowances are related to specific properties, however, and an individual property may be a very small area or even cover an oil sand at a specific depth, with higher or lower sands under a given surface area constituting separate properties for tax purposes.

The dual limitations on depletion as percentages of gross and net income influence operating decisions in mining and oil. Deductible development expenses spent on a property during a year may wipe out any net income from it, which means that percentage depletion is "wasted" during the year. To minimize the time during which depletion is wasted, it is desirable to concentrate deductible expenses into a single year if possible so that a net income and percentage depletion can be restored as quickly as possible on the specific property. Tax planning to minimize any "waste" of percentage depletion calls for close collaboration among accounting, development, production, and tax experts.

Taxpayers are also permitted to aggregate their properties for purposes of computing depletion. This rule is an administrative convenience because it makes it unnecessary to allocate production to the many individual properties which make up a single mine or oil field. But it may also create an opportunity for tax maneuvering. Prior to 1958, a single aggregation could be made within an operating unit, a technical concept which may be larger than a mine and usually is larger than a single oil well. In order to maximize total allowable depletion, high-cost and low-cost properties were aggregated together to try to bring the amount of depletion allowable under the gross income and net income limitations together. In this way, a minimum of allowable depletion under each concept would be "wasted." Aggregations were made on what came to be referred to by those responsible for drafting new tax legislation as the "crazy-quilt" method, and the supposed simplification became just another complication in the tax law but one which permitted tax reductions.

In 1958, a more rational method of aggregation was substituted for mining. Under this approach, if an aggregation is made involving the properties in a mine, all properties must be included; if an aggregation beyond a single mine is made in an operating unit, the aggregation must be of whole mines, not just one mine and scattered properties in other mines. This method seemed reasonable and equitable and eliminated an element of tax maneuvers. The oil and gas industry, however, still may make crazy-quilt aggregations. It should be brought into line and made subject to the same limitations as those applied to mining in 1958.

Two flagrant tax abuses in the extractive industries authorized by lower court decisions were fortunately stopped by recent Supreme Court decisions. They are reviewed here to give an indication of the intricacies and maneuvers with which tax specialists and tax policy officials must concern themselves. The first involved the sale of "carved-out" oil royalties. A carved-out royalty gives a right to a given amount of value or quantity of production to come from a property over whatever period of time is necessary to produce it. It is a horizontal division of a property as distinct from the usual vertical one in which a sale is made of a half or sixteenth or some other fractional interest of all future production. In an established property the horizontal division will have virtually certain value and represent simply the production of the next week or month.

The lower courts held that a sale of a carved-out royalty was a sale of property and entitled to capital gains treatment. This opened the door to a succession of "carve-outs" with the owners of property and those operating it always selling the right to the next few thousand barrels or few thousands of dollars worth of oil and receiving capital gains treatment on the proceeds. The buyers of the carved-out royalties would, of course, receive ordinary income on the margin between purchase price and sale price to compensate for the brief period they might have their money tied up in the royalties, but the bulk of the income would have been realized as capital gain. This seemed like mere assignment of income, but the courts held that it was a sale of property. The Treasury was unsuccessful in getting remedial legislation, but the Justice Department finally secured a review of the lower court decisions and the Supreme Court overturned them.

The second abuse arose from a series of decisions which permitted companies to calculate their percentage depletion on the sale price of brick or tile rather than the clay from which they were made and on finished cement rather than the rock from which it was made. The use of the price of the finished product increased the depletion allowance several times over and, in effect, allowed depletion to be taken on the costs of manufacturing processes rather than the value of the raw product itself.

If a company could take depletion on its finished products rather than on an imputed price for its raw materials, there would be a tremendous inducement for vertical integration in industry. Coke not coal, pig iron or steel and not iron ore, even copper pots and pans would be the desired base for calculating depletion. The controversy arose because of uncertainty as to the point at which mining ceased and processing or manufacturing began and was complicated by an unfortunate phrase "the first commercially marketable product" in the statute. The revenue loss could have run into the hundreds of millions of dollars a year. After several years of uncertainty the problem was resolved almost simultaneously by a Supreme Court decision and remedial legislation late in June, 1960.

The tax savings to the extractive industries from percentage depletion were estimated at 1.25 billion dollars on corporate returns in 1959. A differential tax treatment involving such large sums must be clearly justified on grounds of public policy. Various arguments are advanced from this standpoint, but they have not yet been supported by adequate analysis. Oil and the products of mines are peculiarly subject to international competition. High costs of exploration and production and relatively poor deposits of some products in this country tend to put domestic producers at a competitive disadvantage. It is important for national defense purposes to have domestic supplies of strategically important minerals available. A differential tax treatment may help to assure the availability of supplies. But it is by no means clear that a tax differential is more economical or efficient than an outright subsidy.

It is sometimes proposed to cut back on percentage depletion on foreign production and allow it only on domestic production. This would be consistent with the objective of a strategic reserve, but it ignores the fact that it is probably also of some strategic importance for American companies to own foreign sources, even though the protection given to assure continued ownership may be negligible.

In the absence of percentage depletion, there would be a strong tax inducement for independent owners of oil properties to sell them outright for capital gains. They could thus realize the present value of proved reserves, and operating companies would take cost depletion on the price they paid for the properties. Sales would probably lead to further integration in the industry, the significance of which requires further analysis.

Some of the arguments in favor of continued percentage depletion suggest that an increase in the price of gasoline would be the ultimate catastrophe following a reduction in the depletion allowance. This suggests at least two conclusions, neither of which seems to support the policy of percentage depletion. The first is that the depletion allowance by making possible a lower price to consumers encourages more rapid consumption of an exhaustible natural resource. Stated thus, the result is hardly one that can be defended as in the national interest. The second conclusion is that the saving in tax is not necessary to the industry, since it is passed on to consumers. Higher taxes, accordingly, would also be passed on to consumers, and the industry would adjust to the taxes. This result is very likely not true because of international competition and the importance of world prices. The higher-price-of-gasoline argument indicates the basic uncertainty about the effects of and the justification for percentage-depletion allowances.

Impatient though one may be with the reasons given for percentage-depletion allowances, some caution is needed in changing to a new and reasonable system which would confine depletion deductions to the cost of properties, as is done in all other businesses. Industrial practices and property values have been developed on the percentage-depletion allowances which have been in effect for over thirty years. The extent of disturbance is, of course, uncertain because of the conflicting arguments made by those who support percentage depletion. To the extent that lower depletion would result in higher prices of products, for example, there would be less reason to expect any revaluation of securities. Periodic reductions in the allowances would seem preferable to outright repeal. The interim results could be appraised, and clearer and more systematic analysis might be made of the significance of percentage depletion than has been available thus far.

The oil and gas industry also has an unusually favorable tax treatment through an allowance for current deductions of intangible drilling costs. These may be thought of as the cost of the "hole in the ground" as distinct from structures and other items of tangible property. The intangible drilling costs typically amount to 65 to 70 per cent of the total costs of a well. These intangible costs may be deductible from all other income, including the professional earnings or salary of a person who joins an oil venture syndicate. They are deductible whether the well turns out to be a gusher or a dry hole. Deduction of them has no bearing on subsequent percentage allowances. The effect is to reduce capital costs by about two-thirds through the intangible drilling-cost deduction and then have depletion on top of that.

In a reform of the tax treatment of extractive industries, the current deduction for capital outlays might well be continued as a reasonable concession to the risky nature of investments in it. This is proposed because of a general sympathy for fast write-offs; the concept of intangible drilling costs might even be extended if analogous situations were presented. The fast recovery of a capital cost which will become deductible in due course anyway seems much more acceptable than a severalfold recovery of a capital cost. As long as no more than the actual outlay is recovered tax free, concessions on timing may be appropriate to encourage activity. They are much more appropriate than the right to receive multiples of an investment tax free. Intangible drilling costs give concessions on timing. Percentage depletion gives multiple tax-free recoveries of capital costs.

Small Business

Small business benefits from many special tax provisions, and others, good and bad, have been proposed. Some of the relief is designed to offset directly certain economic disadvantages of small business. In large part, however, the relief is in accord with what seems to be a national policy to maintain as many small businesses as possible, even at the expense of some inefficiency. This sentiment arises from such noneconomic attitudes as a feeling that a small county seat may be a better community to live in if its stores are run by individual merchants who regard the town as their permanent home than if chain stores with transient managers predominate even if chain stores give lower prices.

A preference is given to small corporations by imposing the corporation income tax at two levels, a 30 per cent normal tax on all income and a 22 per cent surtax on income above $25,000. Of all corporations with taxable income in 1957, 82 per cent had income of less than $25,000 and paid only the 30 per cent rate. These corporations had only 6 per cent of the total taxable income. Another 9 per cent of all corporations had taxable incomes of under $50,000 and hence paid the corporate surtax on less than half of their income. This tax relief, being wholly effective for over four-fifths of all corporations, is of great importance to corporate enterprise viewed numerically.

The relief by a split in corporate income tax rates is justified economically because of the heavy reliance which small corporations must place on retained earnings. Until companies reach a fair size, the sale of stock beyond the limited group of original investors is likely to be impossible or prohibitively expensive and long-term loans are not available. A lower rate of tax to permit more earnings to be retained serves to offset this inherent disadvantage.

The relief would be more logical if it were specifically related to retained earnings, but this distinction has never been made for small business even though it was adopted in 1959 for life insurance companies and might be considered for extension. Until 1954, a too vigorous enforcement of a too stringent law on the unreasonable accumulation of surplus penalized small businesses which could not always show an immediate use of funds. Small companies had to accumulate funds in small amounts to build up enough to make the next step in expansion possible. As part of the tax reform in 1954, an accumulation of $60,000 was permitted to be made without regard to purpose (a questionable provision which perhaps invites abuse), the burden of proof was shifted from taxpayers to the government, and administrative officials were directed to ignore the immediacy doctrine which had previously been applied in many instances. The last two of these changes were especially useful to small business.

Though the two rates of corporate income taxation are justified on economic grounds, proposals to convert the corporate tax into a generally progressive tax are without merit. They rest on a false analogy with the individual income tax. The financial problems of small corporations are qualitative. There is no significant difference in access to security markets as corporate income rises from 5 million to 10 million to 100 million dollars. A progressive tax would be a penalty on size alone. Because of the differences in size necessary for efficient operation in different industries, it would also discriminate against specific industries. A company must be fairly large to produce steel or automobiles, but not to fabricate steel products or sell or make component parts for automobiles. A progressive corporation tax would hit minor companies in industries where large capital investments were necessary more heavily than it would a dominant company in an industry requiring smaller amounts of capital.

From the standpoint of equity, a progressive corporate income tax would be likely to be perverse. Many of the largest companies are owned by numerous small investors, while corporations of medium size are frequently owned by wealthy families or small groups of wealthy investors. On the assumption that most of the corporation income tax is borne by the company, and this is certainly the only assumption which justifies any consideration of a progressive corporate tax, the result would be to impose a higher tax on small investors than on wealthy ones, which is surely not the intent of those who propose the progressive corporate tax. Unfortunately, the idea has considerable appeal because it is superficially consistent with the concept of ability to pay, although it violates it fundamentally.

Proposals also are made recurringly either to raise the $25,000 figure at which the corporate surtax begins or to increase the spread between the normal tax and surtax. The former would give no relief to corporations with incomes less than $25,000 (over 80 per cent of all corporations in 1956). The latter method, perhaps by changing the rates to 25 per cent normal and 27 per cent surtax, would give some relief to all corporations and the greatest proportionate relief to the smaller ones. Both are costly in terms of revenue, but either one is acceptable in principle. The introduction of a third intermediate rate should not be considered, however, because this would open the way to a progressive corporate tax, some proposed legislation for which pushes a top-bracket rate to 75 per cent.

In 1958 three new provisions were added to the tax law, following recommendations of the Cabinet Committee on Small Business and endorsed by President Eisenhower. They were intended to assist in the formation, the growth, and the continued independent existence of small business. Two of the three provisions have dollar limitations which might well be increased to make the benefits applicable to somewhat larger companies.

Assistance in financing was given by making any loss by an original investor in a small corporation deductible as an ordinary loss, not a capital loss. A small corporation for this purpose was defined as one in which the total capital stock did not exceed $500,000 and net worth 1 million dollars. The advantages of the ordinary loss deduction were discussed in the section on capital losses in Chapter 5. The ordinary loss deduction is desirable because it gives no outright subsidy and merely has the government share in losses to the same extent that it would share in the income from a successful venture. Though it shares in losses to a greater extent than it would share in a capital gain, it is repeated for emphasis that the sharing in the loss through deduction in computing taxable income is no greater proportionately than the government's share in the income of the particular taxpayers from this and all other sources. The tax relief here is much more limited than that granted in the extractive industries through the intangible drilling-cost deduction. The deduction is permitted there even when there is no loss. On small business investments only actual realized losses are deductible.

Some thought was given in preparing the legislation to attaching the right for an ordinary loss deduction to the first $500,000 of stock and letting it be transferred to subsequent holders, but this was rejected as too complicated administratively. A ceiling of $25,000 per year ($50,000 on joint returns) is imposed on the ordinary loss deduction from stock in small business corporations. This figure might well be increased, since an investor who had put funds into several small business ventures might find that losses developed in more than one of them in a single year.

The second change in the law in 1958 was to permit a deduction of 20 per cent of the first $10,000 invested in depreciable tangible personal property. This was discussed in Chapter 6. Its adoption establishes a useful approach to more rapid depreciation which may well be extended. The original proposal was to permit the use of double-rate declining-balance depreciation on purchases of used machinery and equipment, as had been urged by various small business groups. The House Ways and Means Committee proposed the alternative of an initial allowance which was adopted with the hearty support of the Treasury and the Administration. The percentage and dollar limitations were designed to limit the revenue loss to the amount contemplated in the original proposal and provided for in the Budget.

The third change in 1958 permits a ten-year spread of estate taxes, with interest, on that part of the tax attributable to a closely held business interest in either a corporation or a partnership. This relief measure reduces the tax pressure for mergers which so often exist when the owners of closely controlled businesses die. It is ironic that the estate tax, which is intended to reduce the concentration of wealth, has the effect of increasing the concentration of business because of the need to secure funds to pay estate taxes. As originally proposed, the right to pay the tax in installments would have had a ceiling fixed in dollars consistent with the objective of concentrating tax relief on small business. The House Ways and Means Committee proposed removal of the ceiling. The proposal was welcomed and accepted by the Treasury to convert that part of the bill into a general antimerger relief provision to reduce one of the worst effects of the high estate taxes.

Another part of the law giving relief to small business is contained in the provisions which permit certain partnerships to elect to be taxed as corporations and certain corporations to elect to be taxed as partnerships, often referred to during their discussion in the Congress as the "vice versa" provisions. Theoretically, the second of these options is attractive because the participants in a small business may individually have tax rates lower than the 52 per cent corporate rate and yet a corporation may be necessary to secure investments from outsiders or for other reasons. The optional tax treatment is designed to permit the small business which has to operate under a corporate charter to pay no more taxes than it would under a partnership. This is accomplished by attributing the income of the corporation exercising the option to the stockholders to be taxed to them at their respective individual rates, somewhat as is done with partnership income. The first option is not of particular importance to small business; it was intended to give relief to business which had nontax reasons to operate as partnerships, a problem which at one time existed for firms which were members of the New York Stock Exchange and other exchanges.

Both options were proposed in 1954, and unfortunately only the first one was adopted at that time. The second option, giving relief to small corporations, was added in 1958. Both of them are complicated, especially the one permitting a partnership to be taxed as a corporation. The complications are necessary to prevent abuse by combining the most favorable tax attributes of both categories or switching from one to the other. It is doubtful if the relief is sufficient to justify the complication in the law.

In brief, the tax law now contains substantial relief provisions for small business. Three of them might be extended. This could be done by increasing the spread between the corporate normal tax and surtax, by increasing the amount of loss from investment in the stock of small corporations which can be taken as ordinary loss, and by increasing the amount of immediate deduction which can be taken on business investments in machinery and equipment. The extent of additional relief would depend on the extent to which neutrality in a tax system should be violated to overcome inherent economic disadvantages or achieve social objectives.

It is important also to remember that small business has one tremendous inherent tax advantage. The owner of stock in a successful small business, either an early investor or an organizer, has an opportunity to build up a personal net worth through appreciation of the stock which is almost impossible to match through personal participation or investment in large established companies. This fact has been publicized in the many articles about the glamour companies in 1960. It is notable that the heads of our largest corporations, even with the most generous compensation and stock option plans, cannot begin to acquire the personal net worth of the heads of much less prominent new ventures; prestige and security must compete with potential wealth.

One final point must be made about the differential tax treatment of small business. The split in the corporation income tax rate puts a premium on multiple corporations to carry out a single activity. Each separate corporation saves up to $5,500 a year in taxes (the effect of saving the 22 per cent corporate surtax on another $25,000 of corporate income). Abuse is considerable not only in construction activities but even in ordinary manufacturing or merchandising, where separate corporations may be established for each stage of manufacturing or storage. Legislation is needed to require multiple corporations owned by the same groups to be combined for tax purposes. Certainly there should be no further differentiation between normal and surtax rates on corporate income without a protective amendment of this sort.

Investment Companies

The tax law for many years has given special treatment to regulated investment companies to permit a pooling of funds by small investors to secure diversification. The imposition of the regular corporate tax on an investment company would make an additional layer of tax on the pooled investment, in comparison with direct investment by individuals in ordinary securities. This tax penalty is prevented by removing the corporate tax on investment companies which currently distribute substantially all their incomes to their own stockholders, who pay the full individual tax. The investment companies are regarded as mere conduits and not taxed as separate entities. In addition to current distribution of income the investment companies must also meet certain requirements concerning diversifications of portfolio and minimum number of stockholders to prevent them from being used as personal holding companies. Companies which qualify are treated as "regulated investment companies."

The conduit concept is a reasonable one and if it were not now in the law it should be adopted. Though one may deplore the high commissions given to the individuals and companies selling stock in the investment companies, and the recent public offerings of stock in the companies which manage the portfolios of the open-end investment companies, any problems that may exist in these areas should be approached from something other than the tax laws.

But the conduit concept should not be pushed beyond the point of neutrality, at which a pooled investment fund is given the same treatment as investment by individuals. Any application or modification to give a preferential tax treatment to an investment company raises questions and, in the absence of compelling reasons, should not be permitted. Three relatively new forms of investment companies are questionable from this standpoint: they are certain Canadian investment companies, real estate trusts, and the tax-free formation of investment companies to secure diversification by exchanging individually owned appreciated stock for stock in an investment company. Each of these applications calls for brief comment.

Under the Canadian law capital gains are not taxed. A United States citizen investing individually in securities is always subject to the United States capital gain tax wherever he lives and whatever securities he owns. If he invests in a Canadian investment company, however, that company may sell securities from its portfolio and reinvest the proceeds with no diminution by a capital gain tax, so long as the company is not doing business in the United States. Under the Canadian law the companies may also retain income, subject to a modest tax with no current distributions. These two features clearly go beyond neutrality and give investment through Canadian companies an advantage over individual investment.

The Treasury in 1956 called the attention of the Ways and Means Committee to this situation with an indication that it be corrected in some way. The appropriate change in the law is not clear, however, and no specific recommendation was made at the time. Two possibilities exist. One would be to extend the personal holding company provision to include such companies. This would make it necessary for each United States stockholder to report his share of the undistributed income of an investment company and pay a tax on it. This would be complicated, and the broadened concept of personal holding companies might include some companies which were not created primarily for their tax advantages. The second change would be to specify that any company registered to sell securities in the United States would be deemed to be doing business in this country and thereby taxable on at least some of its income. This change is appealing, but it would still leave open the opportunity for a sufficiently large group of investors to form a Canadian company to avoid classification as a foreign personal holding company while not making any general solicitation or registration in this country. In view of the continued formation of new Canadian companies, extensively promoted for their tax advantages, some action is now called for to restore neutrality with individual investors. An immediate step should be the second proposed change in the law, with possibly some further attention to the definition of the foreign personal holding companies.

Real estate trusts were given special tax treatment in 1960 comparable to regulated investment companies. These trusts, of many years standing, were held to be taxable as corporation before 1940 because of their characteristics of transferable shares and centralized management. It was later argued that the law should be changed to give them special treatment to permit pools of investment funds to be formed without the imposition of a corporate tax to secure neutrality with direct investment by individuals in real estate. The analogy to regulated investment companies does not seem valid, however, because the latter hold securities in operating corporate entities which themselves pay taxes; the relief given waives only a third layer of taxes. Real estate trusts, by contrast, own property directly, and the relief legislation for them waives the basic tax on the business entity holding the income-producing property itself. The Treasury objected to the real estate trust legislation; it was vetoed in the mid 1950s; it failed of passage in 1958; it was finally adopted in 1960. It was argued that as adopted it would not be available for any active operating business. But the line of demarcation between active and passive investment is very tenuous and the applications proposed immediately after passage of the act indicate that this special provision is not well founded and will lead both to abuse and to pressure for additional exemptions. The section of the law should be repealed promptly, before vested interests become established.

Also, in 1960, an ingenious new application was found for two long-standing provisions of the law. A corporation can be formed without tax consequences if those who form the company receive stock in proportion to the value of the property which they contribute to it and if the corporation computes its depreciation and future gains on the tax basis which such property had to its former individual owners. This gives tax postponement, not tax avoidance, and is a desirable feature of the law to remove a tax barrier to business growth when expanding proprietorships and partnerships are incorporated, as they almost inevitably must be, when they need outside capital. The moment of incorporation is typically one when new funds are needed; the imposition of tax on any gain in the value of investment which may have developed up to the time would impede the normal development of successful businesses.

But when tax-free corporations were authorized, no one contemplated that the relevant section of the law would be applied to secure diversification by setting up investment companies. This was what was done in 1960. Since the tax-free exchange is available only on the formation of a corporation, securities are placed in escrow and subscriptions to stock are accumulated up to a specified date when the company is established on a "one-shot" basis, with those subscriptions accepted which will give a balanced portfolio; thereafter the company is operated as a regulated investment company. Management policies will presumably be somewhat different from those in the usual investment company because the original securities have a low tax basis to the company and all sales will create substantial capital gains tax liabilities.

The net effect of the formation of an investment company in the foregoing manner is to secure a tax-free diversification of a portfolio through an investment company which could not be secured by an individual investor operating directly. In this respect, the law goes beyond the neutrality which was intended under the basic conduit concept and it appears that the law should be modified to restore neutrality. This could be done very simply by providing that tax-free incorporations would not be permitted when the property received by the corporation consisted of investment securities. However, it has been proposed in an earlier chapter that tax-free roll-overs be permitted for individual investments. Thus, it appears that neutrality might better be restored by permitting individuals to achieve the same result directly. The new use of investment companies may be regarded as a useful precedent. But if the law is not modified with respect to individuals, neutrality should be restored by denying the right to diversify through the tax-free formation of new investment companies.

Chapter 10 TAXATION OF FOREIGN INCOME

Income from foreign sources is, by definition, subject to two tax jurisdictions. It may be taxed in the country where it arises and in the country to which it goes. The objective of tax policy in most countries is to avoid imposing a discriminatory double tax burden on such income. Domestic legislation in the country from which the income comes (the source country) and the country to which it goes (the country of destination) and international tax conventions determine the taxability of international income.

The tax law in the United States is extremely liberal in taxing income from foreign sources. Though income from abroad is, with few exceptions, subject to our income tax either as it is earned or when it is brought to this country, our law recognizes the primary right of the country where the income arises to tax it and gives an unqualified right to United States taxpayers to offset foreign income taxes against the tax due to the United States. If the foreign tax is exactly equal to the United States tax, there is a complete offset and no net tax is due here. If the foreign tax is less than ours, the difference is due here; if the foreign tax is greater, there is no United States tax due and, of course, no refund or adjustment. Foreign income in this last case is taxed more heavily than United States domestic income, but that is due to the foreign tax law, not to ours. Many other countries are far less generous in recognizing in their basic tax laws the primary right of the country where income arises to tax by giving a full credit for the tax in the source country.

The general policy to avoid a discriminatory double tax may be stated simply, but the application of the basic principles in specific situations may be extremely complicated and lead to much controversy. The most important problems involve the definition of foreign income. When goods are produced in one country and sold in another, how is the profit to be allocated between them? When a lawyer in one country goes to a second country for a conference and then back to his own office to write an opinion which is used in a third country and paid for by the head office of a company in a fourth country, where does the income arise? If a salesman stops to see a prospective customer in a foreign country and the customer later sends an order to the home office of the salesman, where does the income arise and would it have made any difference if the salesman had taken an order and forwarded it to his home office for acceptance? The possibilities of controversy are innumerable. Many of the problems have been largely surmounted by the use of tax treaties which establish common rules and definitions, but the system of treaties is far from complete and new problems arise in each new treaty negotiation in trying to apply common international concepts under the great diversity of national concepts of income.

In spite of our present liberality in taxing foreign income there are numerous proposals, both here and abroad, that we should go further and give a preferential tax treatment to foreign income by making it tax exempt, by applying lower rates of tax to it, or by postponing even more than we now do the taxation of it.

Present Law on Taxation of Foreign Income

The most basic provision in our law on the taxation of foreign income is the statutory right to apply a foreign income tax in full as a credit against the United States tax applicable to that income. Our concept of foreign source income has been developed by rulings, regulations, and court decisions and further refined and developed in our tax treaties. It conforms generally to what have come to be international concepts among the more developed countries and many of the less developed countries. There is little criticism of this provision and few proposals to change it. It seems equitable and removes the tax penalty against foreign income which would otherwise exist.

A second major provision of our law permits postponement of the United States tax on the income of foreign subsidiaries of United States corporations, even wholly owned subsidiaries, until the income is brought back to this country. Income can be earned abroad and reinvested there or in still other foreign subsidiaries without ever becoming subject to the United States tax as long as it is not paid to the United States parent company. The critical factor is the place where the subsidiary is incorporated. If it is a foreign company, it is not subject to the United States income tax unless it actually does business here. If it is a United States corporation, it is currently taxable on all its income even if it operates and is managed entirely abroad. In this respect our law differs from those in many European countries which determine taxability on the basis of a concept of "fiscal domicile" which primarily turns on the location of the center of management. Adoption of this concept is sometimes proposed here.

Individual citizens are taxed currently on their world-wide income regardless of their residence, with two exceptions. United States citizens who are residents of foreign countries are exempt on their income earned abroad, and citizens who are in foreign countries for seventeen out of eighteen months are exempt on income earned abroad up to $20,000 a year.[1] The exemption of income earned abroad, though seemingly simple, has been subject to abuse and to controversy. Does the owner of a ranch or a business "earn" his income or is it attributable to the capital which he has invested in it? The mere fact of salary from a closely controlled corporation does not make the income "earned" income if there is

---

[1] From 1951, when this provision was adopted, to 1953 the exemption was unlimited. This provision, along with the opportunity to use blocked currencies for production costs, gave a tremendous impetus to the making of motion pictures in foreign settings. Income could be earned completely tax-free because it was exempt from United States tax under the seventeen-out-of-eighteen-month rule and not subject to foreign tax because the actors never settled down long enough to become residents abroad. Sometimes the calculations were made too closely. One prominent individual discovered too late that his carefully timed absence was inadequate because it included a voyage on the high seas, which was not the same thing as being present in a foreign country.

a large capital investment and the salary is designed to take out most of the profits. Does a lawyer resident in Europe who handles international tax disputes requiring his presence now and again in New York and Washington earn his income abroad or in the United States? In 1958 the tax law was amended to require information returns on income for which tax exemption was claimed. This involved additional reporting for many people for whom there was no doubt about the legitimacy of the exemption, but there were so many instances of false presumptions of exemption, both innocent and fraudulent, that it was necessary to put tax officials in a position where they could review the facts in specific cases.

It is argued that the exemption of income earned by people who are residents abroad is equitable because the people coming under it have become closely associated with the countries in which they live and do not receive many of the government services provided by the United States. It is further argued that exemption is consistent with national policy by encouraging United States citizens to enter more fully into international affairs and participate in economic development abroad. Some other countries exempt their citizens who reside abroad from taxation on all income except that derived from their country of citizenship and tax that only as they would tax aliens who receive the same income. A subject of the United Kingdom residing abroad, for instance, is not taxable by Great Britain on any income except that which he draws from investments in the United Kingdom, and that is taxed only at the withholding rate applied to all income paid abroad and not to the progressive surtaxes.

A differential tax rate on foreign business income is given to Western Hemisphere trade corporations, which are generally taxable at 38 per cent instead of 52 per cent. The differential rate was given when the corporate tax rate was greatly increased during World War II. Because of our especially close ties with other countries in the Western Hemisphere, a lower tax on companies doing business there was sentimentally appealing and, practically, it made it unnecessary for some companies to convert themselves into foreign corporations which they might otherwise have done to avoid the higher United States tax rate. To qualify, companies must concentrate their business activities in the Western Hemisphere outside the United States.

Though apparently originally designed to apply to companies fully engaged in business in the foreign countries, such as public utilities, manufacturing, or mining companies, the concept was rapidly extended to cover export trade to Latin America or Canada carried out by subsidiaries which confine their activity to the Western Hemisphere. There have been many fine lines drawn in legal opinions as to exactly what can be done and what needs to be done abroad to make sure that income is deemed to arise outside the United States but preferably, of course, not to arise in a foreign country either because then it might be taxable there too. With the growing importance of other parts of the world, there are pressures to extend the differential tax rate to all foreign countries and some resentment in them because they are discriminated against by not being given the same treatment as our hemisphere neighbors. The merits of such an extension are discussed in the second section of this chapter.

The provisions of tax treaties are an important part of our total law on the taxation of foreign income. The treaties establish common rules on the allocation of income. Through treaties the concept of a permanent establishment has been developed with provisions that each country will tax a foreign company only if it maintains a permanent establishment in the country. This permits casual and exploratory commercial contacts in another country without becoming subject to its tax jurisdiction. Under treaties each country usually agrees to allow the income taxes paid in the other country as a credit against its own taxes, a right which we give by statute as well.

Treaties also contain reciprocal provisions by which the countries concerned agree to waive their rights to tax income which they would tax under their statutes. Interest, royalties, and the income of trade apprentices, students, professors, and professional people who are in a country for limited periods may all be made exempt by treaty from taxation in the country of its source, that is, where it is earned. If the two countries have about the same tax rates, this does not necessarily give any net tax reduction to the recipient of the income. The country in which the income is received or of which the recipient is a citizen will usually tax it anyway. Since it is not taxed in the source country, there will be no offsetting foreign tax to apply against the domestic tax in the country of desti-

nation. Taxation is shifted from the source country to the country
of destination. Where income flows are substantially the same in
both directions, total revenues in each country are substantially
unchanged. The principal effect is to relieve taxpayers of the annoyance of having to pay taxes in two countries. International transactions and movement of people are encouraged by removing tax
annoyances even though tax burdens are not reduced.

Proposals for Changes in the Tax Treatment of Foreign Income

Several groups in this country and some foreign governments
urge this country to change the laws to give complete tax exemption to income from foreign sources. The purpose is to encourage
investment and personal activity abroad. Some contend that by
definition double taxation can be eliminated only through such
complete renunciation of the right to take foreign income. Though
this may be a possible interpretation of the phrase, it is not the
meaning as it has been generally developed since World War I. A
more limited objective has been sought in most jurisdictions and
international conferences. Double taxation is thought of as being
eliminated in this sense if there is no greater tax burden on international income than there is on domestic income in either of the
two countries which have tax jurisdiction over it. Unless the tax
rates in both countries are identical, there will inevitably be a
higher tax on international income than the tax on domestic income
in the country with the lower rate.

If a country seeking investment from abroad imposes higher taxes
on income than does the country from which investment is sought,
there will be a tax barrier to the flow of capital. This appears to be a
self-defeating tax policy. More often the countries seeking investment from abroad have lower income tax rates than those in the
capital-exporting countries. This is generally true in Latin America
and in some countries in Asia. Where this is the case, there is no tax
barrier to international investment in the country to which it goes
and no tax penalty in the country from which the investment comes.
The capital-exporting country is neutral and gives no rate differential to encourage investment abroad. It taxes all income of its citizens and residents at the same rate regardless of source. It is the

absence of a rate differential in the capital-exporting countries which is resented in some capital-importing countries. They urge that it is not enough to recognize their primary right to tax all income developed in their jurisdictions. They want the exclusive right to tax it, which means that the country to which the income goes must renounce its right to tax.

In the absence of total exemption, proposals are made for a lower rate of tax on foreign than domestic income, similar to that now given to Western Hemisphere trade corporations, and for a postponement of tax on foreign income earned directly by United States corporations, similar to that now available when foreign income is earned by foreign subsidiaries. Tax relief of this sort is urged by both United States and foreign groups.

More conflicting objectives appear to be involved in the determination of policy in the taxation of income from foreign sources than in any other part of the tax law. Very liberal treatment, up to and including full exemption, is urged to encourage United States investment abroad. Economic development in foreign countries is a basic objective of national policy, as evidenced by our extensive and generous foreign-aid programs. Private investment may to some extent take the place of direct outlays of public funds. More significantly, private investment is especially useful as a catalytic agent in stimulating local private capital and entrepreneurship and, one may hope, in setting standards for high quality, large volume, and low unit profit margins.

The advantages of private investment can be developed at length. It is the form of investment most consistent with our own pattern of development, which we have found to be good and which we hope other nations will find as economically effective and socially desirable as we have. Since development must come largely through local efforts in the countries concerned, it is especially important to stimulate initiative within the countries. Too often there is too much predatory local entrepreneurship in the less developed countries, with emphasis on quick trading profits and monopolistic practices. Though we have by no means outgrown all manifestations of predatory capitalism, the sort of constructive capitalism which is dominant within our own country can be effectively exported through direct corporate investment abroad. Whether the company making the investment operates large retail stores or manufactures automobiles, it can and typically does assist local producers of marketable goods or component parts with technical advice, firm orders, and even financial advances. Small branch plants of our corporations in Asia and Latin America can be a source of real pride, with clean and handsome buildings, well-kept grounds, apparently top wage scales, and quality products which may be as fundamental and simple as tooth paste and sanitary milk.[2] The good impact of such establishments may be offset by manipulators who are even more objectionable abroad than they are at home.

But however one may idealize foreign investment of the right sort, there is a real question as to whether special tax treatment of the income from it can be effective or appropriate. The investment climate in the foreign countries will determine the extent of investment. No conceivable provisions of our tax laws or of the foreign tax laws can alter inherently unattractive situations. The fear of confiscation, currency restrictions, unreasonable administrative interference, or unrealistic requirements for procurement of component parts from local sources may prevent investment. The mere fact of a large population is not a sufficient inducement, nor will exhortation and talk about a moral obligation to invest outweigh unfavorable economic and political policies founded on doctrinaire preconceptions. A bad tax policy in a foreign country might make an otherwise favorable situation unattractive, but the most generous exemption cannot make a bad situation acceptable, nor could our own tax policy push investment out of this country into bad situations abroad, even if it was desired to do so.

Even when it is admitted that favored tax treatment will not induce investment in an unfavorable climate, it is argued that a dramatic change such as tax exemption would so stimulate interest in foreign investment that many existing attractive opportunities would be newly discovered. There is much to be said for this idea. Corporate managements cannot survey all possible uses of available funds at all times. Foreign investment has so many special problems that it is not considered in many companies which after more careful analysis might decide to go abroad. The idea of exemption from

[2] United States companies are by no means alone in these activities. A German department store in Teheran provides an even more impressive contrast to the local bazaars than do the Sears stores in Latin America to the local shops there.

United States taxes, even if it is not so significant as it sounds because of the continued existence of foreign taxes, would stimulate interest and probably some investment.

It is further urged that since other countries have tax rates approaching our own for which we give full credit, our net revenue from foreign income is small and the gain in international good will and in raising the general level of world income would offset this loss. The revenue foregone is also compared with the much larger amounts appropriated for foreign aid, with the conclusion that tax exemption may be more effective especially because it is more likely to encourage development in our own pattern.

Another argument in favor of exemption of foreign income is that our own high tax rate, with the creditability of foreign income taxes, holds an umbrella over tax rates in foreign countries and actually induces them to raise their rates to ours. This makes a strong case against our present system of full taxation of foreign income and unlimited credits for foreign income taxes. Those who favor overwhelming reliance on income tax regard our indirect inducement to other countries as a desirable incidental result of our law, but this attitude is wrong. To the contrary, it seems important to emphasize that the simultaneous existence of high economic development and high income taxation in this country in no sense means that the tax system is the cause of the development. Our problem is whether we can continue effective development in spite of our tax system; it is certainly not something we should encourage others to emulate.

There are numerous instances in which foreign tax rates have been raised because of our high rates and tax credit. United States corporations in some cases have actually encouraged foreign governments to substitute income taxes for alternative charges because the income tax could be fully offset against their United States tax.

We are confronted with a real dilemma in appraising our own policy. The desire to avoid imposing a discriminatory double tax against foreign income has led to the adoption of the full tax credit, but the credit in turn has encouraged higher taxes abroad which hardly encourage investment of domestic capital there. In some instances the foreign countries have been able to develop their taxes to make their higher rates apply only against United States companies and thereby absorb the net tax which would be paid to the

United States Treasury without imposing any new tax burden on either United States or local companies.

Against the proposals for still more liberal tax treatment of foreign income is a fundamental objection to differential rates and rules. Uniformity is generally desirable. In view of all the proposals for special tax concessions for various sorts of domestic activity and investment, it is hard to single out foreign income for special treatment. Our limited experience with exemption on one form of domestic income does not encourage any new uses of it.

It should furthermore be noted that tax exemption places no barrier against removal of foreign income from the country where it was earned while deferral of taxation encourages its reinvestment abroad. This distinction seems obvious once it is mentioned, but it deserves more recognition than it usually receives. Exemption may encourage an original investment, which is particularly important because it provides needed investment in the less developed countries. But retention of earnings is also important abroad as it is here. A combination of low taxes in foreign countries on retained earnings, which is desirable to permit rapid growth of productive capacity by domestic as well as foreign-owned companies, with continued deferral of the United States tax on the income of foreign subsidiaries, would appear to be a useful combination of tax provisions.

For almost fifteen years after World War II, there was general agreement that it was desirable to encourage all forms of investment abroad by United States corporations. But the gold outflow in 1959 and 1960 raised questions as to the best way to adjust our balance of payments. It had already become apparent that there was not a universal and persistent dollar shortage. The attraction of investment in the Common Market was strong, the low-cost high-quality products were available from many countries. Under these circumstances some reconsideration of the previous policy of undiscriminating encouragement of foreign investment was desirable. There was no further need for special encouragement for investments in western Europe. But the underdeveloped areas present a continuing and perhaps a growing problem, and the amounts of private capital which might be expected to go to them even under the most favorable circumstances would probably not have a major impact on our balance of payments. Possible problems in our balance of payments raise new considerations in setting our policy in the taxation of foreign income. The income from wise foreign investments eases the balance of payments.

Any differential tax treatment creates administrative problems and imposes a strain on the definition of foreign income. The lower rate on Western Hemisphere trade corporations encourages manufacturing companies to try to throw as much of the profit into the selling subsidiary, where it is taxed at 38 per cent, and leave as little as possible in the producing company, taxable at 52 per cent. Where there is no basis for determining an arm's length price because of an absence of independent distributors, controversy is likely to arise. Full tax exemption of foreign income would impose an even greater strain on the definition of foreign income.

Another consideration in the special tax treatment of foreign income is the unintended discrimination against small business which may arise. Small companies typically do not establish plants or permanent sales offices abroad; their foreign business is done through casual sales, frequently through brokers or independent exporters. Their larger competitors regularly engaged in business abroad may get the benefit of more favorable United States tax treatment on foreign-source income, which could not be extended to the small companies unless there were an outright tax subsidy to exports which violates international trade agreements. This problem remains unresolved.

It is apparent that many considerations enter into the formulation of our policy on the taxation of foreign income received by United States corporations and citizens. The subject cannot be settled without reference to other international policies and objectives. In no other major area of tax policy does it seem more difficult to strike a balance among the conflicting objectives.

In spite of its political appeal in international relations, tax exemption of foreign business income appears to go too far and to be of questionable economic value. Certainly the argument that this country has no right to tax it is not acceptable; whatever favorable treatment is given should be recognized and accepted as the waiving of a right to tax and an exception to a general tax policy against special treatment made only because of overriding international considerations. Furthermore, any further differential advantage given to foreign income should be confined to income from investments in the less developed countries, to be defined in broad geographic terms. There does not appear to be justification for preferential tax treatment for investment income from Europe and Canada. This exclusion should not be regarded as any reflection on these areas; it is rather based on recognition of their own economic momentum which puts them in a position to share with us the burden of trying to increase growth in other parts of the world.

Lower rates of tax also seem questionable, including the present differential rate on Western Hemisphere trade corporations. The advantages of a lower tax conditioned upon retention of income in the underdeveloped areas, as discussed above, seems preferable. The present 38 per cent tax for Western Hemisphere trade corporations, applying as it does to income from export trade as well as direct investment, does not seem consistent with present policy objectives. Unfortunately, it is unlikely that there could be a dispassionate reappraisal of its effects. It has symbolic importance, and some of the companies benefiting from it would doubtless be able to create enough objection to its discontinuance from some Latin-American countries to make the repeal difficult from a diplomatic standpoint, even though repeal might actually increase reinvestment of earnings in the countries concerned.

Tax deferral is already available for income of foreign subsidiaries. This should be continued, except possibly for holding companies, in tax havens. In a sense it is too bad that both deferral and the credit for foreign taxes are given by statute. If they could be given by treaty, it might be possible to work out some effective arrangement for lower taxes on retained earnings in the countries seeking capital or other desirable provisions. As it is, we have given away by statute what might be two very effective bargaining points in negotiations.

It is proposed to extend tax deferral to United States corporations especially established to carry on business broad. This appears to have many appealing features. Since it can be done through foreign subsidiaries anyway, it seems reasonable to do it through companies under our own jurisdiction. It is questionable, however, if they would really be useful in connection with direct foreign investment. Foreign subsidiaries rather than United States corporations are often desirable and even necessary to operate effectively in foreign countries. This is especially true in joint ventures with local capital.

Unless properly restricted, the principal beneficiaries of tax deferral for United States corporations would probably be exporters and oil and mining companies. Income from our export trade, important though it is in our balance of payments, should not receive a tax advantage. The right to defer tax on income from exports left abroad would actually be an adverse factor in our balance of payments because there would be a tax incentive to seek uses for foreign funds earned through exports rather than making them available for imports. Since we are no longer trying to fill a universal shortage of dollars, a tax policy which had this result should not be adopted. The oil and mining companies now usually operate as United States corporations to get the advantage of percentage depletion which is not available to the dividend income from foreign oil and mining subsidiaries. In the absence of any compelling reason to single out the extractive industries for still more favorable tax treatment, the double advantage of deferral and percentage depletion should not be given to them.

If United States corporations were permitted to defer tax on foreign income, they might be created as holding companies for foreign subsidiaries and used to transfer profits from one country to another. Foreign holding companies established in tax-haven countries are now used for this purpose, though many companies have refrained from establishing tax-haven companies. It would be useful both from a management standpoint and from the standpoint of tax administration to have holding operations brought under United States jurisdiction. If United States holding companies with tax deferral were available, it might be more feasible to tighten the rules applicable to holding companies in tax havens. This probably needs to be done anyway. Any restrictions imposed on tax deferral through United States holding companies should be applied equally to holding companies in tax havens.

The only justification for additional special tax treatment of foreign income is to carry out our policy of encouraging growth in less developed areas. This means that there should be limitations by both the type of income and geographic areas. With the limitations which seem appropriate to protect our own national interest, it seems probable that many of those now urging legislation would lose interest because it would not apply to their particular activities. Properly restricted, perhaps further legislation should be adopted to permit deferral of United States tax on United States corporations on their income from direct investments in less developed areas, but there should be no illusions that it would substantially increase investment abroad. It would have some value for international good will and in drawing attention to possible foreign investment. But the availability of tax deferral on the income of foreign subsidiaries has already provided the most useful tax encouragement which can be given.[3]

The system of tax treaties should be extended. They involve too many technicalities for extensive discussion here.[4] Briefly, treaties can eliminate much of the remaining discriminatory double taxation of international income and reduce tax harassment of international trade, investment, and personal movement. They can also, with proper safeguards, give reasonable recognition, as a matter of international economic policy, to tax concessions granted abroad to encourage economic development and thereby promote international good-will and investment in newly-developing countries.

[3] What is not needed is more special legislation of the sort adopted in 1958 to give a refund to one company which congressional debate identifies as the Westinghouse Electric Corp. The history of the legislation is interesting. Prior to 1958, royalty income from the United Kingdom was subject to double taxation because the British withholding tax was on the British payor rather than the United States recipient and hence was not allowed as a credit against the United States tax on the latter. Westinghouse claimed a credit anyway, which was disallowed. Relief legislation giving a retroactive refund passed the Congress and was vetoed. The Treasury favored abolition of the double tax for the future but wanted a method which divided the revenue loss between the two countries. An amendment to the tax treaty was negotiated in which under some conditions the British waived their tax, leaving the United States tax as the only one, and in all other conditions the United States gave a credit for the British tax. This new concept was approved by all witnesses before the Senate Foreign Relations Committee except a representative of Westinghouse, who opposed it because it did not give retroactive relief to his company. The treaty amendment was adopted, and the new concept in it was later used in other treaties among European countries. But the retroactive relief provision for Westinghouse was passed again as an amendment to an important tax bill which was correctly deemed to be vetoproof. It is found at the end of section 905(b) of the Internal Revenue Code.

[4] For a more complete analysis see: Smith, Dan Throop, "The Functions of Tax Treaties," *National Tax Journal*, December 1959, pp. 317–27.

Chapter 11 ESTATES AND TRUSTS

The taxation of estates and trusts is a vastly complicated subject. Many expert tax practitioners concentrate entirely on this part of the law. Advanced courses in law schools deal exclusively with the subject. In spite of the many complexities in the actual planning of specific family estates, a very few major issues of public policy stand out in the whole area. These are described in this short chapter, with proposals for three major changes. Each of the reforms suggested is a fundamental one. Two of them would ignore for tax purposes the long-established concept of trusts as separate legal entities. Useful and important though trusts are for many practical and legal purposes, their tax advantages are so great that they have been responsible for the establishment of many trusts which were not desired except for tax savings.

The usual proposals to correct admitted tax abuses from trusts would still further complicate the law; the suggestions made in this chapter, though they will be opposed as too drastic by many, would simplify the law as well as make it fairer. They would, above all, remove the present tendency to convert active capital into passive capital and potentially active businessmen into passive rentiers, results which are undesirable from both the economic and social point of view. But the reforms proposed here should be considered on their own merits, and a general reform on other aspects of the law perhaps should not be jeopardized by inclusion of those proposals which will be opposed by groups sympathetic to other aspects of reform. A description of the principal features of the present law on taxation of estates and trusts will indicate the need for reform in this area.

Present Tax Treatment of Estates and Trusts

Estates and trusts are treated as separate entities under the income tax. They are taxed under the progressive individual income tax rates. Estates are allowed a deduction of $600, equivalent to the personal exemption; trusts receive only a $100 or $300 exemption, depending on their nature. Distributions of income to beneficiaries are allowed as deductions in computing the taxable income of estates and trusts, and the distributions are included in the current taxable income of the recipients; trusts are thus taxed only on income which they accumulate. The most significant aspect of the taxation of estates and trusts is that the full range of the progressive rates is applied separately to each one. If property is so divided that the income from each trust does not exceed $2,100, none of the income will be taxed at more than the beginning tax rate of 20 per cent if it is accumulated by the trusts. Each trust receives an exemption of $100; if the income is not distributed, it is taxable to the trust and the entire taxable income falls in the 20 per cent bracket. The advantages of arranging multiple trusts to have them accumulate income subject only to the bottom tax rate are tremendous.

Trusts may come into being either by gifts or under a will. In both cases, if the amounts involved are large enough, either the gift tax or the estate tax will be applied to the transfer of property. Gifts have several tax advantages over bequests by will. The gift tax rates are only three-quarters of the estate tax rates. A combination of gifts and an estate permits the use of the two progressive rate schedules; it is better to have some property paying the bottom-bracket estate tax rates than the top-bracket gift tax rates. A combination also gives dual exemptions, $60,000 for an estate and $30,000 for aggregate gifts plus $3,000 annual exemption per donee; all these exemptions are doubled if as much as $60,000 is left to a surviving spouse and if gifts are presumed to be made jointly by a husband and wife.

Of particular importance when large amounts are involved is the fact that the estate tax is imposed on the entire value of the estate and the tax is included in the tax base. The gift tax, by contrast, is paid only on the actual gift, and the tax is not included in the tax base. A taxable estate of 10 million dollars is subject to an estate tax of a little over 6 million dollars with a minimum marginal rate of 76 per cent on the last 2 million dollars of the estate. The net amount available for heirs is a little below 4 million dollars. If the 10 million dollars were to be transferred by taxable gifts, the calculation is made in a different manner, since only the amount actually received by donees, rather than the total capital sum, is subject to the tax. A total of over 7 million dollars can be given away with a tax of a little less than 3 million dollars, almost doubling the net gift. With the maximum estate tax rate at 77 per cent, there is a great advantage of excluding the tax itself from the base on which the tax is figured by making gifts.

There are, however, two tax disadvantages of transferring property by gifts instead of leaving it in one's estate. The gift tax is due when the gift is made, and this may be many years before an estate tax would be due after death. A family's capital is voluntarily reduced by the amount of the tax during the intervening years and with it the possibilities for income and gain from the amount paid in the gift tax. Also, when property is transferred by gift, it retains as its basis for computing gain the cost to the donor. Property received by transfer at death takes the value at death as its basis. If property has a negligible cost, the step-up in basis by transfer at death will increase its net value to heirs by a third, since the 25 per cent capital gains tax otherwise payable on sale will be avoided. Securities worth 1 million dollars at the time of death can be sold by an executor or heirs for that price with no capital gains tax even if their cost was negligible. If the owner had sold them just before his death, or if anyone receiving them from him as a gift had sold them, the capital gains tax would have been $250,000. This step-up in basis adds to the freezing effect of the capital gains tax. The prospect of a tax-free sale of appreciated property by his heirs can induce an investor to continue to hold property for many years before the end of his life expectancy.

Trusts have two further tax advantages. They may be set up temporarily and the income from the property in them removed from the taxable income of the person who establishes them. To secure this result, a trust must be established for ten years unless the beneficiary is a school, church, or hospital, in which case the period need be no more than two years, though in this case there is no deduction for a charitable contribution. At the end of these periods, the principal amount may revert to the grantor. In the meantime the income is taxable only to the beneficiary, which, in the case of a charitable trust, is tax exempt. For those of us who are not indoctrinated with the concept of trusts as separate legal entities, a temporary trust seems like little more than an assignment of income. If one assigns his pay checks or his dividend checks to someone else for a month or a year or ten years, the income is still regarded as belonging to and being taxable to the person who makes the assignment and not to his beneficiary. The tax law so provides for assignments of income. Trusts are treated differently because the trustee is regarded as the owner of the property, in his capacity as trustee, during the term of the trust.

Most importantly of all from a tax standpoint, a trust may run over several generations, the exact time depending on the state in which it is established. This means that successive generations may receive the income from the trust with no estate or gift tax due when one generation dies and the next one comes into its right to receive the income. An estate or gift tax is due when the trust is originally established; the income is taxed to the recipients if it is distributed and to the trust if it is accumulated, and the final distribution is made to the ultimate beneficiary according to the terms of the trust with no further tax. A trust cannot last indefinitely because of a rule against perpetuities in the law, but the usual rule for its duration is "lives in being plus twenty-one years," which permits an elderly donor or decedent to leave his property in trust for his great-grandchildren with the income to go to the children and grandchildren in the meantime. The advantages of avoiding the gift and estate taxes for the intervening generations are so great that even relatively modest estates are left in trust for as many generations as possible.

The tax planning for an actual estate involves calculations of various combinations of gifts and inheritances with various assumptions about life expentancies, changes in value, probable tax rates applicable to the various individuals concerned, and desires to sell or continue to hold different items of property. Interim income taxes and ultimate total transfer taxes must both be taken into account, with the objective of securing the maximum total of net income and capital value.

The foregoing description of the tax treatment of estates and trusts is a gross oversimplification. It ignores such extremely complex problems as those arising from accumulations and subsequent distributions of income by trusts, the determination of what is income and what is principal, and who is taxed on what when distributions are made from an estate to different beneficiaries. But as long as no one gets the false impression that the application of the concept is simple or that he could work out his own program without expert advice, the oversimplification will do no damage here. The complications and exceptions do not modify the principal economic and social results of the basic provisions of the tax law. It is these economic and social results which justify fundamental changes in the tax law.

Economic and Social Consequences of Tax Treatment of Estates and Trusts

The tax advantages of trusts encourage their use. Temporary trusts are set up to have income go directly to beneficiaries and be taxable to them when an individual is not ready to part completely with his property. Trusts extending over as many generations as possible are likely to be used when one does finally dispose of his property by gift or at death. When income is to be accumulated, numerous trusts, sometimes several hundred, may be used to keep the income in the lowest tax brackets.

The primary objection to the use of temporary and multiple trusts is on grounds of equity. Those who go to the trouble and incur the legal expense of setting up trusts will pay a great deal less in taxes than those who handle their affairs in a more direct and straightforward manner. This comment is not intended to imply that there is anything unethical or underhanded about the use of trusts to save taxes. The law authorizes their use, and one is in a sense negligent if he fails to take advantage of them. The question is whether the law should give such great advantages to a method of holding property which frequently has no reason for existence except tax savings.

There are many good reasons to establish temporary trusts apart from taxation. One may want to give a relative or a friend the assurance that income will be provided regardless of what happens to the donor. This can be done by a trust without losing control of the principal; when the designated period is over, the principal reverts to the grantor or to whatever other person he designates. One may even want to give a favorite charity the assurance of an annual income for a period of years and use a trust for the purpose. These are reasonable and valid reasons to use trusts. They existed long before the income tax even came into existence. The question is not whether trusts should be permitted for these purposes but whether temporary trusts, regardless of purpose, should be permitted to create large tax advantages.

There are no absolute standards against which the fairness of the tax advantages of trusts may be resolved. Legally, trusteed property is owned by the trustee, however temporary the ownership may be. Since the grantor has no right to the present income, it is argued by those who favor the present law that the income should not be taxable to him. For others, the trust device has no more bearing on the taxability of income than the act of cutting the coupons off a bond and handing them to a relative with the remark that it is to be his income and not that of the owner of the bond. One's attitude toward a change in the tax law would depend on whether he feels that a shift in the ownership of income by transferring it through a temporary trust is something substantial and real or is simply a legal fiction which should not be permitted to shift the liability for taxation.

Trusts extending over several generations raise economic and social problems as well as the perennial one of equity. Most trustees are, by law and by instinct, extremely conservative investors. "Legal list" investments often used by trustees do not include new business ventures. Even the most emphatic instructions to a trustee in a trust document to take risks and protect capital against inflation are not likely to make trusteed property become venture capital. Capital in the hands of trustees, especially institutional trustees, is thus likely to be less dynamic than individually owned property, even when they operate under the concept of investing as a prudent man would. From a social standpoint, the beneficiaries of a trust are forced to be rentiers, passive recipients of income with no chance to use the capital as active businessmen or even act as investors in their own right. Successive generations have the assurance of receiving income which will make them independent even if they are wastrels and are subject neither to family discipline nor to the discipline of having to be economically self-reliant.

Trusts extending over more than one generation were used long before there were estate and gift taxes. They are desirable to prevent an imprudent surviving spouse or child from squandering the principal of an estate and depriving himself or his heirs of the expected income. They may increase an heir's happiness by removing the responsibility for investment management. They may protect an heir from fortune seekers by keeping the principal of an estate where it cannot be touched by anyone except direct descendants. All of these are good and valid reasons to create long-term trusts, but the question is whether such trusts should be given very large tax advantages as well. Under the present law, trusts are often created even when the owner of property would prefer to leave it outright to his spouse or children and rely on their judgment to make the right decision on succeeding distributions. But when the total amount available to great-grandchildren can be increased severalfold by the use of trusts, a thoughtful man may be forced to use them even though he finds them distasteful and deplores their nontax consequences.

Here again there are no absolute standards against which to appraise the desirability of the present law. Many will argue that since the intervening generations have no right to use the principal of a trust, it would be unthinkable to tax them on anything other than the income they receive, which is what is done under the present law. Others feel that if one has the right to the income, that is all a prudent man would touch anyway, since even individually owned capital should, of course, be maintained intact for future generations. According to this point of view, a person with the right to income from an estate in trust has for practical purposes all the economic benefits he would have if he owned the property outright and he should be taxed accordingly. It may be further argued that tax advantages for long-term trusts are especially objectionable because of their economic and social consequences in restricting investments and creating passive rentiers. One may favor a change in the law for these reasons even though he does not regard the present law as particularly unfair.

Proposed Changes in Tax Treatment of Estates and Trusts

A good deal of attention was given to the possibility of tighter tax rules on multiple trusts in the late 1950s. A bill making several changes in the taxation of trust and partnership income passed the House and was considered by the Senate Finance Committee in 1960. Among the provisions in it would have been a new rule which would have required the beneficiary of multiple trusts established by the same grantor to pay a tax on the income received from them to the extent that it had been accumulated during the preceding ten years. This would appreciably offset the tax advantages of splitting income among many trusts by bringing it back together again and taxing it to the individual beneficiary as though he had received it when the trust earned it over the preceding ten years. The tax previously paid by the trust would be allowed as a credit against the individual tax. This is obviously a complicated provision, but it would apply only to those who had established multiple trusts, and those who can go to all the trouble of setting them up should not be bothered about keeping track of their results.

This proposal was criticized on the ground that it would not really stop the abuses of multiple trusts but would rather give them legal sanction. It was pointed out that the final tax was due only when the income was distributed to the beneficiary. During the period of accumulation, which might run for twenty or thirty years, only the bottom rate of tax would be applied if enough trusts were created. The postponement of the major part of the tax until distribution, with the additional tax imposed only on the income of the last ten years, was thought to leave too much room for tax avoidance through multiple trusts.

As an alternative, it was proposed by an advisory group of distinguished tax practitioners to the House Ways and Means Committee that the income of all trusts created by the same grantor for a single beneficiary should be consolidated for tax purposes and taxed currently. This procedure also would be extremely complicated and difficult to enforce, since it is not always clear who the actual beneficiary will be (a trust might be established with the income to go to an elderly aunt if she survives to an age of ninety-five and otherwise to one's own son) and neither the trustees nor the ultimate beneficiaries may know of all the trusts established by a deceased grantor. This proposal would continue to treat trusts as taxable entities and merely require that the income of some of them should be consolidated for tax purposes.

The Senate Finance Committee adopted the concept of taxing at the trust level, as though there were one trust, but followed the House approach of waiting until the time of distribution to determine whether one beneficiary had, in fact, received multiple distributions. No legislation was adopted, and the full advantages of multiple trusts are still available.

None of the proposals really seems to get to the heart of the matter on the taxation of trust income. The following proposal is made as a desirable ultimate solution to be applied to trusts created in the future.

Trusts should be ignored for income tax purposes. Trust income should continue to be taxed to the person establishing the trust unless the transfer is sufficiently permanent and complete to make it taxable to another individual or charity. This is the first major change proposed. A transfer to be sufficiently complete to shift the liability for income taxation would be subject to either the gift or estate tax on the principal amount. When one has a sufficient interest in the income from property to be taxable on it, that is, when someone else has made a sufficiently firm transfer of property to be *not* taxable on the income from it, the property would then become subject to estate or gift tax when it or the right to receive income from it was permanently transferred on to still another person. This is the second major change. To permit discretion and flexibility in handling property for a surviving spouse or minor children, an estate might be permitted to continue as a single taxable entity for some period of time, perhaps up to twenty-one years or for the life of a surviving spouse, whichever is longer, with income from any property not definitely transferred to heirs taxable to the estate.

The results of this proposal would be to wipe out completely the tax advantages of multiple trusts or even single trusts which accumulate income, as well as the multiple-generation trusts. It would not in any way destroy the usefulness of trusts for purposes other than taxation. They could continue to be used as they have been, but they would no longer receive major tax benefits which are so great as to force their creation even where trusts are not desired for other reasons.

In its simplest terms, this set of rules would provide that a person is taxable on the income from his own property and would continue to be taxable on it until he made a complete and final transfer of the property to another person. He could not get out of his tax liability by a temporary transfer to anyone else whether the other person is an individual or a trustee. To shift liability for income taxation, he would have to make a transfer of the property to another individual, with the transfer subject to the estate or gift tax if applicable. An irrevocable transfer to a trustee would qualify if a definite beneficiary were established. If the income were to go to any one of several beneficiaries at the discretion of the trustee, the transfer would not be complete and the income would still be taxable to the person establishing the trust or to his estate.

This does not seem an unduly stringent rule for tax liability. Certainly if a person left his bonds in several safe-deposit boxes with instructions to his surviving children to go to the boxes once a year to clip the coupons and divide them up in whatever way they chose for tax purposes, with the additional right to leave some of the coupons in the boxes, each of which thereby became a separate taxable entity to be taxed on any unclipped coupons, there would be a general outcry against tax avoidance. But that is exactly the result achieved by trusts, with a trustee taking the place of the safe-deposit boxes and making them legal taxable entities.

Property could still be left in trust for as many generations as the trust law permits, but when each life interest or other definite interest was terminated, the principal amount from which the income was paid would be subject to gift or estate tax. This would not curtail the usefulness of trusts for nontax purposes; they could and would still be established to prevent a squandering of capital and to assure continued income to several generations in the future, but there would be no tax advantages over normal outright bequests. We may revert again to the analogy of the safe-deposit box. If a person could leave bonds in his boxes with instructions to his children to clip the coupons but never take out the bonds except to exchange them for other bonds to be placed in the boxes, with further instructions to leave the keys to the boxes to their children who would continue the process for their lifetimes and then turn the keys over to their children who would be the great-grandchildren of the person who rented the safe-deposit boxes in the first place—if all this could be done with only an original transfer tax when the bonds were put in the safe deposit box, there would be objection to avoidance of intervening gift or estate taxes. But that is just what can be done now if one thinks of each safe-deposit box as a trustee. Trustees have all the tax advantage of the hypothetical safe-deposit box and many other advantages, because a trustee can exercise his judgment and change investments and even pay out some of the principal to maintain a customary standard of living or meet some other specified objective.

Drastic though it may seem from some standpoints, the inclusion in one's estate of the principal sum from which one receives income seems fair and reasonable if one has not been brought up to think of trusts as separate legal entities. If a person unfamiliar with them were to hear them proposed as a new device to conserve property and permit an original owner's desires to be carried out after his death, he would probably react sympathetically and regard the proposal as a good one as long as it did not create an area for tax avoidance. What is proposed here is to unravel and wipe out the entire fabric of tax maneuver that has developed around trusts and in many instances has been the sole reason for their creation.

The new rules as a matter of fairness should be applied only to trusts created in the future. As a practical means of handling property left at death for varying uses, an estate might be permitted to be continued for a considerable period as a taxable entity. A person, in a sense, would be permitted to project himself in time as a taxable entity but not to proliferate himself into a group of new nonpersonal taxable entities. Income would be taxable to the estate until the property from which it came was transferred to an heir or to a trust with sufficiently definite terms to make the income from it and the capital sum attributable to a specific individual. Estates would not be given deductions as they now are for income distributed here and there on an interim basis to various heirs, any more than a living person can shift the liability for tax on his income by distributing the income year by year to his children and prospective heirs. The law would be no more strict on an estate than on the person whose property went into the estate. It would, to repeat, permit an individual to continue himself, through his estate, as a single taxable

294 Federal Tax Reform

entity but deny the possibility of creating other new nonpersonal entities.

There would doubtless be many administrative problems in working out this new concept. It is proposed here as an objective for major reform. If the concept is accepted, exceptions should be made only to avoid impossibly complicated provisions covering special situations. The approach should be to bring all aspects of the tax law into conformity with the general objective, not to make minimum changes in the tax law to give recognition to the objective while maintaining as much of the present substance as possible.

The revenue gained from the elimination of future trusts as separate taxable entities should be regarded as available to finance other aspects of tax reform, especially the reduction in the top-bracket individual tax rates and estate tax rates. A revision of individual rates with a tightening of definitions is a first objective of tax reform. The burden of the tighter rules on trusts would fall primarily on those whose incomes are in the middle and upper brackets. The proposal made here may be regarded as one aspect of the tightening in the definition and concept of taxable income.

A third major change in the estate tax would be to convert it into an inheritance tax. This is proposed for consideration, though with less assurance that it would be a major reform than is possible on the two preceding proposals concerning trusts. The revenue from the estate and gift taxes fluctuated between 700 million and 1.4 billion dollars during the 1950s. It is obviously not a major source of revenue and is widely recognized as having been adopted and continued primarily for ulterior social purposes. The breaking up of large accumulations of wealth to prevent their perpetuation over many generations has become a part of our social policy. The estate tax is the means to that end. An inheritance tax would appear to be more effective and fairer.

One's attitude toward the social objective of taxation to reduce inheritances will be determined by his appraisal of the way people with inherited wealth behave. The escapades of some receive extensive publicity and create an understandable distaste for the idle rich. But "leading families" do seem to perform useful functions in both urban and rural communities when their responsible members take independent leadership as they so often do in community activities and in setting the tone for discreet social conduct and cultural interests. Such action is less newsworthy and receives less publicity. It is unfortunate that trusts help to keep the notorious group active. Perhaps the removal of the tax advantages of trusts, by discouraging their use, will make it more likely that those who are irresponsible in their personal conduct will soon lose their inheritances through financial irresponsibility. This would be a desirable incidental result of the change in the tax law. On the basic social objective of gift and estate taxation, the position taken here is to accept, though with some regret, the present total tax burden on gifts and estates and to consider ways to make the taxes fairer and more likely to produce desirable social and economic results. A change to inheritance taxation would seem to be a desirable reform.

An estate tax is imposed on the entire estate of a decedent regardless of the number of heirs. The tax is the same on a 10-million-dollar estate whether it is left to an only child or divided up with 1 million dollars to each of five children and $500,000 to each of ten grandchildren. An inheritance tax is imposed on the amount received by an individual heir. Thus the greater the concentration of ownership in property among heirs, the higher the tax would be under a system of inheritance taxation.

The Federal government uses estate taxation exclusively. The states rely principally on inheritance taxation but use estate taxes on a supplementary basis, usually to make sure they receive the full amount of a credit allowed for state taxes under the Federal estate tax legislation of 1926. Many of the states have found the inheritance tax administratively difficult because of the problem of placing valuations on future interests in trusts, but under the plan proposed here future interests will be much less common and that problem will be reduced.

An inheritance tax seems fairer than an estate tax because the conscious burden falls on the live heir rather than the deceased owner of the property. The sacrifice involved in a reduction of capital by a tax can be conceived of most clearly in comparison with what individual heirs would have received in the absence of a tax. There would appear to be more psychological sacrifice involved if each of ten heirs has his 1-million-dollar bequest reduced by $700,000 than if one heir has his 10-million-dollar bequest reduced by 7 million dollars, but the estate tax takes no account of the number of heirs or the size of their individual bequests. An inheritance tax would make it possible to relate the tax burden to the amounts received by individuals.

An inheritance tax would also actually encourage a maximum distribution of large fortunes at any given level of total taxation, because with progression in rates starting all over again for each individual heir there would be a tax advantage in leaving one's estate to as many heirs as possible. With the splitting up of large aggregations of capital a principal reason for the existence of death taxes, a form of tax which encourages division would seem to be the desirable one. When the estate tax was first adopted, the rates were low and the impact was not great. The estate tax was somewhat easier to administer and to explain. Subsequent increases in rates have been made with no fundamental review of the form of tax imposed at death. It seems desirable that there should be reconsideration now, especially when the inheritance tax appears to be preferable as regards both equity and social purpose. If a change were to be made, it could be done with a readjustment of rates designed to bring in the same total revenue.

A proposal frequently made in the past has been to integrate the gift and estate taxes, applying a single set of exemptions and making the estate tax rates depend on total transfers during life as well as those at death. A 1-million-dollar estate, if it followed 2 million dollars of gifts, would be put in the 2-million- to 3-million-dollar bracket and taxed at rates applicable to this bracket. The purpose is to raise the total tax burden in order to increase the effectiveness of transfer taxes in reducing the transmission of property between generations. Some people actually regard the existence of separate taxes on gifts and estates as a form of loophole.[1] This concept and the proposed change are not adopted here. The integration of the taxes would not deal with trust problems which seem to require corrections. Nor is the idea accepted here that bigger transfer taxes are automatically and by definition desirable for social purposes.

The present estate tax law contains one capricious feature which should be corrected to make the law fairer. When split income was authorized for income taxation in 1948, a marital deduction was also

---

[1] It is interesting that in England there is no gift tax, in spite of very high death duties. If one can correctly guess the sequence of deaths in a family and make gifts far enough in advance to outlive a presumptive contemplation of death rule, property can be transmitted without transfer tax.

established in the estate tax. This allows up to half of an estate to be left to a surviving spouse without being included in the taxable estate of the first decedent.[2] It is, of course, then included in the estate of the surviving spouse unless it is passed on by gift previously. Under the marital deduction, an estate may be split in two, with each half starting the progression in the tax rates afresh, provided that the spouse who owns the property dies first. This is a critically important proviso. If the spouse without property dies first, the marital deduction can never come into operation and the total tax on the undivided estate is much larger. This is the capricious element in the present law. The total tax on the transfer of property from parents to children varies greatly with the happenstance of which parent dies first.[3]

The most reasonable and equitable change in the law would be to permit some sort of credit for bequests to children if a marital deduction is not available. Legislation has been introduced in the Congress to give a credit or deduction for property left to children to supplement the marital deduction. It would appear to be especially justified if the marital deduction cannot be used or if adapted to give a greater benefit for that part of an estate which did not come under a marital deduction. A limitation to bequests to children would appear to be appropriate because property left in this close relationship is often not thought of as a windfall but merely a

[2] Prior to 1942, the estate tax law had given a great advantage to some families in community-property states by recognizing the community-property concept under which half of the total property acquired by a married couple was presumed to belong to each spouse, with no tax on the half of the estate going to a surviving widow. This advantage was withdrawn in 1942, and all property was treated as being in the estate of the person who had acquired it; the same action should have been taken in connection with the income tax. The marital deduction in 1948 in effect went back to pre-1942 law for the community-property states and gave the same advantages for bequests to spouses in other states.

[3] This point can be dramatically if gruesomely emphasized for a class by posing the problem of what a feeble and elderly man with 10 million dollars of property can do to increase the net estate going to his heirs as he sits by the bedside of his dying wife. Students typically propose all sorts of remote possibilities but seldom think of the one obvious answer that if he commits suicide and dies a minute before his wife does, the net estate for the children will be slightly above 5 million dollars, while it will be slightly less than 3 million dollars if his wife dies first.

transfer of title to what has always been regarded as family property.

The attitude of many protagonists of high death taxes that all inheritances are windfalls seems quite wrong as a generalization. In many families, property is thought of as being jointly owned and only temporarily in the possession of the older generation. Far from an inheritance being regarded as a windfall, any tax at death is regarded as a capital levy on the family group which accentuates the economic loss of the earning power of the decedent and the division of the property among the children. An inheritance tax thus has a further advantage over an estate tax in that the rates of tax can be adjusted to take account of the degree of relationship with a decedent, which typically has a bearing on the attitude of the heir and hence on the psychological burden of a tax. The windfall bequest from the distant uncle would seem to have more taxpaying capacity than the equal bequest from a father to a son or daughter in a closely knit family group.

Chapter 12   EXCISE TAXES

A full discussion of the many inequities and complexities in the present system of selective excise taxes would be quite extensive. Some appreciable improvements on technical points, but with some new complications, were made in 1958. This legislation was based on extensive hearings before the House Ways and Means Committee in 1956, the printed record of which extended to 1,107 pages. There will be no attempt here even to indicate all the problems which arise under selective excise taxation. The principal proposal for change is simple but fundamental. It can be described very briefly and is contained in this separate chapter only because the subject is distinct from all those discussed in previous chapters.

The desirable reform in excise taxation is to substitute a single broad-based excise tax for the present selective excises. A rate should be selected which will bring in the same amount of revenue as the present excises; a 2 per cent general tax, subject to the qualifications below, would be sufficient to replace the present selective taxes other than tobacco, liquor, and highway taxes, which produced 3.9 billion dollars in fiscal 1960 and are mostly at 5 and 10 per cent rates. Since the present excises are not confined to luxuries, there would be no significant change in the burden at different income levels. Two qualifications should be made to the proposal for a single broad excise tax. First, the present rates on tobacco, liquor, and highway taxes should be maintained. High taxes on liquor and tobacco have been traditional in this country, as they are in virtually all other countries. These taxes are steady producers of substantial amounts of revenue, estimated at 2.0 billion dollars from tobacco and 3.2 billion dollars from liquor in fiscal 1961. There is little feeling that selective relief should be given in this area or that this tax burden should be shifted to other items of consumption.[1] The highway taxes, estimated at 3.0 billion dollars in fiscal 1961, are now fortunately used to finance the highway program and for reasons previously discussed should be kept at or raised to whatever level is needed to meet the requirements of the program.

The second exemption to a broad-based excise tax should be the adoption of whatever exemption is necessary to permit the shift from selective to broad excises without a significant change in excise tax burden at different income levels. An exemption of medicine and food would probably be sufficient for this purpose. It may also be desirable to exempt goods consumed or used in further production, to the extent that it is administratively feasible to do so, in order to prevent pyramiding of the tax and to avoid giving a tax advantage to vertically integrated companies which produce their own components or equipment. On the other hand, with the growing importance of the service industries, consideration should be given to extending the tax to them to avoid any discrimination between the consumption of intangible and tangible goods.

All forms of excise taxation (except those on liquor and tobacco) are opposed by some people on the basis of a logical fallacy which occurs too frequently in popular discussion. There is general acceptance of the proposition that taxation which bears more heavily on people with small incomes and wealth than on those with large incomes and wealth would be unfair and bad. It is also true, as a minor premise, that a general excise and most selective excises bear more heavily on small than on large incomes. This is so because more of the larger incomes are saved or spent on services which are hard to reach by excise taxation. But it does not follow, as is often alleged, that excise taxation is therefore bad. The general proposition has meaning only with reference to a system of taxation, not to a single part of it. As long as the system of taxation does not impose

[1] Some representatives of the liquor industry have argued for special relief on the grounds that with changing patterns of consumer expenditure "the product" has not maintained "its share" of total consumer outlays, but tax reduction to maintain liquor consumption has not yet been proposed publicly by the industry, nor does it seem likely that it will be.

greater burdens on smaller incomes and accumulations of wealth, there is no injustice if one part of the system is regressive.

Any single form of taxation will have its imperfections and inequities. With the requirements for total revenue as high as they are, sole reliance on any one tax would magnify the impact of its shortcomings. With a combination of taxes, the inequities of each component may offset one another. With personal exemptions in the income tax at $600 and rates going even as high as 50 per cent, there would be substantial progression in the tax system as a whole, especially when the individual tax itself produces more than half of the total Federal revenue.

Each exemption in an excise tax produces border-line cases, with discrimination among products. Even the exemption of food, which presumably would not include candy, would discriminate in favor of "sweet baked goods." How thick must the chocolate coating be on a cookie to make it a form of candy, and how much dough can be put in the center of a piece of candy to make it tax-exempt food? Much of the objection to the present selective excise is based on discrimination, not on the existence of the tax. Why should cheap fur coats be taxed while expensive cloth coats are exempt? How should luggage be defined to give certainty about taxability to manufacturers and prevent unfair competition from comparable untaxed items? Should the tax on jewelry be applied to amateur lapidaries, and if it is not, how can there be assurance that amateur stonecutters will not make a business of their hobby? The unfair competition from untaxed articles is, to repeat the point, the basis of much of the objection to excises. The fewer the exemptions, the less the possibility of discrimination.

It is also desirable to have an excise tax imposed as close to the retail level as possible. Our selective excise taxes imposed on manufacturers have produced unintended discrimination between manufacturers who sell directly to consumers and those whose products pass through several intermediate distributors before they reach consumers. A flat rate of tax on both will put a greater tax burden on the former, since his price will have to be higher to cover many distribution costs which are not borne by the second manufacturer. To meet this sort of problem, presumptive or adjusted prices have been established, but any departure from an actual price invites controversy. There is also uncertainty as to the point at which manu-

facturing stops and distribution begins. The manufactured ingre-
dients of a cosmetic product or a soft drink may be a negligible part
of the final price. If a separate corporation puts it in packages and
advertises and distributes it, which company is the manufacturer?
The tax base of the first company may be a minor fraction of the
second, and there is a tax inducement to split up operations artificially.

A retail tax gives minimum opportunity for controversy on price
and the definition of a taxable sale, but it imposes administrative
burdens on a large number of business establishments. The retail
sales tax has also been preempted by the states and municipalities.
Unless the state and local governments wanted the Federal government to enter the field and provide centralized and uniform administration, a national retail tax should not be imposed. But a
wholesaler's tax, that is, a tax on sales to retailers, might be preferable to a tax at the manufacturer's level. It would minimize, but not
eliminate, proposals for presumptive and adjusted prices, and it
would largely remove the tax incentives to pretend that manufacturing included only the physical production of a commodity. More
extensive inquiry into experience in other countries is needed to
give a final judgment on the relative advantages of taxation at the
manufacturer's and wholesaler's levels.

Too frequently, the arguments of representatives of industries
against selective excises have been so broad that they have increased
the opposition to all excises. This shortsighted policy has been
modified in recent years. The objections of the more responsible
and farsighted business groups have been made to discrimination
in the selection of commodities and services to be taxed rather than
to the principle of excise taxation. After all, taxes have to be collected some way, and the vehement opposition of a few groups to
taxes on their products or services makes the development of a
balanced tax system more difficult. But the combined results of the
opposition of a few business groups, along with the fallacious
argument against any excise taxation discussed above and the sentimental attachment to income taxation in much of the tax literature,
have brought about a situation where excise tax reform will be
difficult. Here, too, it seems preferable to consider tax reform in
this area as a separate topic and not make reform in other parts of
the tax law more hazardous by bringing in additional opponents.

In the meantime, there should be renewed efforts to prevent a continued whittling away of this important source of revenue. The too effective lobby groups in some industries have led to eliminations and reductions of some taxes with revenue losses which might better have gone to some of the needed basic reforms in the income tax. The revenue loss from the elimination of the freight tax in 1958 would have been sufficient to bring all surtax rates down to 55 per cent from the present level of 91 per cent. The agitation for repeal of the tax on local telephone service estimated to yield 463 million dollars in fiscal 1961 will doubtless continue. The revenue loss would be even larger than that from the freight tax, and the telephone industry has no conceivable basis for urging relief because of untaxed competition or a depressed industry, as was true for the railroads. The House Ways and Means Committee and the House of Representatives have prevented further inroads on the revenue from excises. Their position should receive full support.

CONCLUSIONS

The discussion in the preceding chapters has covered many aspects of Federal tax policy. Technical tax matters, theories of tax incidence and corporate finance, and comments on social and political issues have been included; they are all relevant to tax policy.

An attempt has been made to describe the most controversial parts of the present law and the possible changes in them. On some of them, it is concluded that proposed revisions would make the law worse rather than better. On others, reform is needed, with varying degrees of urgency.

Reform is itself controversial. It often involves a removal of special privileges, and the opposition of those who stand to lose their special privileges can be vigorous. As a practical political matter, a series of reform packages would have a greater chance of success than a single reform bill because there would be less concentrated opposition from groups with special interests.

There is no prospect for a substantial budget surplus in the next several years which would permit a combined program of tax reduction and tax reform. Each reform package accordingly should be substantially self-financing. Such reform packages could and should be considered without reference to the budget position. If they are basically sound, any net gain of revenue would be welcome in view of total prospective expenditures. Any net loss of revenue would be shortly recouped by a more vigorous economy and greater collections from improved taxpayer morale.

The changes which would increase revenue generally should be adopted only as parts of reform packages. Each package has at least one feature which involves an immediate loss in revenue. If such items stand alone, they are likely to be unacceptable politically even though they are sound in principle. It is fortunate that so many aspects of reform will increase revenues. This fact permits the development of substantially self-financing packages which make general tax reform possible even without a budget surplus for general tax reduction.

With reasonable tax reform, the tax system could be made to produce more revenue than it now does with less damage to the economy. This opinion should not be regarded as an open invitation to higher government expenditures. Though some government expenditures are essential for a good society and a dynamic economy, the wrong sorts of public outlays can undermine personal initiative and the sense of private responsibility. When they do this, they are worse than foolish individual consumption, which, while deplorably wasteful, is seldom destructive.

But tax reform is needed regardless of one's views on spending programs. Total revenue requirements will remain very high whatever changes may occur in total government expenditures. With a large tax burden, it is especially important to keep the inequities, the complexities, the uncertainties, and the inherently repressive effects of taxation at a minimum. If the tax system is not sound, the adverse effects of taxation may more than offset the benefits of even the most soundly conceived program of expenditures.

Taxpayer morale is weakening under our present tax laws. Without tax reform it may degenerate seriously to the point of undermining the whole system of self-assessed income taxation. In the minds of many, the indefinite continuation of the confiscatory high-bracket wartime rates in the individual income tax justifies elaborate and devious maneuvers, including illogical special relief amendments to the law to avoid the tax. We are still short of a situation where outright fraud is socially acceptable except in limited groups, but a decline toward this ultimate collapse of fiscal morality is not impossible. In the absence of tax reform, one may at least expect that special relief provisions will become more numerous, with ever-increasing complexities, and that tax shenanigans short of fraud will be widely condoned. Some tighter rules on individual deductions are important to cleanse the atmosphere, even though the direct revenue gains may not be large.

There seem to be two approaches to tax reform. Some of those concerned with the subject give primary attention to tighter definitions and broader concepts of taxable income while recognizing, perhaps regretfully, that the confiscatory tax rates will have to be reduced. Others believe that a reduction of the rates should be the primary objective in order to improve morale, restore equity, and make it again more significant to increase income than to create deductions. The imposition of stricter rules and the removal of special privileges, though desirable in themselves, are especially useful because they should make reform packages involving rate reductions acceptable. The latter approach is the one adopted here. The issue is not how much rate reduction will have to be granted in order to close loopholes, it is rather how much rate reduction can be achieved while closing loopholes.

The major proposals for tax reform made in this book can be summarized briefly in the following reform packages.

Individual Income Tax

1. Revise middle and upper bracket rates to restore a situation where it will be more important to earn income than to save taxes.
2. Tighten definition of taxable income by
   a. Stricter treatment of employees' expense accounts and professional and hobby expenses of the self-employed
   b. Improved taxation of interest and dividends, by withholding if necessary but preferably by better enforcement
   c. Elimination from capital gains category and taxation as ordinary income of such things as lump-sum withdrawals from pension plans, stock received under stock options which is not held for quite long periods, and coal royalties
   d. Stricter rules on charitable contributions of appreciated art objects and elimination of charitable deduction for used personal possessions
   e. Elimination of deduction for interest and taxes on owner-occupied homes
   f. Elimination of tax exemption on future issues of state and local securities. (A plan to reimburse state and municipal borrowers for higher interest costs probably must be included; even if this is done, this reform item should be considered separately if it would jeopardize a reform package.)

3. Consider, as an ultimate reform in the interests of simplicity and equity

   a. Complete elimination of the deduction for taxes and interest, except when incurred in a trade or business

   b. Allowance of deductions for charitable contributions, casualties, and medical expenses only when they substantially exceed an average figure

   c. Elimination of optional standard deduction, which would become unnecessary in view of items *a* and *b* above

   d. Reduction of bottom-bracket rate to the effects of the reduced deductions in items *a*, *b*, and *c*

The net effect of this ultimate change would be a great simplification both in personal record keeping and in the preparation and auditing of tax returns. By an adjustment of rates, those now using the optional standard deduction would pay exactly what they do now. There would be greater equality between homeowners and those who rent, and itemized deductions would go only to those whose medical expenses, losses, or contributions are unusually large.

Depreciation

1. Establish depreciation rates on broad categories of property to permit recovery of capital outlays over periods which recognize the probability of high obsolescence and the desirability of encouraging rapid replacement.

2. Tax profit on sale of depreciated property as ordinary income, instead of capital gain, up to original purchase price.

3. Require depreciation taken on books to be at least as large as that claimed for taxes.

4. Permit taxpayers to justify higher depreciation rates than those generally authorized where special circumstances justify them.

5. Consider adoption of larger deductions in year of acquisition of depreciable property to stimulate capital investment. This is of much less importance than the preceding four items.

Capital Gains and Losses

1. Tighten definition of capital gains, as described in 2*c* above under individual income tax package.

2. Reduce rate on very long-term gains, over ten years, to 12½ per cent, and increase rate on short-term gains, under two years, to 37½ per cent.

3. Lengthen minimum holding period for capital gains to one year.

4. Increase allowance for deduction of net capital loss from ordinary income from $1,000 to $5,000.

5. As a preferred alternative to 2, 3, and 4 above, permit tax-free roll-over of long-term investments, with carry-over of basis, and tax any net gains not reinvested as ordinary income. This will remove the tax barrier to shifts of long-term investments and increase the supply of stocks and real estate on the market to mitigate excessive price rises during speculative booms. The law also will be more equitable if it taxes as ordinary income those gains which do not continue to be embodied in a capital fund and at the same time remove those applications of the tax which now make it more of a capital levy than an income tax.

Corporation Income Tax

1. Tax cooperatives on net retained earnings, allowing deductions only for cash distributions to patrons and members.

2. Tax cooperative financial institutions on net increases in surplus reserves after allowance of deductions for bad-debt reserves which are more closely related to those permitted to ordinary taxpaying corporations than is now the case.

3. Tax all corporate income and gains at the same rates by not giving corporations a differential rate on capital gains.

4. Tighten the law to prevent abuses of tax advantages from multiple subsidiary corporations or multiple corporations owned by the same group of investors.

5. Eliminate the concept of percentage depletion over a period of years unless it can be justified on better grounds than have been advanced thus far. Whatever change is made in the depletion allowance for corporations should also be made for individuals.

6. Use revenue received from preceding changes to reduce the corporate normal tax rate, thereby giving relief to all corporations with the greater proportionate relief to smaller corporations.

Trusts and Estates

1. Ignore trusts established in the future as separate taxable entities, making the income of them taxable to the donor or to the estate unless the right to income is definitively transferred to an individual beneficiary.

2. When income of a trust or estate becomes taxable to a beneficiary instead of to the donor or an estate, under the preceding rule, the principal of the trust or estate will be deemed for tax purposes to belong to the beneficiary and an additional gift or estate tax will apply when the recipient of the income dies or the income is shifted to another beneficiary.

These two changes will remove the tax benefits of multiple trusts within a generation and of trusts extending over several generations without impairing their use for nontax purposes. An estate should be permitted to continue as a taxable entity for a substantial time; an individual could continue himself in time after death but could not proliferate himself into numerous artificial taxable entities either during life or after death.

3. The revenue gained from the two preceding points should be used to reduce the estate and gift tax rates and, since much of the gain will come from higher income tax revenue over the years, to reduce the income tax rates as proposed in the first tax reform package.

4. Substitute an inheritance tax for the estate tax; this is a separate package by itself.

Excise Taxes

1. Substitute a single broad-based excise at the manufacturer or wholesaler level for the present illogical selective excises on a variety of products and services while keeping the liquor and tobacco taxes at least up to present levels. Keep gasoline and other highway use taxes high enough to finance the highway program.

These six tax-reform packages could reasonably be considered as separate items of legislation, though they are somewhat interrelated as noted in their descriptions. The reforms in the individual tax and in depreciation allowances are the most important of the six. The depreciation reform is the simplest and should be the least controversial. Its prompt adoption in 1961 may also be especially timely, both to encourage economic expansion and to permit reductions in costs which will improve the international position of the dollar. For these reasons, it should be treated separately.

In addition to the items in the six reform packages, numerous other proposals for change were made in the foregoing chapters. They are not repeated here because a mere listing of them would make tax reform seem more formidable than it should be. They may be adopted as separate items of legislation or included as additional items in the reform packages provided that their inclusion does not clutter up and endanger adoption of the basic elements in the reform program.

Federal Individual Income Tax Exemptions and First- and Top-bracket Rates, 1913–1960

Income year	Personal exemptions					Tax rates			
	Single	Married				First bracket		Top bracket	
		No	Dependents			Rate, %	Amount of income	Rate, %	Income over
			1	2	3				
1913–1915	$3,000	$4,000	$4,000	$4,000	$4,000	1	$20,000	7	$500,000
1916	3,000	4,000	4,000	4,000	4,000	2	20,000	15	2,000,000
1917	1,000	2,000	2,200	2,400	2,600	2	2,000	67	2,000,000
1918	1,000	2,000	2,200	2,400	2,600	6	4,000	77	1,000,000
1919–1920	1,000	2,000	2,200	2,400	2,600	4	4,000	73	1,000,000
1921	1,000	2,500a	2,900	3,300	3,700	4	4,000	73	1,000,000
1922	1,000	2,500a	2,900	3,300	3,700	4	4,000	56	200,000
1923	1,000	2,500a	2,900	3,300	3,700	3	4,000	56	200,000
1924	1,000	2,500	2,900	3,300	3,700	1½b	4,000	46	500,000
1925–1928	1,500	3,500	3,900	4,300	4,700	1⅛b	4,000	25	100,000
1929	1,500	3,500	3,900	4,300	4,700	⅜b	4,000	24	100,000
1930–1931	1,500	3,500	3,900	4,300	4,700	1⅛b	4,000	25	100,000
1932–1933	1,000	2,500	2,900	3,300	3,700	4	4,000	63	1,000,000
1934–1935	1,000	2,500	2,900	3,300	3,700	4c	4,000	63	1,000,000
1936–1939	1,000	2,500	2,900	3,300	3,700	4c	4,000	79	5,000,000
1940	800	2,000	2,400	2,800	3,200	4.4c	4,000	81.1	5,000,000

1941	750	1,500	1,900	2,300	2,700	10[c]	2,000	81	5,000,000
1942–1943[a]	500	1,200	1,550	1,900	2,250	19[c]	2,000	88	200,000
1944–1945	500	1,000	1,500	2,000	2,500	23	2,000	94[e]	200,000
1946–1947	500	1,000	1,500	2,000	2,500	19	2,000	86.45[e]	200,000
1948–1949[f]	600	1,200	1,800	2,400	3,000	16.6	2,000	82.13[e]	200,000
1950[f]	600	1,200	1,800	2,400	3,000	17.4	2,000	91[e]	200,000
1951[f]	600	1,200	1,800	2,400	3,000	20.4	2,000	91[e]	200,000
1952–1953[f]	600	1,200	1,800	2,400	3,000	22.2	2,000	92[e]	200,000
1954–1960[f]	600	1,200	1,800	2,400	3,000	20	2,000	91[e]	200,000

[a] If net income exceeds $5,000, married person's exemption is $2,000.

[b] After earned income credit equal to 25 per cent of tax on earned income.

[c] Before earned income credit allowed as a deduction equal to 10 per cent of earned net income.

[d] Exclusive of Victory tax.

[e] Subject to maximum effective rate limitation: 90 per cent for 1944–1945, 85.5 per cent for 1946–1947, 77 per cent for 1948–1949, 87 per cent for 1950, 87.2 per cent for 1951, 88 per cent for 1952–1953 and 87 per cent for 1954–1958.

[f] Additional exemptions of $600 are allowed to taxpayers and their spouses on account of blindness and/or age over sixty-five.

Source: *The Federal Revenue System: Facts and Problems*, p. 189. (Materials assembled by the Committee Staff for the Joint Economic Committee, Congress of the United States, 1959.)

Estimated Cumulative Number of Taxpayers, Their Taxable Income, and Tax Distributed by Taxable Income Brackets for Calendar Year 1960

Taxable income bracket, $000	Tax rate % *	Cumulative number of taxpayers, thousands †	Taxable income ‡ millions of dollars	Tax from 20% basic rate, millions of dollars	Tax from rates above 20%, millions of dollars	Total tax § millions of dollars
Not over 2	20	84,420	116,919	23,384	. . . .	23,384
2–4	22	32,398	36,397	7,279	719	7,998
4–6	26	8,186	10,854	2,170	646	2,816
6–8	30	3,597	5,263	1,053	520	1,573
8–10	34	1,987	3,247	650	451	1,101
10–12	38	1,290	2,141	428	382	810
12–14	43	846	1,478	295	338	633
14–16	47	638	1,071	214	286	500
16–18	50	475	869	175	257	432
18–20	53	375	718	143	235	378
20–22	56	315	591	118	211	329
22–26	59	264	909	182	352	534
26–32	62	173	870	174	363	537
32–38	65	113	542	108	243	351
38–44	69	774	345	69	168	237
44–50	72	54	239	48	123	171
50–60	75	31	268	59	146	200

60–70	78	19	160	32	92	124
70–80	81	12	100	20	60	80
80–90	84	9	72	14	46	60
90–100	87	6	53	11	35	46
100–150	89	5	120	83	24	107
150–200	90	1	56	11	20	51
Over 200	91	1	324	65	230	295
Total.........	....	....	183,606	36,780	5,967	42,747

* Rate shown is that applicable to all taxpayers other than heads of household. Therefore, multiplying rate by taxable income would overstate the tax by about 50 million dollars.

† Married couples filing joint returns are counted as two taxpayers, each with one-half the combined income.

‡ Does not include 1,130 million dollars of long-term capital gains subject to the alternative rate.

§ Excludes 565-million-dollar alternative tax and is before deduction of the effect of the 87 per cent limitation of 3 million dollars, the dividends received credit of 330 million dollars, and the retirement income credit of 98 million dollars.

APPENDIX C

Reconciliation of Personal Income with Adjusted Gross Income and Derivation of Individual Income Tax Base, 1959
(In billions of dollars)

Personal income	383.3
Deduct:	
Transfer payments	27.0
Other labor income	10.1
Personal income in kind	1.9
Food and fuel consumed on farms	1.6
Imputed rent	7.0
Noncorporate, nonfarm inventory valuation adjustment	−0.1
Value change in farm inventory	0.5
Imputed interest	10.0
Nontaxable military pay and allowances	2.0
Net accrual of interest on government bonds (savings)	0.3
Tax-exempt interest not accruing to corporations	0.7
Fiduciary income not distributed	1.4
Dividends excludable from gross income	0.3
Sick pay excludable from gross income	0.6
Income of pension funds and other tax-exempt organizations	1.6
Dividends reported as capital gains	0.5
Total deductions	65.4
Add:	
Employee contributions for social insurance	7.8
Net capital gains of individuals	7.0
Adjusted gross income of individuals in Hawaii and Alaska	1.3
Miscellaneous income of individuals	1.8
Annuities and pensions	1.4
Total additions	19.3
Net deductions	46.1
Personal income adjusted	337.2
Nonconceptual differences:	
Specifically estimated items:	
Income received by individuals not required to file (income less than exemptions)	3.4
Income eventually disclosed by audit	3.8
Estimated dividends not accounted for on tax returns	1.2
Estimated interest income not accounted for on tax returns	4.4
Total specifically estimated items	12.8
Remaining unexplained reporting gap and statistical discrepancy	16.4
Total nonconceptual differences	29.2
Adjusted gross income—all returns	308.0
Adjusted gross deficit	1.0

Adjusted gross income—returns with adjusted gross income 309.0
  Adjusted gross income—nontaxable returns 20.4
Adjusted gross income—taxable returns 288.6
  Personal deductions (standard and itemized) 40.9
Net income 247.7
  Personal exemptions 81.6
Taxable income of individuals 166.1

SOURCE: U.S. Treasury, Tax Analysis Staff. Published in *Panel Discussions on Income Tax Revision,* before Committee on Ways and Means, House of Representatives, November and December, 1959, p. 104. (Figures revised to show subsequent revisions in national income data.)

Itemized Deductions by Adjusted Gross Income Classes, 1958

(Dollar amounts in millions)

Adjusted gross income class	Adjusted gross income	Contributions	Interest paid	Taxes	Medical and dental expenses	Other deductions	Total deductions
Under $1,000	184.3	16.6	10.0	22.1	28.3	9.2	86.2
1,000 and under 3,000	6,215.3	346.0	242.2	403.5	572.8	216.4	1,781.0
3,000 and under 5,000	22,214.1	957.0	1,001.0	1,184.6	1,120.6	662.5	4,925.8
5,000 and under 10,000	66,010.1	2,316.0	3,408.4	3,415.0	1,832.0	1,660.8	12,632.2
10,000 and under 20,000	25,008.0	859.9	998.8	1,266.0	470.6	577.5	4,172.7
20,000 and under 50,000	15,671.9	535.0	372.0	744.0	187.6	338.5	2,177.2
50,000 and under 100,000	5,823.4	254.9	129.1	263.7	53.5	159.2	860.4
100,000 and over	4,231.9	408.5	107.6	181.3	18.2	146.8	862.4
Total, all returns with itemized deductions	145,359.0	5,693.8	6,269.2	7,480.3	4,283.5	3,771.0	27,497.9

Percentage distribution

Adjusted gross income class	Adjusted gross income	Contributions	Interest paid	Taxes	Medical and dental expenses	Other deductions	Total deductions
Under $1,000	0.1	0.3	0.2	0.3	0.7	0.2	0.3
1,000 and under 3,000	4.3	6.1	3.9	5.4	13.4	5.7	6.5
3,000 and under 5,000	15.3	16.8	16.0	15.8	24.2	17.6	17.9
5,000 and under 10,000	45.4	40.7	54.4	45.7	42.8	44.0	45.9
10,000 and under 20,000	17.2	15.1	15.9	16.9	11.0	15.3	15.2
20,000 and under 50,000	10.8	9.4	5.9	9.9	4.4	9.0	7.9
50,000 and under 100,000	4.0	4.5	2.1	3.5	1.2	4.2	3.1
100,000 and over	2.9	7.2	1.7	2.4	0.4	3.9	3.1
Total, all returns with itemized deductions	100.0	100.0	100.0	100.0	100.0	100.0	100.0

SOURCE: Internal Revenue Service, *Statistics of Income, Individual Income Tax Returns for 1958.*
NOTE: Figures are rounded and may not add to totals.

INDEX

Note: The letter n following a page number refers to a footnote.